D1084538

WITHDRAWN

# OUTLINES
## OF A SYSTEM OF
# POLITICAL ECONOMY

# OUTLINES

OF A SYSTEM OF

# POLITICAL ECONOMY

WRITTEN

WITH A VIEW TO PROVE TO GOVERNMENT
AND COUNTRY

THAT

## THE CAUSE

OF THE

THE PRESENT AGRICULTURAL DISTRESS

IS

ENTIRELY ARTIFICIAL

AND TO

SUGGEST A PLAN FOR THE

MANAGEMENT OF THE CURRENCY

TOGETHER WITH THE FOURTH EDITION OF AN ESSAY ON
*THE PRINCIPLES OF BANKING*

BY

THOMAS JOPLIN

[ 1823 ]

REPRINTS OF ECONOMIC CLASSICS

AUGUSTUS M. KELLEY · PUBLISHERS
*NEW YORK 1970*

First Edition 1823

( London: *Published by* Baldwin, Cradock & Joy,
1823 )

Reprinted 1970 by
AUGUSTUS M. KELLEY · PUBLISHERS
*New York   New York   10001*

.   .   .   .   .   .   .   .   .   .   .

*S B N   678 00590 7*

*L C N   68 30530*

.   .   .   .   .   .   .   .   .   .   .

PRINTED IN THE UNITED STATES OF AMERICA
*by* SENTRY PRESS, NEW YORK, N. Y. 10019

# OUTLINES

OF A

## SYSTEM

OF

# POLITICAL ECONOMY;

WRITTEN

WITH A VIEW TO PROVE TO GOVERNMENT
AND THE COUNTRY,

THAT

## THE CAUSE

OF THE

PRESENT AGRICULTURAL DISTRESS

IS

ENTIRELY ARTIFICIAL;

AND TO

SUGGEST A PLAN

FOR THE

MANAGEMENT OF THE CURRENCY,

BY

WHICH IT MAY BE REMEDIED NOW, AND ANY RECURRENCE
OF SIMILAR EVILS BE PREVENTED IN FUTURE:

TOGETHER WITH THE

FOURTH EDITION

OF AN

ESSAY

ON THE

## PRINCIPLES OF BANKING.

BY T. JOPLIN.

London:

PUBLISHED BY BALDWIN, CRADOCK, AND JOY.

1823.

# PREFACE.

As its title imports, this Essay is but the Outlines of the subject on which it treats. It has also been rather hastily written, and is not so perfect as the Author could have wished. As an apology for its imperfections, therefore some account of its origin may not be unnecessary.

Most writers imagine that they add something to the general stock of knowledge; and the Author is not without his hopes, that there are views in this Volume, which may be useful. But it is the matter, and not the manner in which they are conveyed, upon which he founds any claim they may possess, to the reader's attention. He is a man of business, to which he was early brought up; and he has not possessed those advantages which are usually considered necessary to good writing; nor is it probable, that in the present stage of his life, he would have written at all, except for a practical object.

His motive for writing the Essay on the Principles of Banking, the fourth edition of which this Volume contains, was entirely interested. If the charter of the Bank of England is altered, and Joint Stock Companies, on the principles he recommends, are established, he proposes to take such a share in each of them as individuals are allowed to hold ; and requests each bank to open an account with him, hold his share as security, and charge him interest upon the advance required. He might open an account with some one or more banks, and get them to take up the shares for him, as they must upon the average be ample security for their original value; but if the banks which may be established acknowledge any obligation to him, he has not any apprehension that this will be necessary.

Having thus, however, a practical object in view, the Author did not allow his pamphlet to sleep in the hands of the booksellers, but at once made a considerable distribution of it in Newcastle, the towns comprised in the plan, and in the counties of Durham and Northumberland, and sent copies to leading persons in other places.

It was quite clear from what had been said by ministers upon the subject, that they only desired some plain business view of the question, by any one whose situation in life enabled him to give it, in order to make some change in the present system of Banking. But the change recommended struck very deep at the interests of a powerful body ; and it appeared extremely desirable, if it were practicable, that the public should express their wishes on the subject, in order to shew ministers that if they did put their shoulders to the work, and procure an alteration of the charter of the Bank of England, Public Banks would actually be set up in consequence.

The pamphlet made as great an impression as could have been wished, and the principal persons in New-castle seemed disposed to meet and petition Parliament immediately; but a leader was wanting: no person seemed willing to do any thing but second. It was thought that some country gentleman ought to take the chair. Parliament, however, had assembled; most of the gentlemen were out of the county, and none that remained seemed willing to do so except one, and he afterwards declined.

The argument against moving in the business, generally used by merchants is, that they are so intimately connected with the Banks, that they cannot be seen in it, and that the subject ought to be taken up by the country gentlemen; and with the country gentlemen, that it ought to be taken up by the mercantile men, who have so much to do with Banks, and are more immediately interested in the question.

In the county of Durham, however, there was less difficulty. Five Banks out of seven had failed within a few years, and Lord Barrington, though he in general declines to take any lead in public matters, thought the establishments recommended so obviously desirable, and even so absolutely necessary in that part of the country, that on being applied to, he did not hesitate to take the chair at a meeting of county gentlemen held on the subject. At this meeting a committee was appointed, and the resolutions were passed, which will be found in the Appendix.

A few of the principal men in Liverpool were disposed to take up the question. By the accounts of gentlemen from Northumberland who were in Liverpool after the pamphlet had been published there, it appears that it had produced a great sensation. Some meetings took place in consequence, and resolutions were passed and published, and ministers memorialized upon the subject.

A gentleman of talents and great perseverance, though not of sufficient influence to take a lead, undertook to establish the principles of the pamphlet at Manchester. This he did so completely, that it seems if the bank charter had been altered last session, three Banks, by different classes of persons, would have been started immediately. No expression of public opinion, however, took place. But were it necessary, more reliance might perhaps be placed on Manchester than any other town. The manufacturers are in general rich and independent; and it has one of the best Chambers of Commerce in the kingdom. During the session of Parliament, this chamber meets regularly to discuss all questions relative to trade and commerce, but more especially those which relate to the trade of Manchester, and it takes steps to carry the result of its deliberations into effect. A very important act of Parliament was obtained by it last session, for the registering of warrants of attorney; and the transactions of the Banks, so important to commerce, receive its particular attention. It resisted the issue of local notes, by calling the meeting of the inhabitants of Manchester for that purpose, mentioned in the Essay on Banking; and it makes other regulations respecting them whenever it is necessary for the interests of commerce. A measure of this importance, therefore, could not consistently be overlooked by it. Almost all of its members are known to think well of the scheme, and some of them to be very desirous of promoting it. It is therefore expected by the people of Manchester, of whom they are the commercial representatives, that they will take such steps as might be expected from the town of Manchester, in such a question.

Although there is no place where a public Bank is more desired, yet this does not arise from any dissatisfaction with the existing Banks. Messrs Jones, Lloyd, and Co., and Messrs Heywood and Co. are both liberal and wealthy bankers; but the principle of the Scotch Banks is preferred by all commercial men, as well in Manchester as in every other place.

The Author made some attempts to bring the subject into notice in other commercial towns, but his endeavours were not successful. Banks, it was said, would be set up when there was liberty to do so, but no encouragement was held out that any public steps would be taken in order to procure that liberty.

Ministers, however, soon rendered the exertions of the Author perfectly unnecessary. They made an arrangement with the Bank of England for an alteration of its charter; and there seemed no doubt that it would be completed as a matter of course. During the dependance of the question, the Author was in London for a couple of months, and after his return, addressed the following Letter to the Editor of The Newcastle Courant, in order to explain how the matter stood:—

## THE PROPOSED PUBLIC BANK.

SIR,—As this has become a question of considerable local interest with this part of the country, the following information respecting it, may, perhaps, not be unacceptable to the public:—

Your readers, who have given attention to the matter, are, no doubt aware, that two or three months after the publication of the Essay on Banking, the question was taken up by government, without any petitions to parliament, which that Pamphlet recommended. It had been circulated very freely in Lancashire, and had produced a considerable sensation there, as well as here; of this, the ministers were fully apprised, not only by communications constantly forwarded to them, but by a deputation of bankers interested in the matter, having waited upon the Chancellor of the Exchequer, to ascertain the views of government upon the subject.

At the commencement of the session, ministers proposed, that four millions should be advanced by government to the agriculturists, but that plan was dropt, and the alteration of the bank charter, with a view to the establishment of public banks, adopted, as a much more effectual application of that mode of relief, as well as being an improvement imperatively required in the banking system of the country.

A bargain was made with the Bank of England, by which, in consequence of allowing the immediate establishment of public banks, in the country, at a distance exceeding 65 miles from London, its charter was to be renewed for 10 years longer. This arrangement was confirmed by a general meeting of proprietors, and a bill was to have been submitted to parliament, by ministers, accordingly.

In the mean time, however, considerable difficulties arose. It was contended, by the opposition, that the bargain with the bank was improvident. It ought to have given up its privilege for nothing; what was gained by it was only worth having, but not worth paying for. Lord Grey stated, that "as far as he could learn, there was no call for the measure; at least, in the part of the country with which he was more immediately connected, there was no complaint respecting the stability of banks, nor any distrust as to the property by which their credit was sustained." Truth, however, requires it to be stated, that, at this very time, Sir Francis Blake, Reeds, and Co.'s bank had stopped payment, for nearly half a million of money, and their notes were then at a discount of from 5s. to 7s. in the pound. There are, however, so many bankers, and such banking interest in parliament, that this doctrine went very well down with a great majority of both sides of the house. And it is extremely probable, that had ministers brought the measure forward, they might have had some difficulty in carrying it; more especially, as they themselves thought that the bank ought to have consented to the alteration without purchase.

At the same time, the bank directors also had as little relish for the matter, on their part, and would, by no means, consent that the arrangement should be concluded on any thing like a sensible basis. No public bank can be set up without a law to render it liable only for the acts of its directors. As the law of partnership now stands, any partner, if there were a thousand, could either raise money or indorse bills, or do any act of that kind, in its name; and if fraud could not be *legally* proved and brought home to the holders of the bills or other securities, the bank would be bound to pay them. That the privilege, thus necessary, should be granted, however, the directors would not consent, which put an end to the business, and rendered the meeting of the bank proprietors and the whole proceedings, quite a nullity.

A correspondence that took place in the Times paper, which exhibits the peculiar views or the apology of the directors in this extraordinary proceeding, you have below; and though long, it will probably possess interest to those who feel an interest in the subject.

In consequence of the representation of the merchants of Liverpool, who had stated their views in a memorial to Lord Liverpool, ministers thought it expedient that charters to a limited extent should be granted, to which the bank had previously objected; and they proposed to the directors, that a more limited extension of their charter, with the power of conferring charters where it appeared necessary, and the other regulations required, should be granted. This also fell to the ground; and the Chancellor of the Exchequer stated in parliament, that when the bank applied for a renewal of its charter, the proposed extension of it would be made.

That the bank directors should offer such opposition, seems almost incredible, and yet it is at least tacitly avowed in the subjoined correspondence. It is not unlikely, however, that finding the interested feeling and probable difficulty the measure would encounter in parliament, even amongst their own friends, ministers were disposed to wait until public opinion was more decidedly expressed in its favour. Besides the measure had assumed a new character,—merely throwing open the charter, so that banks might have whatever number of partners they thought proper, involved none of that time, attention, and consideration, which would be necessarily required, if charters were to be granted; and at the late period of the session, when this alteration of the views of ministers took place, they probably could not, with the business they had on hand, give that attention to the subject it required. Hence any opposition or apology for putting it off would perhaps be the more readily embraced.

Next session of parliament, it is probable that petitions from different places, will be set on foot, and the measure will be again brought forward by ministers, who are not only pledged to carry it, but have an honest conviction of its utility, and a sincere wish to see it adopted, as friends to the true interests and welfare of their country.

Of its necessity and advantage, the public are universally convinced; and if Lord Grey will enquire, he will find that his statement in parliament was not at all correct.

It need not, however, be expected, that any petitions to parliament, will be very generally signed by that class of persons who, having most to do with the banks, are most interested in the question. This class will much more readily subscribe to a bank when about to be set up, and they do not hesitate to say so, than do the slightest act that might seem to imply dissatisfaction with those at present established. But as this will be obvious to parliament, the very deficiency of such signatures will prove the trammels of the country, and be an argument for the alteration of the law which inflicts them.

There are some other circumstances also which render it extremely probable that the opposition of the bank directors will be considerably abated next session of parliament; independent of which they will be under the necessity of applying early for a renewal of their charter, in order to keep up the value of the bank stock. Were any difficulties to arise respecting the renewal of the charter, the stock would necessarily fall. It is now at 252, and its intrinsic value, were the charter not to be renewed, including any reserved fund or savings which the bank may possess, is not probably more than 110 or 120.* It is the soundest policy, as well as the practice of the bank, to get its charter renewed in good time. The present charter was granted in 1800, 12 years before the last expired, and this has now not more than 11 years to run. Any further delay in getting it renewed might be dangerous, and, on the part of the directors, inexcusable. Public opinion is making rapid inroads into the territory of that prejudice, which, as a national institution, has run rather high in favour of the Bank of England; and though the directors may be at the head of a

* This value, it appears, is too low by at least twenty or thirty per cent.

regiment of clerks, the nation would prove too strong for them, were they to provoke an encounter, or injudiciously court it, by leaving the policy of renewing their charter open to that freedom of enquiry which is taking place on the subject.                                    T.

[The letters from The Times referred to, will be found in the Appendix to the Essay on Banking.]

The high character of Lord Grey leaves no room to doubt the purity of his motives; or the truth of the statement quoted from his speech in the above letter, so far as his lordship's knowledge went. The probability is, that as Sir Francis Blake, Reeds and Co.'s bank, which had not been in the best credit for some time, had stopped payment, his lordship presumed that all the rest were now good. This presumption was perfectly correct. But when his lordship stated that there was no distrust as to the property by which their credit was sustained, he proved that he had not a very accurate local knowledge on the subject. It is one thing to say that a bank has good credit, and another to say that it has property enough to sustain it. Its credit may depend upon the known prudence with which it is managed, more than upon the property with which it is sustained. It may be perfectly safe to take a single voyage in a bad ship well navigated, while it would be madness to engage to do so annually for twenty years, whether it was well navigated or not. The fair way to put the question is this: would Lord Grey, or any other person, think it prudent to guarantee the stability of all the present banks in Northumberland and Durham, for that time, respectable as they at present undoubtedly are?

The Author does not mean to say, that so far as he could learn, the opposition generally were against the principle of the measure; he believes, on the contrary, that the majority were very decidedly in its favor. It is probable that even Lord Grey merely thought that the bank had too good a bargain; but to contend that the country ought to be afflicted with the present system ten or twelve years longer, in order to punish the bank, was evidently pushing the argument too far.

With respect however, to the present Essay: the Author, when in London, had an interview with Mr Huskisson, on the bank subject; at which he ventured to state, that he entertained some opinions on the cause of the present agricultural distress, which he had arranged in the form of propositions; and that if Mr Huskisson wished it, he would leave them to be considered at his leisure, should he find them worth his attention. He consequently left those which follow :—

*A few consecutive Propositions in Political Economy, which are capable of Proof.*

### CONSUMPTION.

1. That the monied income of society is and must annually be spent.

2. That all income is derived from the soil.

3. That the produce of the soil, and the demand for it are upon the average equal.

4. That it is the supply which creates the demand, and not the demand which creates the supply.

5. That the cost of all commodities, though it may be nominally stated to consist of profits, taxes, &c. as well as materials and labour, does consist of materials and labour solely.

6. That the relative prices of the produce of the

soil are determined by labour, and if the soil was 20 times more productive than it is, it would preserve the same relative price to labour and other commodities which it does at present.

From this chapter it ought to appear, as a matter of course, that with respect to the national prosperity, the taxes are neither an evil nor a good.

### CURRENCY.

7. That every state of prices which is average and general, is determined by the amount of currency in circulation.

8. That it is thrown into or abstracted from circulation through the medium of an increased or diminished consumption.

9. That the total value of currency in the world cannot be altered by an alteration in its quantity.

10. That its value depends upon the exchanges it is required to perform.

11. That the same is the case with any particular nation. By an importation or exportation of gold, the price of it is altered, but no difference is made in the total value of the money in the country.

### FOREIGN TRADE.

12. That the foreign trade of a country consists in an exchange of its commodities for those of other nations.

13. That the value of such commodities is computed in money.

14. That if the commodities of any nation are superior to those of others, the demand of the other countries for its commodities will be superior to its demand for theirs, and the balance will be paid in money. That prices will in consequence be raised in the country to which the balance is paid, and reduced in the countries by which it is paid, and by this means, the demand for commodities will be reduced on the one hand and increased on the other, until they are equal in money, though more unequal in quantity.—That in proportion to this inequality in the amount of commodities exchanged will be the advantage of the nation in which prices are high, over those with which it deals.

15. That if a country with great manufacturing superiority, were to prevent the importation of provisions, and were to confine its foreign trade to the importation of such commodities as it required for the population which its own soil would support, the exchange might be conducted on very advantageous principles.

16. That if the importation of foreign provisions were freely admitted, the effect would be merely an increase of manufacturing population.

17. That both an increase of population, and an advantageous exchange may be produced by a tax upon foreign provisions judiciously imposed.

18. That the amount of this tax must be determined, not by an enquiry into the cost of production by our agriculturists, but into the extent of our manufacturing superiority.

19. That a tax upon foreign provisions would not in the least degree be a tax upon the people of this country, nor upon the countries where they are produced, except to the extent of actual British labour or produce received in return for them; but upon the fo-

reign consumers of the produce of British soil and labour all over the world.

20. That the corn bill alone would not have produced the effects to which it has led, unconnected with other causes.

21. That the present state of the country is the effect of the want of consumption, produced by the sudden change in the value of property from the altered value of the currency; and by the reduction of the expenditure of government.

22. That the reduction of the expenditure of government creates the evil which it is intended to cure.

23. That the present situation of the country could not have been brought about with a metallic currency, or with a paper currency upon different principles.

24. That the economy of the nation and government has no other effect at present than to contract the circulation, and instead of reducing the interest of money, to reduce the price of provisions.

25. That this might be prevented by such alterations in the principles upon which paper was issued, as would put it upon the footing of a metallic currency.

These propositions appear to have been thought by Mr Huskisson to possess matter of some interest. He returned them in a few days with a note, which the author will crave his indulgence for inserting, as it will serve for a warrant to the reader that the following attempt to develope the principles they contain may be at least worth examination :—

" Mr Huskisson presents his compliments to Mr
" Joplin, and having had an opportunity of looking
" over the propositions on Political Economy, which
" he left with him for perusal when he had the plea-
" sure of seeing him a few days ago, now begs to re-
" turn the several papers herewith.

" Mr H. is persuaded Mr Joplin must be aware
" that the propositions in question comprehend a very
" extensive and important range of subject, combined
" with matter of great general interest, and will re-
" quire the utmost attention and consideration to
" their developement; but he is not prepared at pre-
" sent to offer any conclusive opinion upon the points
" adverted to.

" *Whitehall Place, 6th July,* 1822."

It was not until two months after this, that the Author determined upon undertaking the work at the
present moment. It will be afterwards seen by the
reader, that the arrangement of these propositions is
imperfect. The first and second form the subject of
the eighth and eleventh chapters of this work, and the
fifth proposition is erroneous. Consequently his views
were more obscure, and the undertaking more difficult,
and likely to require much more time and attention
than he could conveniently give to it. When, however, the arrangement which has been adopted occurred to him, and he discovered that deduction which
he has termed the Fulcrum of the Argument, the difficulty seemed at once to vanish, and the undertaking
become more practicable.

In order to have it out before the ensuing session of
Parliament, if possible, as well as for the purpose of
forwarding it to Mr Huskisson, the chapters were

sent to the printer as they were written; but owing to constant business interruptions, which tend to disturb the current of thought, and of course to retard a work of this description, at the end of two months not more than a third of it was completed.

The Author, however, had, by this time, sent the first eleven chapters to Mr Huskisson. His object was to render his views, if they were true, as useful as possible; and as ministers, he was aware, were preparing some plans to submit to parliament the ensuing session, any light that could be thrown upon the subject would of course be desirable. Mr Huskisson, he had no doubt, would at once see whether or not his general principles were correct, and if so, deduce from them measures of practical utility, and if not, no harm could arise from submitting them to his consideration.

As, however, the Author got slowly on with his work, which, if his views were correct, ought to be out by the meeting of Parliament, he now absented himself from business altogether for a short time, and in six or seven weeks of perfect seclusion, was enabled to complete it.

The brevity with which he has discussed many of the principles laid down, renders it necessary for him to state, that he considers himself only addressing such as possess some previous knowledge of the subject, or will take the trouble to understand him. The multitude can never be political economists. But if his general principles are approved by those who are capable of appreciating them, he will probably at some future period of leisure, endeavour to furnish a more enlarged and elementary work on the subject.

This Essay, thereore, having been hastily written by

an unpractised writer, and sent to the press as the chapters were completed, by which any corrections, alterations, or improvement that must always suggest themselves in the course of a work of this nature, were prevented, considerable allowances ought to be made by the critical reader. It is the author's object to show, that the present agricultural distress might have been prevented by a different system of currency, and may now be cured; and if he has done that, he has done all he aimed to do; though he may have deemed it requisite to go through a wider range of subject than might at first appear necessary.

Since this work was completed, and even printed, all but three or four pages, the Author has read, for the first time, Mr Ricardo's Pamphlet on Currency, entitled "The high Price of Bullion, a Proof of the Depreciation of Bank Notes." He was not before, nor does he believe, that the world in general are sufficiently aware of the obligation they are under to that gentleman for this able little production. Treating merely of general principles, it has been smothered in the discussion to which it gave rise. He is anxious to explain that he had not before seen it, perchance it should be supposed that some of the ideas contained in the following work, had been taken, without acknowledgment, from that, so far as the subject is developed, perfect theory, of the currency.

# CONTENTS.

PAGE

PAGE

# OUTLINES

OF

# 𝔓𝔬𝔩𝔦𝔱𝔦𝔠𝔞𝔩 𝔈𝔠𝔬𝔫𝔬𝔪𝔶.

## CHAPTER I.

*Definition of a few Terms employed in the following Essay.*

I⊤ is generally admitted that political economy is a science not yet fully understood. In which case, nothing is more natural than to suppose that terms may be required to express discriminations of meaning, which, in fact, may never before have been made. I trust, therefore, that there can be no objection to my adopting language to express such distinctions, as it may appear in the course of this Essay either necessary or desirable to establish, or even, for the sake of precision, to define for myself the meaning in which I may employ words already in use. The following are a few terms that I shall take the liberty of using in the sense which they are explained to convey:

VALUE, in common language, has two meanings : it either refers to the price of a commodity, or its usefulness. Water, though not worth money, is valuable ; such a person is also a valuable man, &c. In this sense it has no reference to price. On the other hand, it is usually said, that the value of a thing is what it will bring : we value our goods at the price for which we think they will sell. In this case it is synonymous with price. Value, in use, however, is not a term required in political economy, which treats only of the exchangeable value of commodities, while price expresses exchangeable value as well as any other term. I shall, therefore, use the term value, to express the cost of a commodity, in labour, materials, profit of capital, &c. ; the price at which it can be produced to indemnify the cultivator or manufacturer, after paying for the labour, rent, profit, and other charges incident to it; or in speaking of any thing not the produce of materials and labour—such as land, I shall employ it, as it commonly is used, to express its price at par, or its average value according to the interest of money, or by whatever general principles its value is determined. A person will sometimes give more for an estate than it is worth, or may sometimes purchase it for less. Its value, however, by judges, is estimated according to the current price of land. If a person choose to give more, or take less for an estate than it is worth, that does not alter its real value. Also in mentioning money, value is used. We never speak of the price, but always of the value of money.

PRICE.—Commodities are very seldom sold for their precise value in the market, according to the foregoing definition; though they may be so upon the average. They are continually fluctuating, like the pendulum of a clock, on one side of their value or the other, and yet constantly gravitate towards it. The market value of a commodity we shall, therefore, term its price; thus distinguishing it from value, the cost of its production: the price and value being the same only when the commodity is at par, and sells for the fair remunerating price necessary to pay its producer. By the same rule, the price of an estate is what it sells for; its value, what it is worth; and only when it sells at its value, is its price and value the same.

COMMERCIAL CONSUMPTION.—It is of no importance to the manufacturer or grower of a commodity what becomes of it after he sells it. It is, so far as regards the commodity sold, as much consumed to him if put into a warehouse as if it were put into the fire; consequently all commodities in the hands of merchants, shopkeepers, &c. so far as he is affected, are consumed. That demand which influences his production has taken place; and to distinguish this from *actual*, I have termed it *commercial consumption.*

PRE–EXISTING MATERIAL PRODUCE.—The materials of which the manufactures and commodities that we consume are composed, are of two descriptions: those which are the produce of the soil, and those which pre-exist in nature, and are abstracted from it by labour or art. All experience points out that the former is the basis of wealth, and the latter its superstructure. The richest mineral productions are of no value in a country with a barren soil, except in so far as they will exchange for the productions of one more fruitful. In political economy their value is of course determined by different principles; hence it will not be improper to give them separate designations. Those materials, therefore, which pre-exist in nature, and are by some mechanical or chemical application of labour or art, extracted from it, are termed *pre-existing materials,* or *pre-existing material produce.*

VICTUAL PRODUCE.—The produce of the soil may be divided into two descriptions: that which is used for food—such as corn, beef, rice, coffee, sugar, fruit, &c. and those materials which form the basis of manufactures, and other articles of convenience—such as hemp, flax, cotton, wool, wood, &c. In speaking of the former, it is not unusual for political economists to express them under the general head of corn. In doing this, however, a particular explanation is always necessary, to avoid which, the term *victual produce* is employed.

MATERIAL PRODUCE consists of those materials, the produce of the soil, which form the base of manufactures as above described, and which are thus distinguished from victual produce on the one hand, and pre-existing material produce on the other. Material produce also naturally divides itself into animal and vegetable. This distinction, however, is not necessary for the purpose of our argument.

# CHAPTER II.

## *Use of Money.*

MONEY is not wealth. It only conveys the power of obtaining those things which compose it. Wealth consists in the necessaries, comforts, conveniences, and enjoyments of life. This nation is the richest in the world, yet the principal part of its money consists of a paper currency, which is intrinsically not worth the ten-thousandth part of the value it represents. When in its greatest prosperity, it had the least amount of the precious metals in circulation. Paper, however, answered the purpose quite as well, and proves, if proofs were wanting, that wealth does not consist in gold and silver. This country was never more rich and flourishing than a few years ago, when it had the least of them. If wealth had consisted in gold and silver, instead of the richest, we must then have been one of the poorest nations in the world. No nation, not entirely barbarous, had at that time less of them than we had. We still, however, have an itching palm for gold; we parted with what we had reluctantly, and are extremely desirous to have it back, though we are certainly not the richer since it became more plentiful.

The wealth of a country consists in the abundance which it may possess, of those necessaries and conveniences, the produce of land and labour, which furnish the support, and contribute to the enjoyments of life. That part of the aggregate wealth of a nation which forms the wealth or income of each individual, consists of some particular description of the labour or produce, of which the whole is composed. The income of one person is derived from land which produces corn, another from land which produces cattle. One has a tin mine, another a mine of coal, one man makes nails, another shoes, &c. Thus the income of each individual is generally derived from contributing to some particular want of a great many different persons. On the other hand, the necessaries and luxuries which each individual requires, take some portion of the labour and produce of as great a variety of persons to supply. And it is necessary for him to exchange that in which his income consists, with all those who may desire a part of it, in order that he may procure from them that portion of each of their labour or produce which he requires for himself. In order to facilitate these exchanges, money is necessary. " When

" the division of labour" (says Smith, in his
Wealth of Nations) " has been once tho-
" roughly established, it is but a very small
" part of a man's wants, which the produce of
" his own labour can supply.  He supplies the
" far greater part of them by exchanging that
" surplus part of the produce of his own la-
" bour which is over and above his own con-
" sumption, for such parts of the produce of
" other men's labour as he has occasion for.
" Every man thus lives by exchanging, or be-
" comes in some measure a merchant, and the
" society itself grows to be what is properly a
" commercial society.

" But when the division of labour first began
" to take place, the power of exchanging must
" frequently have been very much clogged and
" embarrassed in its operations.  One man, we
" shall suppose, has more of a certain commo-
" dity than he himself has occasion for, while
" another has less.  The former consequently
" would be glad to dispose of, and the latter
" to purchase a part of this superfluity.  But
" if the latter should chance to have nothing
" that the former stands in need of, no ex-
" change can be made between them.  The
" butcher has more meat in his shop than he
" himself can consume, and the brewer and
" the baker would each of them be willing to
" purchase a part of it. But they have nothing

" to offer in exchange except the different pro-
" ductions of their respective trades, and the
" butcher is already provided with all the bread
" and beer which he has immediate occasion
" for. No exchange can in this case be made be-
" tween them. He cannot be their merchant, nor
" they his customers, and they are all of them
" thus mutually less serviceable to one another.
" In order to avoid the inconveniency of such
" situations, every prudent man, in every pe-
" riod of society after the first establishment
" of the division of labour, must naturally have
" endeavoured to manage his affairs in such a
" manner as to have at all times by him, be-
" sides the peculiar produce of his own indus-
" try, a certain quantity of some one commo-
" dity or other, such as he imagined few peo-
" ple would be likely to refuse in exchange for
" the produce of their industry.

" Many different commodities, it is proba-
" ble, were successively both thought of and
" employed for this purpose. In the rude
" ages of society, cattle are said to have been
" the common instrument of commerce ; and
" though they must have been a most inconve-
" nient one, yet, in old times, we find things
" were frequently valued according to the
" number of cattle which had been given in
" exchange for them.

" The armour of Diomede, says Homer,

" cost only nine oxen; but that of Glaucus
" cost an hundred oxen. Salt is said to be the
" common instrument of commerce and ex-
" changes in Abyssinia—a species of shells in
" some part of the coast of India—dried cod
" at Newfoundland—tobacco in Virginia—su-
" gar in some of the West India colonies—
" hides, or dressed leather, in some other coun-
" tries; and there is at this day, a village in
" Scotland, where it is not uncommon, I am
" told, for a workman to carry nails instead of
" money to the baker's shop, or the alehouse."

" In all countries, however, men seem at
" last to have determined, by irresistible rea-
" sons, to give the preference, for this employ-
" ment, to metals, above every other commo-
" dity. Metals can not only be kept with as
" little loss as any other commodity, scarce
" any thing being less perishable than they
" are; but they can likewise, without any loss,
" be divided into any number of parts, or, by
" fusion, those parts can easily be united again,
" a quality which no other equally durable
" commodities possess, and which, more than
" any other quality, renders them fit to be the
" instruments of commerce and circulation.
" The man who wanted to buy salt, for exam-
" ple, and had nothing but cattle to give in
" exchange for it, must have been obliged to
" buy salt to the value of a whole ox, or a

" whole sheep at a time. He could seldom
" buy less than this, because, what he was to
" give for it, could seldom be divided without
" loss ; and if he had a mind to buy more, he
" must, for the same reasons, have been obli-
" ged to buy double or triple the quantity, the
" value, to wit, of two or three oxen, or of two
" or three sheep.

" If, on the contrary, instead of sheep or
" oxen, he had only metals to give in ex-
" change for it, he could easily proportion the
" quantity of the metal to the precise quantity
" of the commodity, which he had immediate
" occasion for. Different metals have been
" made use of by different nations for this pur-
" pose. Iron was the common instrument of
" commerce among the ancient Spartans—
" copper among the ancient Romans—and
" gold and silver among all rich and commer-
" cial nations."

By a modern improvement, however, in commerce, a paper currency, founded upon public confidence, is found to answer the same
purpose as the precious metals, and in this and
other countries has been principally substituted for them.

The comparative value of commodities is determined through the medium of money, on
the axiomatic principle, that things which are
equal to the same thing are equal to each

other. Thus if my labour or commodity be worth a pound, it is of equal value, and will, through the medium of the pound for which I sell it, exchange for any other commodity worth a pound, which I may require. The object of every individual, therefore, is to get as much money for his labour or commodity as he can, not that the money is of itself of any value, but that the exchangeable value of his commodity or labour is thereby determined. If it is equal to, or worth, a given sum of money, it is equal to, and will command any other quantity of labour or commodities of the same value in money, whether such quantity be great or small. Hence, as most people have a general idea of the present value in money, of such commodities or luxuries as they require, by ascertaining the value in money, of their own produce or labour, they can form a tolerably correct estimate of the share of the general wealth of society which they possess.

Money is thus a scale by which wealth is estimated, and though it is not wealth, more than a barometer is weather, yet it is our only mode of computing it, and nothing, perhaps, is more natural than that the shadow should sometimes have been over-valued, or even taken for the substance.

## The Money in the World is always sufficient for the Use of it.

If there were twice the quantity that there is at present, it would not purchase more commodities than the amount now in circulation ; or if there were but half the quantity, it would not purchase less. No alteration in the amount of money in the world, can alter its total value in that which composes wealth, the necessaries, comforts, and conveniences of life. If there were twice the quantity, the nominal price of commodities would be altered ; they would be twice the price all over the world. It would take double the sum of money to purchase the same quantity of wealth ; but that being the case, the whole money in circulation would only then be worth the same commodities as now. By the same rule, if there were but half the present money in the world, commodities would be half the price, and it would still command precisely the same amount of the enjoyments of life. The world, in neither case, would in the slightest degree be either richer or poorer.

What is the case with the world at large, is also the case with any particular nation, in so far as the commodities of that particular nation are concerned. As the quantity of money increases, the value of it depreciates, and the prices of the national commodities rise; the additional quantity of money brought into circulation, merely altering its nominal value. In countries, also, where the quantity is reduced, its nominal value is increased, and its total value, with respect to the commodities of the country, is the same.

In neither case are the respective nations richer or poorer by the stock of money increased or reduced, in so far as the value of the money itself is concerned.

Such alterations, however, continually take place. They are generally produced by the foreign trade of nations, and though with respect to the produce of the respective countries in which such changes take place, the effect is a mere alteration of prices, yet it is attended with important consequences, in regulating the trade of nations with each other, which will form the subject of the next chapter.

# CHAPTER III.

*Balance of Trade.*

T<small>HE</small> monied price of the produce of a nation determined by the quantity of money in it, not only affects the price of that which is consumed at home, but that which is sent from home and consumed by foreign nations. In trading with each other, nations compute the value of their respective commodities in money the same as individuals. The commerce of nations is, indeed, merely a number of individual transactions. In the international account, the value of commodities, whatever the respective quantities may be, is only known by their monied price.

Dr Smith says, " though at distant places " there is no regular proportion betwixt the " real" (which he establishes to be their value " computed in labour) " and the money price " of commodities, yet the merchant who car- " ries goods from one to the other has nothing " to consider but the money price, or the dif- " ference between the quantity of silver for " which he buys them, and that for which he " is likely to sell them. Half an ounce of sil-

" ver at Canton, in China, may command a
" greater quantity both of the labour and of
" the necessaries and conveniences of life than
" an ounce in London. A commodity, there-
" fore, which sells for half an ounce of silver at
" Canton, may there be really dearer, or of
" more real importance to the man who pos-
" sesses it there, than a commodity which
" sells for an ounce at London, is to the man
" who possesses it at London. If a London
" merchant, however, can buy at Canton for
" half an ounce of silver a commodity which he
" can afterwards sell at London for an ounce,
" he gains a hundred per cent. by the bargain,
" just as much as if an ounce of silver was at
" London exactly of the same value as at Can-
" ton. It is of no importance to him that half
" an ounce of silver at Canton would have
" given him the command of more labour, and
" of a greater quantity of the necessaries and
" conveniences of life, than an ounce can do
" at London. An ounce at London will al-
" ways give him double the command of all
" these, which half an ounce would have done
" there, and this is precisely what he wants.
  " It is the nominal or monied price, there-
" fore which finally determines the prudence
" or imprudence of all purchases and sales."
  The profits of trade, however, are equal upon the average, and are determined by the

capital employed, in importing the commodity, which is again determined by its original cost in money. If commodities, therefore, sell for little money at home, they sell proportionably low all over the world.

### *The Trade of Nations, upon the Average, balances.*

The commodities which go out of a country pay for those which come in. The value of its exports and imports are equal ; when they are not so, the balance is paid in money. By this means, as we have already stated, the price of commodities is raised in the country by which the balance is received, and reduced in that from which it is sent.

The prices of commodities influence their consumption ; when they are high, their consumption is reduced ; when low, increased. Consequently by the diminished value of money and increase of prices on the one hand, and increased value of money and decrease of prices on the other, the demand is reduced on one hand, and increased on the other, until computed in money, they become equal. To illustrate this principle we shall imagine an extreme case, by way of example.

Suppose a nation was to forbid, entirely, the importation of foreign goods, but to allow the exportation of its own, for payments in money ; and the nations trading with it were still, under these circumstances, to allow the trade, on their parts, to be continued, the effect, it is obvious, would be, that, in time, the prices of all commodities would rise so high in the exporting country, that the trade would be put a stop to by their mere exorbitancy.

The policy or impolicy of admitting a trade under such circumstances, would never enter into the calculations of the merchant. So long as the goods which could be bought in one country for money, could be sold for money in the other with a profit, he would continue the trade. While he could gain money by any one commodity, he would continue to export it from one country to the other.

Such a trade, however, must come to an end at last, or in time the whole money of the one nation would be sent to the other.

By the operation of this principle, the trade of all nations is brought to a balance. Should a country possess manufacturing superiority, and a greater demand exist for its commodities than it has for those of other nations, it creates a balance of trade in its favour. This balance is paid in money, by which a rise is produced in the price of its manufactures, and this rise progressively continues until they are sufficiently high to reduce the demand for them to a level with that demand, which it has for the commodities of other nations. Thus the manufacturing superiority of this country elevates its prices above those of every other. Our consumption of foreign commodities is restricted to the wants of our own population, while the demand of all the world for our manufactures can hardly be said to have limits except those which are imposed by price.

The general state of prices at which the foreign trade of a nation balances, we shall term its *National Prices*, in contradistinction to *Market Prices*. The average market price of a commodity is of course its national price. But according to the scarcity or abundance of the supply, the market price continually diverges from, and gravitates towards the national price, which has reference to the quantity of money in the country, and not to superabundance or scarcity in the markets.

*The Accounts of Nations, and their National Prices, have only Reference to Metallic Money.*

When the trade between countries balances, or those payments, when that is not the case, which are not made with the precious metals, are settled by means of bills of exchange, a merchant of one country, who ships goods to his correspondent in another, if he does not order his correspondent to ship for him goods to as great an amount in return, draws a bill upon him for the value of the commodities which he ships. This is sometimes done by the merchants of both nations. Bills are drawn indiscriminately at both ends, as with this country and Holland; and sometimes it is the practice to draw from one end only, as in the trade with America.

In the former case, there are foreign bankers or dealers in foreign bills, at both places, who have correspondence with each other. To these bankers the bills at both ends are sold, and remitted by them to each other to be received. If the bills drawn at both ends are of the same amount, saving the banker's profit for his trouble, they are worth the value in money for which they are drawn, and the price of bills, or exchange as it is called, is at par. But if the bills drawn in one country are of greater amount than those drawn in the other, the banker who purchases them will have to receive the balance in money. The expence of transporting this money, however, will amount in freight, insurance, &c. to 4, 5, 6, or 7 per cent. Independent, therefore, of the regular discount for his trouble, he cannot purchase the bills, without he has them for as much less as will cover the expence of importing the money to be received for them. The variation in the exchanges or price of bills can never, of course, much exceed the expence of transporting money from one country to the other. When there are, to any extent, more goods ordered of a nation than by it in return, bills upon it usually attain this premium. The exchanges are stated to be in its favour, and money is remitted in settlement of the national balance, until from the increased price of commodities, a check is given to that demand for them by which it was created, and bills fall below that price at which money can be remitted.

When there are no regular bankers established in countries trading with each other, the bills are all drawn one way. In the trade between this country and America, bills are all drawn upon England. In that case, one bill settles two transactions. A. in New York, ships a quantity of flour to A. in Liverpool, without ordering goods in return. B. in Liverpool, also, without receiving goods in return, ships an equal value of British manufactures to B. in New York. The established practice being for all bills to be drawn upon England, A. in New York draws on Liverpool for his flour, and sells the bill to his neighbour B. who remits it to Liverpool, in payment for his goods. If bills are scarce, B. in New York

might have to remit money at a certain expence, in payment of his goods ; he will, therefore, rather give as much extra price for a bill
as this expence amounts to, than incur the
trouble of sending money. If they are plentiful, and cannot be sold, A. may have to be at
the expence of transporting the money from
Liverpool to New York, for which his flour
sells. Rather than do this, he will also take as
much less for his bill, as the expence of transporting the money amounts to. If, however,
the shippers at both ends were to draw bills,
and there were no bankers to buy them, neither
of the bills would sell. Wherever, therefore,
bankers are not regularly established, all bills
must necessarily be drawn only one way.

Thus the exchange is the price of bills, and,
the weight and fineness of the coins of different
countries being determined, it is at par when a
bill will sell in the country where it is drawn,
for as many pieces of money of whatever denomination, as shall be equal or equivalent in
weight and fineness, to the number of pieces of
money for which it is payable in the country
upon which it is drawn. Thus we shall say, if
six silver rix dollars, current in St Petersburgh,
have as much value of silver in them as one
pound sterling, a bill drawn in St Petersburgh
upon England for £100, will sell, when the exchange is at par, for 600 rix dollars. Should,
however, the coin of St Petersburgh become

clipped or defaced, and reduced in weight by wear, it may take $6\frac{1}{2}$ or 7 rix dollars to make one pound sterling; consequently, before a remittance of such money could be made to England, bills upon England must not only be at such a price as would cover the expence of transporting the money with a profit, but make up this deficiency in the weight of the rix dollar also. The real par of exchange would be 650 or 700 rix dollars for £100, as it would take that quantity coined into English money to make one hundred pounds sterling. The par of the exchange, however, having been previously determined, before the rix dollars were defaced, at six to the pound sterling, in all tables of exchanges, the exchange would nominally appear to be in favour of England, by the amount of this depreciated value of the Russian currency. The same is the case when the bills are drawn payable in a paper currency, which does not bear the value it represents. During the existence of the bank of England restriction act, bank notes, in which all payments were then made, became considerably depreciated in value, compared with metallic money. The consequence of course was, that a bill upon England, drawn in St Petersburgh, would sell in St Petersburgh for as much less in metallic money, as the paper currency, in which it was payable, was depreciated below the value of metallic money in England.

By these means, the original par, as determined in books, tables, &c. often ceases to be any measure of the actual par of exchange, and only serves to embarrass and confuse the subject. The proper way to come at the true state of the exchange, is to ascertain what weight of gold and silver a bill is really worth in the country where it is drawn, and the weight of gold and silver it is worth where it is payable ; and the comparison of its value will exhibit how the exchange really stands. In determining also the national prices, it is necessary to ascertain whether the currency, if paper, is worth the metallic money it represents, or if gold and silver, whether it contains its original weight in bullion, and if not, to make an allowance accordingly.

*The Effect of an Importation of Money into a Nation being merely to raise the Price of Commodities in that Nation, until the Demand for them is checked, and the Trade brought to a Balance, this might be just as well done by the Price of Commodities being raised in any other Way.*

The Money of a country may altogether consist of a paper currency, though convertible into gold. As banks increase, the issue of their paper they diminish the value of money generally. If a guinea note will answer the purpose of one guinea, two guinea notes will answer the purpose of two; and if there are two guineas in paper and gold in circulation before, by adding another, the value of money would be depreciated, and prices increased above the national standard, just the same by the issue being paper as if it were gold. A reduced foreign demand for commodities would follow, and the balance of payments would be determined against the country, which would continue until prices were again brought down to the national level, by gold being sent out of the country, equal to the increased issues of paper that had taken place. This might continue until almost all the gold was sent out of the nation; but when it had nearly disappeared, the banks would be compelled to make their advances with greater caution. Any demand which their issues might create for gold to be sent abroad, for want of gold they would be unable to supply. While there was plenty of it in the country, they might increase them with confidence. But when the principal part of the gold had left it, any increase of issues, which would elevate prices above the national level, would create a demand for gold in exchange for their notes, which they could not answer without loss, and which would render a contraction of their issues, so as to reduce the prices to the national standard, necessary.

With such a tendency in the banks to increase their issues as far as could be done with safety, a balance of trade, in favour of the country, would not be the means of bringing much money into it. The effect would be to allow the banks the opportunity of increasing their issues without producing a balance the other way. By elevating the standard of the national prices, it would admit and produce an increase of local currency. Prices would rise more rapidly, and the trade would be brought to a balance without any considerable, if any, addition to the precious metals in circulation; or if such addition were made, in the first instance, it would be forced out of the country again, by a subsequent issue of bank paper, which would raise prices still higher. The same tendency in the banks to increase their issues, which would render gold unnecessary to the circulation of the country, would also expel it.

If in this manner the trade might be brought to a balance without the aid of the precious metals, or without their continuing in circulation, it might be much more easily done by the state of the exchanges. We will suppose, for example, that with all nations, the transit of money is so effectually prohibited, that it could not be exported from one country to another.

This being the case, any balance of trade would produce an excessive demand for bills. No transportation of the metals being allowed, the national prices would remain, in both nations trading with each other, unaltered. The respective demands, therefore, of the two countries for the goods of each other, so far as their original cost determined it, would preponderate as before. This preponderance, however, would be checked, and the trade brought to a balance by the price which the bills would attain; and as any reduction in the price of bills, by which this check was produced, would again create the original preponderance of demand, the bills would remain at the price to which they had risen.

Thus if, in the trade between this country and Russia, we suppose the demand for British manufactures to far exceed our demand for Russian produce, instead of bills drawn in St. Petersburgh upon England being worth, upon the average, six silver roubles per pound sterling, they might rise to perhaps twice that, and remain at that price, so that a merchant in St. Petersburgh, importing goods which cost £100 in England, would have to sell them for twelve hundred silver roubles in St. Petersburgh, independent of what would cover his profit and expences, in order to enable him to purchase a bill upon England with which to pay for them. In this transaction there would be nationally no more gain or loss than with an interchange of payments in a metallic money ; for, if the inhabitants of Russia, or other parts of the world, would rather give such prices for British goods, as this state of the exchanges would bring them to, than want them, the national prices in Great Britain, from the balance of payments, produced by such a demand, would necessarily rise to precisely a corresponding level.

While by this state of the exchanges British goods would be double the price in St Petersburgh which they cost in England, Russian produce would be half the price in England which it cost in St Petersburgh. A merchant shipping Russian produce to England, would be enabled to sell the bill he drew for it, for twice the money which the goods cost him. Consequently, if he got half the price in England which they cost in Russia, besides what was necessary to cover his profit and expences, it would pay him.

In the case thus supposed, the national prices would not be altered, while the price of foreign commodities would. Instead of the national prices doubling in this country, the prices of foreign commodities would be reduced one half. Whereas in Russia the consumers would, perhaps, know no perceptible difference, and it would be perfectly immaterial to them whether the high price of British goods arose from the price of bills upon England, or the general state of prices in it.

When the national prices of any particular country are raised by an importation of gold and silver, they will be met by a corresponding reduction in the price of commodities in the countries trading with it. But, as with England, which trades with all the world, its national prices might be raised very high, by the importation of the precious metals, without any perceptible reduction in the prices of all the world. Hence, it is probable, that in the case supposed, there would be no perceptible difference between the prices at which British goods would be sold in Russia, whether they arose from the metallic currency of the rest of the world being poured into Great Britain, or from the state of the exchanges.

If, by any improvement in the monied systems of Europe, paper currencies were altogether substituted for metals, the commerce of the respective countries would be brought to a balance in the manner described. The national prices would remain steady, and the fluctuations of foreign trade would merely affect the prices of foreign commodities.

By the foregoing, it at least clearly appears, that the foreign trade of nations always, upon the average, balances. The exports of every country pay for its imports.

Now, if I were to make a piece of cloth, which took me the labour of a month, and exchanged it with another person for any other commodity, having made the best exchange I could, it would be of no importance to me whether the commodity I purchased took six months, or six days labour, to produce it. Its cost to me would be one month's labour. The same with the produce of land. Were I to exchange a given quantity of the produce of my land for a given quantity of any other produce of land, the cost to me would not consist in the land and labour which the commodities I purchased took to produce them, but of the land and labour which it cost me to produce those commodities which I gave in exchange for them. Did I make these exchanges through the intervention of money, it would be the same as if by direct barter of commodity for commodity.

What is the case with individuals is also the case with nations. The original cost of foreign commodities, in the land and labour which it took to produce them, is no part of their cost to the nation importing and consuming them. Their cost, to it, is the produce of its own land

and labour, with which they have been purchased. Consequently, in consuming foreign commodities, a nation does but indirectly consume its own.

The expenditure of a country is regulated by its income in money, and every individual in this country who consumes one pound's worth of foreign commodities, consumes one pound's worth of British land and labour, which was given in exchange for them.

Hence, in the reasonings of political economy, it is unnecessary, in computing the expenditure and consumption of the income of a nation, to refer to its consumption of foreign produce, which is only an indirect consumption of its own. In speaking, therefore, of the expenditure of British income, we speak of the consumption of British produce, which, though indirectly, is, in reality, as much consumed when we consume foreign commodities as if we had no foreign trade and foreign luxuries, but consumed the produce of our own land and labour at home.

# CHAPTER IV.

### *The Fulcrum of the Argument.*

It is the produce of the land and labour of a country, in which its wealth consists.

Dr Colquhoun sums up the annual income of the nation, expressed in money, at a scale of value corresponding to 70s. 6d. per quarter for wheat, in the following table :—

*Property created in Great Britain and Ireland, in the Year 1812—13.*

| | |
|---|---:|
| Agriculture, in all its branches - | £216,817,624 |
| Mines and minerals, including coals - | 9,000,000 |
| Manufactures, in every branch - | 114,230,000 |
| Inland trade, in all its branches - | 31,500,000 |
| Foreign commerce and shipping - | 46,373,748 |
| Coasting trade - - - | 2,000,000 |
| Fisheries, exclusive of the Colonial Fisheries of Newfoundland - - | 2,100,000 |
| Chartered and private bankers - | 3,500,000 |
| Foreign income remitted - - | 5,000,000 |
| | £430,521,372 |

Without subscribing to the perfect correctness of this estimate, as we cannot see how banking profits are a creation of national property, whatever they may be of individual, we shall, for the sake of argument, assume the statement to be true.

Now, the first thing necessary to the annual production of any commodity is, that there should be an annual consumption and demand for it. Its production is, in fact, a proof of its consumption. Without consumption no demand could exist, and no production would take place. Demand, on the other hand, proceeds from income. Without income, the inclination to consume may be strong enough, but not being accompanied with the power of purchase, the inclination is not sufficient. It is, therefore, from the expenditure of income only, that this demand arises.

This conclusion is, therefore, obvious,—that if to the existence of an annual income of 430 millions, an expenditure of 430 millions be necessary, in order to cause that demand which gives rise to it, and there is no other source of income from whence this consumption can proceed, every shilling of the 430 millions must be annually spent.

# CHAPTER V.

## *National Wealth not increased by National Economy.*

IF the whole income of society must be **spent,** and if the whole annual produce must be consumed, in order to its being produced, no increase of national wealth by mere accumulation can take place. There must, no doubt, at all times, be a stock of commodities in the hands of the merchant, manufacturer, and dealer, in order that consumption may be regularly supplied. This stock, however, must have been accumulated previous to the establishment of that consumption to which it administers. Thus, cotton, which comes from the East and West Indies, has to go through such various manufacturing processes, that with the voyage, and the time occupied in preparing it for use, a second crop, in all probability, will be off the ground before the first reaches the consumer. Hence, of necessity, there must be generally a stock equal to one crop on hand, before consumption can take place. This stock may be sometimes larger, and sometimes less. But it must always be sufficient to supply consumption, and can never, to any very great extent, exceed the amount necessary for that purpose. A merchant or manufacturer very soon discovers when his stock is too large, by his being unable to dispose of it. He consequently ceases either to import, or to manufacture what he cannot sell. It is the same with every other commodity. A stock of it must exist previous to consumption, and though it may vary in amount, can never very far exceed the limits that the object for which it exists prescribes to it. Not only will it not pay to have capital invested in an unsaleable stock, but most commodities are perishable, and if they do not entirely spoil, lose their saleable value by keeping. Thus there can be no great accumulation of national wealth by the saving of stock on its way to consumption. Neither can there be any saving of buildings and machinery. They must also exist previous to the consumption which they aid in supplying. The manufacturing machinery at any one time in use, is generally equal to supply the demand to which it administers, and if no improvement take place in it, no very considerable stock of machinery beyond what is wanted can accumulate. By an improvement in machinery, an additional capital is sometimes rendered necessary. This, however, is not the result of an accumulation of capital, but of ingenuity; and sometimes by simplifying machinery, less capital is rendered necessary, as well as more. When, however, an additional capital, in consequence of any such improvements, is required, it must accumulate before consumption through the medium of the new machinery can be supplied, and when a sufficient quantity of it for that purpose is set agoing, no further increase can take place. The same may be said of almost every other description of what economists call productive capital. Its wear and tear will require to be kept up. This forms part of the annual expenditure of a nation, but it never can materially increase beyond the demand for it.

That this is the case will be sufficiently evident upon an examination of the amount of productive capital which this country is estimated to possess. The following is from Dr Colquhoun's Tables, and includes Great Britain and Ireland :—

Mines and Minerals. ——This valuation, I apprehend, not only includes the capital which they cost, but their value, according to the rent or profits which they yield, which, with the best mines, must far exceed their cost,   -    -    -    -   £75,000,000

Carried forward   -    -   £75,000,000

| | |
|---|---:|
| Brought over - - - - - | £75,000,000 |
| Canals, tolls, and timber, estimated probably upon the same principles, - - - | 50,000,000 |
| Dwelling-houses, including warehouses and manufactories, £400,000,000, one quarter of which we shall suppose to constitute the value of the warehouses and manufactories, | 100,000,000 |
| Manufactured goods in a finished state, deposited in manufactories, warehouses, and shops for sale, - - - - - | 140,000,000 |
| Foreign merchandise, deposited in warehouses, shops, &c. either paid for, or virtually paid by debts owing to this country by foreigners, - - - - - | 40,000,000 |
| British shipping of every description employed in trade, including vessels on the stocks, | 27,000,000 |
| Agricultural property, consisting of grain, hay, straw, cheese, butter, and other productions of farms, including implements of husbandry, - - - - - | 45,000,000 |
| Animals, viz. horses, horned cattle, sheep, hogs, goats, asses, deer, wild animals, and poultry, - - - - - - | 183,000,000 |
| | £660,000,000 |

This table contains all that description of capital, by the accumulation of which, according to the theory of Dr Smith, the wealth of society is, and may be increased ; yet it is little more, by Dr Colquhoun's calculation, than equal to one year and a half's amount of property annually created, though it has been accumulating from the first dawn of civilization. That such capital is necessary and essentially conducive to national wealth, there can be no question. A spade is necessary and essentially conducive to the annual produce of the garden which is dug with it. But, that public wealth can be increased by any parsimonious savings of it, is quite impossible. When you have spades enough, and to spare, more would not be wealth but waste. If you build a mill upon your estate, it may improve its value. If you build another, with only employment for one, you throw away so much money. You do not increase your wealth by it. The same with a nation. A stock of goods, machinery, &c. is necessary, in order to the production and advantageous distribution of wealth, but no merely parsimonious increase of it can be of any service. This country has much more rapidly improved, and increased its stock of this description of wealth, during the last thirty years, than at any former period of our history; yet during the principal part of that time, we have been engaged in expensive wars, which have drained the country of its surplus capital. Little or none was left to accumulate and spread over the land, to irrigate its agriculture and commerce, according to existing theories. No deficiency of capital, however, has been observed: it has always been found where it has been wanted. And from this it may, perhaps, not be incorrect to infer, that where the spirit of improvement and enterprise, (which are the children of freedom and intelligence,) exists, want of capital is seldom experienced. It may, at least, be very safely assumed that it never can accumulate where it is not wanted ; and that national parsimony, to any extent, is neither particularly advantageous nor possible.

# CHAPTER VI.

## *National Wealth composed of Annual Income.*

A FINE house, fine furniture, a good stock of cloaths, and other consumable commodities, are the usual symptoms of wealth; but we should not consider an individual rich who had no other property. We should think him, on the contrary, excessively poor, for the show he exhibited. He would only be rich in proportion to this appearance, if his annual income corresponded with it. A nobleman with a splendid house and no estate, would be an exceedingly poor nobleman. He would, in fact, be only worth what his house would sell for, and purchase him in annual income. If he could not sell it, and purchase annual income with the produce, he would be worth nothing.

What is the case with an individual, is the case also with a nation. Its buildings, furniture, stock in trade, manufactures, shipping, &c. though important instruments and undoubted proofs of wealth, form but the surface of it. It is the annual amount of commodities produced for actual consumption in which the wealth of a nation principally consists. Though stock, manufactories, canals, &c. like a mill upon an estate for grinding its produce into flour, warehouses for storing it, and conveyances for carrying it, are necessary for preparing and distributing its wealth for consumption, yet as it is the corn, and not the mill, warehouses, carts, &c. which constitutes the value of the estate—for without the estate they would be worth nothing,—so is it the annual produce of a nation, which forms its wealth, and not the instruments by which that produce is fitted for consumption.

# CHAPTER VII.

## *Real and Nominal Income of Society.*

THE income of society, as expressed in money, may be divided into two descriptions, the nominal and the real. A person with an estate, which will yield him ten thousand pounds per annum, may have it mortgaged to half its value : his income, however, will still be ten thousand pounds per annum, though the mortgagee may receive one half of the rental for the interest of his mortgage. The two incomes united, in that case, would amount to fifteen thousand pounds per annum, while the income from which they were derived would only be ten thousand pounds. The proprietor might, with the remainder of his income, and the mortgagee with his share of it, employ servants and labourers, purchase commodities which represent labour, materials, and profits of manufacturers and tradesmen, hire teachers, reward players, go journies, &c. and those persons who thus received the money might in their turn do the same. By passing in this manner from hand to hand, it might entirely compose the

incomes of many, and form a part of the incomes of many more; and were the whole added together, would present an enumeration of
income to many times its original amount. The
real income, however, from which the whole
proceeded, would be that which was, in the
first instance, derived by the owner of the
estate from the produce of the soil.

# CHAPTER VIII.

*The Income of Society is consumed.*

In whatever way a person acquires the money he receives, he must do one of three things with it. He must either hoard it, lend it at interest to others, or expend it himself.

If he hoard it, he contracts the amount of currency in circulation, and reduces the prices of commodities below the national standard. All changes of price are produced by an increased or diminished demand for commodities in the market, and the effect of hoarding is in the first instance to reduce the demand for commodities to the extent of the money hoarded. By this means their price is reduced; and by this reduction the foreign demand for them is increased, and the surplus quantity which the money hoarded left without a demand, is carried off. A balance of payments is thus created in favour of the nation, and a quantity of money brought into it equal to that which by hoarding was abstracted from circulation. When the money that has been hoarded is brought into circulation again, precisely the opposite effects are produced. Hoarding money, therefore, does not diminish the ultimate demand for commodities, it only alters the channel of their consumption.

If he lend it to others at interest, they give him interest for it, either to expend it commercially or actually. They employ it either in building houses or ships, or digging mines, &c. from which an annual profit is expected, or in the manufacture of goods, or in the purchase and sale of them, or in some way in which the transit of commodities from their first production to their final consumption is promoted, in all of which commercial or actual consumption is produced; or otherwise they expend it in the actual purchase, consumption, and enjoyment of the necessaries, conveniences, and luxuries of life.

If he expend it himself, it must either be in actual or commercial consumption as above described : so that whether he saves the money, or whether he spends it, consumption is equally produced.

# CHAPTER IX.

## *Capital.*

CAPITAL, in common language, is understood to be money. By political economists it is defined to be not only money but stock, buildings, and machinery. Properly, however, it is neither money nor stock, buildings and machinery.

In speaking of capital, we say that it is invested in stock, buildings, and machinery; but we equally say that it is invested in land. It would be evidently improper to say, of the latter, that capital was land, or land capital— and it is equally so with respect to the former.

Neither is it proper to term money capital. We speak of a miser's money, but not of his capital. It is only capital when it bears interest, or is otherwise profitably employed. Before it can be so designated it must be spent, or lent to others who will spend and consume its value either commercially or actually.

It is the power of acquiring the means of annual consumption which gives value to property, and money is the medium by which this power is conveyed. Hence the value of all property is computed in money. If two persons wish to exchange properties, they each estimate how great a quantity of consumable commodities they will command, that is, how much money they will sell for, and they regulate their bargain accordingly.

The value of money varies both with respect to the commodities it will command, and the interest which is given for it; the former being determined by the quantity of money in circulation, the latter by the demand for it on the part of those who wish to borrow, compared with the supply by those who have it to lend.

If property were subject to no changes of value, from alterations in its own powers of production or means of administering to the enjoyments of mankind, it would be constantly subject to fluctuations in value, as computed in money from the variations in the value of money itself. When money will only command $2\frac{1}{2}$ per cent. interest, an estate is worth twice the sum that it is when money will command five; and when money is depreciated in value, the price of the annual produce of the estate being increased, its total value in money is increased with it, and *vice versa*. Hence the value of money, and of property, the annual value of which is not regulated by the value of money, continually varies. Houses and property created by the expenditure of money, progressively change their value with it.

Many of those who save money have no desire to purchase property; partly because they do not wish to incur the trouble of managing property, the nature of which they probably do not understand, and partly because they think they can get better interest for it than any property that they can purchase will afford. They prefer, therefore, lending their savings at a given rate of interest to those who will engage to repay them in money when it shall be required; and as they, at all times know the value of money in property, by knowing the amount of the obligations which others are under to them, that is, the money which they have out at interest, they know the property they are worth.

On the other hand, men of landed property are seldom willing to sell their estates until they are so much in debt that they cannot avoid it. They will rather pay a rate of interest for money somewhat higher than the income of their estates will leave, compared with their value in money. For the repayment of this money when it is required, and the interest of it in the mean time, they pledge their estates. By this means, though they have virtually disposed of as much of them, as at their value, would be required to discharge the mortgage, yet they still retain them in their own hands, with the power of discharging it at their pleasure, possess the entire management of them, and lose or gain by any alteration which may take place in their value. The lender has no further concern with them than to know that they are a sufficient security for the principal and interest of his loan. Dwelling-houses, buildings of different kinds, mines, and property of a commercial nature, generally possess a greater annual value than the common rate of interest; and the owners of such property, rather than sell it, will often prefer borrowing money when in want of it, as they find it will be more profitable to do so.

The money thus acquired amounts virtually, on the part of the borrower, to a sale of property to the value of the sum borrowed, and the lender of the money, if his security be good, is actual possessor of as much property as it would take, computing its value in money, to satisfy the debt. But it has no reference whatever to the particular nature of the property pledged for its security. Mortgages are merely a precaution to which creditors think it necessary to resort, in order to prevent persons getting into more debt than their property will redeem, or from the state of the laws, which make it difficult to compel a person to surrender his estate for the payment of his debts, if he be not in trade, without he does so voluntarily. If the lender has no particular security, the property of his debtor, to the value of his debt, is still virtually his.

The debt which an individual contracts has reference to his property generally ; and it is not unfrequent in trade to credit individuals to considerable amounts, without a guarantee of any kind ; but it is always upon the presumption that they have property sufficient to meet their engagements. After the money is borrowed, it is spent and disappears, and the produce of it is either totally consumed, and the property of the party, to the value of the debt, is virtually sold to the lender, or an accumulation of stock, buildings, machinery, or some property of value takes place, which is pledged, with the general property of the borrower, for the repayment of the money when it is called for. But whether the money be spent in actual or commercial consumption, is quite immaterial to the lender, if there be only property of one kind or other to repay him. If his security be good, it is the same to him whether the property of his creditor consists of stock, of buildings, or of land.

Money thus lent, is, properly speaking, capital. Capital is to property what a pound sterling is to money. Though there is no such coin as a pound sterling, its value in money is clearly understood. An obligation to pay a pound sterling, is an obligation to pay its amount in British coin. In the same manner there is no such identical property as capital. It is the value of property expressed in money, and a person with capital possesses either directly or indirectly property equal to its value.

Capital, no doubt, often exists without representing any property that is tangible, and yet is still capital. Thus tradesmen often have considerable sums in book debts, due by persons who depend upon their labour, or life incomes alone, for the means of repaying them; yet if these debts are safe and will be repaid, they are as much capital to the tradesman to whom they are owing, as if the amount of them were vested in lands, buildings, or stock, or rested on the most unquestionable securities. In this case, however, the laws give the tradesman a mortgage upon the future labour or incomes of the persons thus credited. His capital becomes vested in the lives of the parties he trusts; the same as capital is vested in slaves, who out of their labour repay the principle and interest of their cost. He has a life interest in the labour or income of his debtors, the same as they may have in estates or other property.

Money lent by banks in their own notes becomes capital on the same principles. It is employed in actual or commercial consumption by those who borrow it, and their personal labour, stock in trade, debts, or property of whatever description, is mortgaged for its repayment, independent of any particular mortgage or sureties which may be given.

Tradesmen, merchants, manufacturers, miners, &c. in estimating their capital, pay no respect to whether it consists of book debts, stock, buildings, machinery, money, or land, if land be necessary to their business. The value of each description of property in money is estimated, the whole is summed up together, and the total is the capital employed.

Nothing, perhaps, has contributed to greater confusion of ideas, than the want of a proper definition of capital. To common observation, it appears to be a mixture of property and credit, which eludes description. It is one thing to-day, and another to-morrow. Its value is better understood than its nature. Upon looking into political economy, however, for an analysis, it is found to be stock, buildings, and machinery. Whereas it is very well known, that many great capitalists have neither stock nor machinery, nor even buildings. " It has been usual," says a political economist of great celebrity, to whom the world is under great obligations, " in speaking of that portion of the national " revenue which goes to the capitalist in re-

" turn for the employment of his capital, to
" call it by the name of the profits of stock.
" But stock is not so appropriate an expression
" in this case as capital. Stock is a general
" term, and may be defined to be all the mate-
" rial possessions of a country, or all its actual
" wealth, whatever may be its destination;
" while capital is that particular portion of
" these possessions, or of this accumulated
" wealth, which is destined to be employed
" with a view to profit. They are often, how-
" ever, used indiscriminately; and, perhaps,
" no great error may arise from it, *but it may*
" *be useful to recollect that all stock is not, pro-*
" *perly speaking, capital, though all capital is*
" *stock.*"

This is the generally received definition of capital by political economists, and I only give it in the language of the author I have quoted, because it is briefly and clearly stated. Nothing, however, can be more erroneous. Stock is the particular, and capital the general term. The stock of a tradesman is the commodities he has for sale. The stock of a farmer is the produce which either is ready, or is preparing for sale. The stock of a manufacturer the same. A stock of cattle must be kept up, in order to consume the herbage of the land on which they are fed; so must a stock of raw materials by the manufacturer, in order to keep his men and machinery employed. In both cases, however, they are a stock preparing for consumption. When we speak of a person's stock simply, we always mean the stock which he has on hand, of the commodities he deals in, or produces for sale. It is also applied to machinery, to implements of husbandry, &c. but, in that case, the particular articles to which it refers, are mentioned. We thus say, his stock of implements of husbandry, his stock of machinery, his stock of carts and horses, &c. We also, no doubt, speak of a person's stock in trade, by which we mean his capital, or the value of his property in trade, but this is an abuse of the term, which political economists have aided to perpetuate.

Stock has reference to the quantity, capital to the value of the commodities. A tradesman's stock of commodities may be large, while the capital, which his stock is worth, is small; whereas if a scarcity of the particular commodity he deals in, were to occur, his capital might be rendered comparatively large, while his stock was small. Thus stock is the term of particular application, while capital is the general term; and so far from their being in the least degree synonymous, they are in direct opposition to each other. There is no manner in which the term capital is more correctly applied than to the capital of a public bank, while there is nothing unreasonable in the supposition, that such capital might be lent out altogether upon the security of land, in which case it could have no reference to stock of any description ; yet by an abuse of language we call the capital of such banks their capital stock, and instead of joint capital, we call them joint stock companies. It might not be improper to speak of the stock of capital possessed by a bank, but in that case stock would be synonymous with quantity.

Capital is not usually applied to land, except it be to express the interest which the mort-gagee may possess in it. That, however, per-haps, principally arises from its not being so fre-quently bought and sold for money, as the pro-perty of tradesmen, and from the value of its annual produce not depending upon the rate of interest. But a person's capital in land, is the value of his land in money, the same as a tradesman's capital in stock is the value of his stock in money. A person may employ a ca-pital by speculating in land, the same as by spe-culating in stock, and some do so. In which case it is evident that the amount of their capi-tals must be determined by the value of their stock in land.

Hence capital is an abstract term. When we speak of a person's capital, we speak of his pro-perty, but it is his property valued or expressed

in money.   Money itself is not capital until it
is converted into property, or exchanged for it,
by loans upon the security of annual income,
or by the purchase of it.

Neither is land, nor stock, buildings and
machinery, capital.   Capital is their value in
money.   It is merely the term by which their
value is expressed ; and when we speak of any
description of property, with respect to the
capital it contains, we say that we have invested so much capital in it.

# CHAPTER X.

*Principles which regulate the Saving of Money.*

As all the income of society is, and must be, annually consumed, all the money which is borrowed, in order to be spent by one person, class, or body of individuals, must be necessarily saved by another.

If every person himself spent the share which he received of the 430 millions of national income, there would be no money to be lent. Those who are enabled to lend money, or purchase the property of others, are those who have first saved it out of their incomes ; and if nobody did save, to borrow would be impossible.

On the other hand, if no one consumed more than his annual income, to lend money, and acquire property by saving it, would be equally impossible. No person would dispose of his property, either by borrowing money upon it, or by selling it, if he did not want the money, which he thus gave up his annual means of subsistence to acquire ; and if he neither expended, nor wished to expend more than his annual income, he could not want it. In this case, no person could acquire property by saving money. He could only hoard the produce of his economy.

In all countries, however, possessing good laws; where every person may do with his property as he thinks proper; and where the fruits of every man's industry and economy are secured to him, there always is a demand for money, more or less, and hoarding is very little practised. As the whole income of society must be spent, it is, therefore, equally clear, that the demand for money on the one hand, and supply of it on the other, must be equal. The amount of the savings by those who do not spend their annual incomes, must be precisely equal to the wants of those whose expenditure exceeds them.

A demand for money is produced by four different causes. By the necessity which exists in an improving country for an increased stock of buildings, machinery, commodities, &c. in order to supply the increased population and consumption which its increased fertility creates. By losses in trade and commerce. By the excess of expenditure of those whose expences exceed their incomes; and by the wants of government.

In the cases just supposed, in which we have stated that no demand for money could exist, we, of course, presume the fertility and population of the country not to be advancing, but stationary. In an improving country, there always is, however, a demand for money, for the purpose of increasing its stock of commodities, &c. by which to supply the consumption of its increasing population. But, comparatively speaking, this demand can never be very considerable. The productive capital, as it is termed, of this country, does not exceed, by Dr Colquhoun's calculation, six hundred and sixty millions: little more, as we have before stated, than a year and a half's income. When we consider the immense time that this stock has been in accumulating, we cannot suppose the annual demand for it to have been very considerable. Had this kingdom been a barren waste six hundred and sixty years ago, and the whole had accumulated since then, it would still only prove a demand for money of one million per annum upon the average—equal to the saving of one pound a year in an income of four hundred and thirty. I apprehend, no individual, whose demand for capital did not increase at a greater rate, would ever imagine that any great effort of saving would be necessary, in order to supply himself. Nor does it seem possible, that with a nation, any very material demand for capital can arise from this cause.

A demand for money is produced by losses in trade. A stock of goods in the hands of the merchant, manufacturer, &c. is necessary, in

order to supply consumption, and this stock
has its natural limits. If, however, a manufacturer produce and sell his goods to a loss, or a
merchant import and sell his commodities for
less than they cost him, he reduces his capital by increasing the consumption of the country, and a demand for the savings of others, to
make up his loss, is produced. If a person sell
his commodities for half what they cost, the
amount of his loss is saved by the purchaser,
whose general consumption is increased in that
proportion, or the saving is lent and consumed
by others. The commodity, however, still
costing the same to produce, requires twice the
money to replace it for which it sold. Hence
a demand arises for the savings of others equal
to this deficiency; which the losing party must
either borrow, sell property to acquire, or otherwise, by reducing his trade, allow other persons
who have saved money equal to his loss to step
in with it, supply his customers, and increase
their trade in proportion as he is compelled to
reduce his. Losses in trade, therefore, which
diminish the price of the commodity to the
consumer, are indirectly an expenditure beyond
income equal to the loss sustained, and a demand for money continually arises from this
source.

In the third place, a demand for money is
produced by the expenditure of those, whose

expences exceed their income, and who are consequently compelled to borrow money, or dispose of their property for money, in order to supply this excess of expenditure; and lastly, by government, who often raise money by loans, and pledge the property and annual income of the nation for the payment of the interest of them.

On the other hand, the supply of money must arise from the inclination to save; and the power to save by those who have the inclination.

By far the greater part of the community have no inclination to save. Those whose incomes are derived from labour, find them in general too small to supply their customary wants; and those whose incomes are derived from property, being secure of the annual receipt of their incomes, and in consequence removed from any anxious cares respecting the future, live in general to the full extent of them. The economists of society principally consist of the mercantile classes, who, being dependant upon trades of precarious profit for their support, learn the inclination of acquiring money from the habit of doing so. It is necessary for every tradesman who means to do well, to save money, in order to provide against a future evil day, which the uncertainty of trade often produces. This necessity, the desire of independence, and the ambition to be rich, which the pursuits of trade usually generate, render this class, in general, economists, and the savings of society are principally made by them.

The amount of savings by this class must, however, altogether depend upon their power to save. When the interest of money, and profits of trade are large, their power of saving is necessarily greater than when the profits of trade, and interest of money are small. When their income is great, they can of course save more than when it is little.

Now, the profits of trade are regulated by the interest of money, and the interest of money by the demand for it.

When the supply of money is greater than the demand, it falls in price ; and rises when it is less. If a person have money, and he cannot get five per cent. interest for it, he must take four ; if not four, three, &c. Any rate of interest, with good security, will be better than hoarding it. On the other hand, if an unusual demand for money arises, the only way to procure it, by those who have the means of doing so, is to give a higher rate for it; and those who are willing to give most will have the preference. Thus the rate of interest fluctuates with the supply and demand, upon the same principle as with other commodities.

The effects are also precisely similar. An increased demand for other commodities produces an increased supply, and a reduced demand diminishes the supply. And with money, when the demand is reduced, the power of production, or of saving it, is also diminished; and when the demand is increased, the power of production or of saving is increased with it. The interest of money and profits of trade, by which the power of saving is determined, rise and fall accordingly.

" As the market rate of interest varies in any country," says Dr Smith, " we may be as-
" sured that the ordinary profits of stock must
" vary with it, must sink as it sinks, and rise
" as it rises."

He also says, " As capitals increase in any
" country, the profits which can be made by
" employing them necessarily diminish. It be-
" comes gradually more and more difficult to
" find within the country a profitable method
" of employing any new capital. There arises,
" in consequence, a competition between diffe-
" rent capitals, the owner of one endeavouring
" to get possession of that employment which
" is occupied by another. But upon most oc-
" casions he can hope to justle that other out
" of his employment by no other means but
" by dealing upon more reasonable terms."

On the other hand, profits are raised with the demand for money, by part of that money being lent for consumption, which would otherwise have gone to replace the stock of the dealer. By this means the consumptive demand is increased, and the prices of commodities raised; while, by the diminished capital in trade, stocks are kept low, and the prices kept up. Much of the capital employed in trade is borrowed of bankers, and others, by persons in trade, at the market rate of interest; and the first effect of any increased demand for money, is to induce these bankers to abstract it from its ordinary channels, in order to lend to those who offer better terms for it.

Thus, with the increase or decrease of the demand for money, do interest and profits of trade rise and fall, by which the power of economizing, in order to supply the demand, is exactly proportioned to it.

The savings of a nation, therefore, diminish the power to save. The incomes of those being reduced, who are the principal economists of the country, their power of economizing is reduced with the excessive supply of money, by which the value of it is diminished.

The Dutch are the most saving people in Europe; and with them the profits of trade, and interest of money, are always at a very low ebb. When the bulk of a nation are economists, the difficulty of making money becomes excessive; and the commercial part of it are ground down to penuriousness by the national parsimony.

Precisely opposite are the effects produced by an increase of national expenditure. The profits of trade are good, and a free stile of living pervades the mercantile classes ; they not only save more money, but they also spend more.

Such an unusual increase of expenditure as to raise the interest of money, rarely, however, perhaps never, happens from the expenditure of individuals. It mostly, if not always, arises from the demands of governments.

The government of this country has, during war, not unfrequently borrowed thirty or forty millions of money, in one year ; whereas during peace, instead of borrowing, it has been usual to discharge some part at least of the debt, which during the war had been contracted. The interest of money, and the profits of trade, have, of course, corresponded with this wide difference in the acts of government. Interest of money has been double at one time what it was at the other; and the profits of trade even more than double. It is not unusual for 3 per cent. consols to be at from 95 to 100 during peace. They have been even at 106, as will be seen by a table in the Appendix ; while during the war, when these great loans were contracting, they have been at or under 50. That is, interest of money on the security of government, is often 3 per cent. in peace, and 6 per cent. in war.

The average profits of trade are affected in even a greater degree. The legal rate of interest in this country, is 5 per cent. ; above which individuals are not allowed to receive. When 3 per cent. stock is, therefore, under 60, and government pays more than the legal rate of interest, individuals cannot give equal terms. The expectation of profit by the future rise in the funds also holds out temptations so great, that the country is almost drained of its capital, in stock, to supply the demands and consumption of government. When this is the case, trade is greatly carried on upon credit, and its profits far exceed that proportion to the interest of money which they regularly preserve when interest is below the legal rate. Most persons who have been in trade within the last dozen years, will be able to vouch for these facts.

Government securities are not now so high as at any previous interval of peace of the same duration ; but this has arisen from a cause which we shall hereafter explain.

At the same time that the power of saving is greater or less, the power of spending in those who have the means and inclination, will be affected in an inverse ratio. When the interest of money rises, the value of land falls. An estate which would be worth forty years purchase with the interest of money at $2\frac{1}{2}$ per cent., would be worth only half that with the interest of money at five, and would only have half the spending in it. For this reason, as the demand for government increased, the power of spending by individuals would be diminished. On the contrary, when there is a superior tendency in a nation to save, either by the economy of its government, or of individuals, temptations to expenditnre are held out by the increased value of landed property. If a person will run through his estate, with money at 5 per cent, when it is comparatively so easily done, he will be much more disposed to do so when there is so much more spending in it, and his ruin is at so increased a distance : or if living to a small extent above his income will not materially affect it, many may be tempted to exceed a little, who would be restrained when the interest of money was high, and land of comparatively small value. With small profits, the employment of a greater capital in trade also becomes necessary, and leaves room for a greater accumulation. When profits are high, credit is very generally given and received, and merchants are often enabled to make money on transactions in which no capital is employed. They will often be able to purchase on credit, and effect sales of the commodity so purchased in sufficient time to enable them to meet the payment with the proceeds of their sales. This credit, which is attended with risk, must be paid for, and must be recovered in the price for which the commodity finally sells. By a general system of credit, which a universal scarcity of money is the means of establishing, a tradesman is thus enabled to conduct his business with less capital than would be otherwise necessary. If he get four or six months credit upon all his goods ; in some trades wherein the sales are quick, and principally for money, they may be almost carried on without any capital; but in all trades less capital is necessary than where payment must be made in money.

When, however, capital becomes plentiful, credit is neither required, nor can be afforded. The profits are so small, that they will not cover the risk attending it ; while, from the superabundance of capital in trade, which cannot be better employed, credit is not required. The tradesman with capital finds it more to his interest, by way of employing it, to pay money for his goods, which he gets cheaper in consequence. He is disposed also to hold larger stocks. By these means he is able to undersell his poorer competitor, and in every respect has the advantage of him. Tradesmen without capital are, therefore, finally superseded by those who have it.

Very little business is done in Holland upon credit. Capitals are required in every trade; and the experience of most persons now in business will enable them to say, that, taking trade in all its branches, there is a greater quantity of capital employed for the value turned over, than there was a few years ago— larger stocks on hand, and less credit given, at least among merchants and traders, with each other.

It is very usual to consider, that when the profits of trade are good, the nation is flourishing ; and it cannot be denied, that to the superior education and intelligence which wealth has disseminated, and the spirit of speculation and improvement to which success in trade has given rise, the advancement of this country to its recent state of commercial and agricultural prosperity must be attributed. But, it is evident, that the profits of trade, which fall upon the price of commodities, must be nothing more than a tax paid by the ultimate consumers of them, and that just in proportion as the tradesman flourishes the consumer suffers. If the whole income of society must be consumed, it is only a different mode of arranging that consumption, and nationally there is no greater prosperity with great profits than with small ones. Capitalists, however, principally reside in towns, and the profits of trade influence every department of business. The newspapers, the organs of public opinion, feel the goodness of the times as well as any other description of traders, and express themselves accordingly. Both feeling and seeing the great difference which a change in the profits of trade produces, they are apt to imagine that the nation is going to ruin when they are small, and that it is prosperous when they are high; because, in the one case they, their friends, and neighbours are making money; and in the other, a general depression exists, and they and their neighbours are losing it, or making less than before.

# CHAPTER XI.

*Corn creates its own Demand.*

In well-populated countries, the earth is made
to produce to its utmost ability, by the best management, which, according to their skill in
agriculture, its inhabitants can apply to the
cultivation of the soil : yet, if we, at each re-
turning harvest, examine the barns, granaries,
and stack-yards throughout the country, we
shall generally find that the produce of the past
year has been consumed. After a year of more
than usual abundance, we may, no doubt, occasionally see here and there wealthy farmers
holding their crops over to another season;
but, by taking an average of two or three
years, we shall find that the annual produce is,
upon the average, annually disposed of.

When the harvest is an average one, this is
more particularly the case. Provisions are then
at an average price. There is no temptation
to hold, unless there is a prospect of the ensuing harvest being particularly bad ; and as this
is happily not very frequent, the farmer generally disposes of one crop before the other is
fit for the market.

In those seasons the prices of provisions are at that level to which the means of expenditure are accommodated. There is sufficient for all who enjoy their accustomed means of paying for it, according to the existing supply and wages of labour; and while there is nothing deficient, there is nothing to spare.

Those countries which regularly export or import corn may be said to afford an objection to this rule. They, however, always import or export a corresponding quantity of commodities representing labour, by which, as we shall hereafter more particularly show, the rule, as it affects the internal production and consumption of a country, is not infringed. But if we take inland countries, where exportation or importation is physically impossible, we shall find this proportion of the consumption to the supply, with respect to the principal articles of food, uniformly preserved.

The provision of nature, by which this parallel is maintained, might, at first sight, appear wonderful. There are thousands and millions of people in every country, many of whom are not restrained by any pecuniary consideration from consuming what they think proper. They eat and drink three or four times a day, without practically, at least, taking any thought whether the crop will last to the end of the year or not; and yet, when an average one, it does last to the end of the year, without any material surplus, at least, and without any deficiency having been experienced.

There are very few families that could previously undertake to determine their consumption for the ensuing year with any such exactness; yet if nature, in any country, were to make a mistake in its calculation of but one day's provision in twelve, that is, of one month in the year, and the country were to run short, the inconvenience that would result may be conceived, when it is considered that the greatest supply of provisions which was ever imported into this country in years of the severest scarcity, never exceeded a month's ordinary consumption of its inhabitants.

With all commodities, however, the supply and demand must, upon the average, be equal. As we have already stated, production is a proof of demand, and would not take place without it. But between food and other commodities there is this difference, that with the former the supply is produced without reference to the demand, and yet the demand is exactly equal to it, while with the latter the supply is regulated by the demand.

With all commodities, except food, great fluctuations in the quantities cultivated or manufactured constantly take place. The supply produced is sometimes much larger, and sometimes much less than is required, and it is from the alteration in prices produced by this fluctuation that they are ultimately accommodated to each other.

Of every article of general consumption there are naturally a great many growers or manufacturers, who have no connexion with each other, and no knowledge of the quantities which each intends to produce. Neither in general have they much knowledge of the consumption; their only mode of knowing the state of either, with any degree of practical certainty, being from the state of the market. When the market is too full, sales cannot be made, and when it is short in quantity, they can. By this criterion the producers regulate themselves. When there is a brisk demand, prices get up, and more land or more labour is turned to the production of the commodity, until the demand is satisfied and the market over-stocked. While this glut continues, that which is grown or made cannot be sold, the prices fall, and the quantity produced is again diminished until it is reduced below the regular demand. The over stock is consequently again taken out of the market, and a brisk demand succeeds as before.

From these fluctuations, it will be obvious that it is the supply which accommodates itself to the demand. But this cannot be the case with corn, or similar effects would be observable. Sometimes without a particularly favourable season, the supply would be too great, and sometimes without a bad season, the supply would be too small. Whereas we find the agriculturist applies his utmost art and labour to the cultivation of the soil, which he renders as productive as he possibly can, and he always finds a demand equal to the supply which he is enabled to produce. It is, therefore, the supply which creates the demand, and not the demand as with other commodities, which creates the supply.

The skill with which the soil may be cultivated in different countries, may not be the same, and one country, without greater natural advantages, may be made to produce infinitely more than another: but this equality of demand with the supply, is the same, whatever the fruitfulness of the soil may arise from.

Any considerable variation from an average crop, is also accompanied by a corresponding alteration in the demand. When the crop is great, the demand is greater; when it is small, the demand is less. This is produced by an alteration in prices, which the alteration in the supply creates. When it is abundant, the prices fall; when deficient, they rise; and in every fully populated country, a corresponding variation in consumption takes place, with the

variations of price. High prices compel its population to reduce their consumption, and low
prices enable them to increase it. Unless,
therefore, it is the pleasure of the growers or
speculators to hold their stocks over to another
season, it can always be consumed within the
year. This the experience of every farmer and
corn dealer will enable him to substantiate.
Whatever theories he may entertain upon the
subject, or however he may account for it, he
will be enabled to state, that there never was
a year in which he could not have sold at the
market price; or that he could, from his own
observation, perceive any want of consumption,
however he may have lamented the lowness of
price.

That the consumption is always equal to the
supply, even when the demand for labour appears to be considerably reduced, is evident
from last year's experience. The necessities of
the farmers, and the little prospect of advantage by holding, together with the prospect of
an early and abundant harvest, could not but
have the effect of inducing them to bring their
corn to market; and this it appears they have
done. Messrs Cropper, Benson, and Co. of
Liverpool, who possess the only information
that can be relied upon respecting the crops,
and who may be considered perfect authority
upon the subject, in a most important circular

which they have lately issued on the state of the cotton trade, have stated with respect to corn, as follows :—

" Last year's crop of corn is generally esti-
" mated not to have supplied the country more
" than eleven months ; and though the present
" crop is less than the preceding, and the con-
" sumption going on at a greater rate than
" ever known, still the price is lower than ever
" remembered. If the present unmercantile
" feeling of holding no stocks is to continue to
" prevail, we may be quite run out of all these
" important articles before people are general-
" ly aware."

The reason, no doubt, for the consumption going on so rapidly, is, that the farmers cannot hold, and are forcing their corn into the market, and the consumption, on the principles stated, keeps pace with the supply. I do not mean from this to infer, that the present general low state of prices arises from abundance of supply : the above extract shews that not to be the case, but merely that there is always a demand equal to the supply at the existing prices, even though some may for want of employment be starving ; and if the prices are sufficiently reduced, the supply will be taken of.

Thus while in average seasons the demand and supply are equal, the fluctuations in demand which abundance or scarcity produces, by which to accommodate it to the supply, support the general principle that it is the supply which creates the demand.

This reasoning only applies of course to well populated countries. In new countries, such as the back settlements of America, where the population is thin, the production of corn is checked by the want of demand. But even then the demand steadily increases. There is no fluctuation similar to what is observed in other commodities, and when the supply becomes stationary, the average demand will become so too.

The agricultural committee of 1821, have laid down a principle in their report to which the above is in direct opposition, and proceeding from such authority, some notice of it becomes necessary. The report says,—

" In the article of corn, however, there is
" one consideration to be constantly borne in
" mind, most material to enable the house and
" the country to arrive at a sound and safe
" conclusion on this important subject, name-
" ly, that the price of corn fluctuates more
" than that of any other commodity of exten-
" sive consumption, in proportion to any ex-
" cess or deficiency in the supply.

" The cause which produces this greater
" susceptibility in the corn market, cannot be
" better explained by your committee, than in

" the following extract from the answers of
" Mr Tooke, one of the witnesses who was
" particularly examined on this point. Why
" should a different principle apply to corn
" than to any other general production? Be-
" cause a fall in the price of any other commo-
" dity not of general necessity, brings the ar-
" ticle within the reach of a greater number of
" individuals; whereas in the case of corn the
" average quantity is sufficient for the supply
" of every individual; all beyond that is an
" absolute depression of the market, for a great
" length of time, and a succession of either
" two or three abundant seasons, must evident-
" ly produce an enormously inconvenient ac-
" cumulation. Is there not a greater consump-
" tion of corn when it is dear than when it is
" cheap, as to quantity? There may be, and
" possibly must be a greater consumption; but
" it is very evident, that if the population was
" adequately fed, the increased consumption
" from abundance, can amount to little more
" than waste; and this would be in a very
" small proportion to the whole excess of a
" good harvest or two. The whole population
" of this country and others do not subsist up-
" on wheat, therefore when wheat becomes
" cheap, those who were formerly fed upon
" other corn, may take to feeding upon wheat:
" my remark was general as applying to corn.

" There is no doubt that if there is one de-
" scription of corn applicable to human food,
" which is abundant, and another that is defi-
" cient, then the principle does not apply;
" my principle applies to corn generally as ap-
" plicable to human food. It may be observ-
" ed, that abundant seasons generally extend
" to the leading articles of consumption, and
" that it seldom happens in what are common-
" ly called good years, there is a complete fail-
" ure in any one great article."

" In the substance of this reasoning your
" committee entirely concur; and it appears
" to them, that it cannot be called in question
" without denying either that corn is an arti-
" cle of general necessity and universal con-
" sumption amongst the population of this
" country, or that the demand is materially
" varied by the amount of the supply. This
" latter proposition, except within very narrow
" limits, altogether disproportioned to the fluc-
" tuations in production, is not warranted by
" experience. The general truth of the ob-
" servation remains, therefore, unaltered by
" any small degree of waste on the one side,
" or of economy on the other; neither of
" which are sufficient to counteract the effect
" which opinion and speculation must have
" upon price, when it is felt how little demand

" is increased by redundancy, or checked by
" scantiness of supply."

The first principle thus laid down is quite
erroneous. Precisely the reverse is the truth.
" Why should a different principle apply to
" corn," says the report, " than to any other
" general production? Because a fall in
" the price of any other commodity, not of
" general necessity, brings the article within
" the reach of a greater number of indivi-
" duals."

Now the fact is, that there is no such difference in the supply of other commodities, or the
fluctuations would be greater. Our merely acquired habits of consumption do not so quickly
change. The demand for commodities gene-
rated by habit is pretty uniform, and the cost
of their production is known. When, therefore, the prices fall below it, it is common
sense that those will hold who can, it being
certain that a diminished supply must follow,
since the prices will not pay for the production. If an increased quantity of some articles,
which must be sold, as is the case with corn,
were thrown into the market, they would sell
for hardly any thing.

" Whereas in the case of corn," it is further
stated " the average quantity is sufficient for
" the supply of every individual."

Now this means nothing, if it does not mean

that in average seasons every labourer has employment, and wages sufficient to purchase food that will fully supply the wants of himself and every individual of his family. As this, however, as much depends upon the supply of labour as of corn, it cannot go thus far, and therefore must go for nothing.

" All beyond that," the report goes on to state, " is an absolute depression of the mar-
" ket for a great length of time, and a succes-
" sion of even two or three abundant seasons
" must evidently produce an enormously in-
" convenient accumulation."

On this principle, therefore, whether the existing low prices arose from excessive supply might have been at once determined, by ascertaining the fact of whether or not there was an enormously inconvenient accumulation. This, however, the committee neglected to do, or, it is probable, they would have discovered the error into which they and Mr Tooke had fallen.

It next says, " Is there not a greater con-
" sumption of corn when it is cheap, than when
" it is dear, as to quantity? There may be,
" and possibly must be a greater consumption
" of corn when it is cheap, than when it is
" dear, but it is very evident that if the popu-
" lation was before adequately fed, the increas-
" ed consumption from abundance, can a-

" mount to little more than waste ; and this
" would be in a very small proportion to the
" whole excess of a good harvest or two."

This last clause widens the principle of inconvenient accumulation, by laying it down as impossible, that the excess of a good harvest or two, could be consumed. If Mr Tooke, and the committee, would pardon an attempt to smile at their expence, we have fairly a right to assume, that they never rise from table, until they are so satisfied that they can seldom take another mouthful themselves, and being, as they conceive, adequately fed, innocently imagine that the rest of the population have as little room left in their stomachs for more, as they have.

Whether it might be waste or not, we shall not pretend to say. But this I think we may venture to state, that whatever may be the case with the committee, the labouring classes, including their families, can consume half as much more, if not twice as much, as they have the means of doing in average seasons, with the present redundancy of our population. And that in populous countries, there never was a harvest so abundant, that it was not very easily consumed, without producing either surfeit or apoplexy.

In the substance of Mr Tooke's reasoning, the committee, it will be seen, entirely concurred, denying that the proposition, that the demand is materially varied by the amount of the supply, except within narrow limits, altogether disproportioned to the fluctuations in supply, is warranted by experience.

What experience is here referred to, I am unable to discover. It is from our every-day experience, that we are compelled to draw the opposite conclusion.

My object in making these observations is to eradicate an erroneous opinion which has the weight of authority with it ; not any wish generally to find fault with the report, which altogether is evidently far the most sensible and able document which has appeared upon the subject.

From the foregoing, it will at least appear, that it is not the demand for food which creates and regulates the supply as with other commodities, but that it is the supply which creates and regulates the demand. In every country the supply has created an average demand equal to itself, and when any temporary variation takes place in consequence of superabundant or deficient crops, consumption is increased or diminished in equal proportion, by a rise or fall in prices.

# CHAPTER XII.

## *Labour.*

### *Corn can only create its own Demand by furnishing Mouths to consume it.*

Mʀ Malthus, in his admirable essay on the principles of population, has shewn, that it always keeps pace with the means of subsistence. When labour is scarce, wages high, and families easily maintained, population increases; and when population is too great, and labour too plentiful, wages fall below what is necessary to support a family, and population decreases.

These principles are perfectly natural; but the genius of Mr Malthus has rendered them obvious. Without this, indeed, the right application of principles can seldom be either seen or safely adopted. Men are animals, and propagate their species in the same manner as other animals. Were all to marry at the age of puberty, each couple would, on the average, it has been calculated, produce not less than eight or ten children. If food and cloathing

were as plentiful, and acquired with the same
ease at that age by men, as by other animals, it
is probable that we should act like other animals
in that respect. The feeling or sentiment of
love is, perhaps as strong, if not stronger, at
sixteen or seventeen, than at any other period ; and if, at that age, persons could provide for themselves and families, plenty of
food, shelter, and cloathing, without care or
foresight, there can be little doubt but they
would marry, and multiply as other animals do,
under the same circumstances. At this rate,
population would necessarily increase four or
five fold, every twenty or thirty years.

Men, however, do not marry at this age ;
and for this very obvious reason,—they could
not provide for themselves and families if they
did. Though they are animals, they are en-
dowed with reason, which has rendered this
evident. In an advanced state of society, to
provide for a family requires in general all the
forecast and exertion of a mind and body at
full maturity.

In no state of society, however, could men
marry so early as at the age mentioned. If the
means of human subsistence were ever so plentiful, it is never acquired, as by other animals,
without labour. Both labour, and the exercise of
knowledge and experience in its application, are
necessary to the production of the necessaries of

life ; for which, the strength, neither bodily nor mental, at the ages of sixteen or seventeen, is sufficiently matured. As it is, population, under favourable circumstances, will double itself in twenty-five years, as has been proved in America, if not even in much less time.

When population has arrived at that point beyond which it can advance no further,—when the world, or any particular nation, has as many people as it can produce food to support, more children cannot be reared, than are necessary to supply the waste of life among its existing inhabitants. Instead of eight or ten to each couple, which mankind are capable of producing, there cannot be more than two brought to maturity, upon the average of the whole community. This renders a prudent restraint with respect to marriage absolutely necessary.

Mr Malthus has shewn, that when this prudence is departed from, the children which are brought into the world, perish for want of proper nourishment. In many countries, where such restraint is not practised, disease, pestilence, and famine are the periodical consequences ; and in all countries, its neglect is attended with the most baneful effects.

Having, on the other hand, shewn the beneficial results of a prudent restraint with respect to marriage, he recommends the practice of it ; and condemns our present poor laws, the effects of which are to create the evils which they are intended to cure.

As the law now stands, if a man cannot provide for his family, the parish must. This removes the fear of starving, the only check to early marriages which exists. The consequences of this are, that more children are brought into the world than can be supported—a great part of the lower classes is reduced to a state of pauperism—and the parishes are at a great annual expence in dealing out a scanty and insufficient support to those wretched beings, who are rendered so, by the miserable and mistaken system of laws, under which the charity they receive is granted.

" Poverty," Dr Smith states, " though it " no doubt discourages, does not always pre- " vent marriage. It seems even to be favour- " able to generation. A half-starved High- " land woman frequently bears more than 20 " children, while a pampered fine lady is often " incapable of bearing any, and is generally " exhausted by two or three. Barrenness, so " frequent among women of fashion, is very " rare among those of inferior station. Lux- " ury in the fair sex, while it inflames perhaps " the passion for enjoyment, seems always to " weaken, and frequently to destroy altogether " the powers of generation.

" But poverty, though it does not prevent

" the generation, is extremely unfavourable to
" the rearing of children. The tender plant
" is produced, but in so cold a soil, and so se-
" vere a climate, that it soon withers and dies.
" It is not uncommon, I have been frequently
" told, in the highlands of Scotland, for a mo-
" ther who has borne 20 children, not to have
" two alive. Several officers of great experi-
" ence have assured me, that so far from re-
" cruiting their regiment, they have never
" been able to supply it with drummers and
" fifers from the soldiers' children that were
" born in it. A great number of finer chil-
" dren, however, is seldom seen any where
" than about a barrack of soldiers. Very few
" of them, it seems, arrive at the age of 13 or
" 14. In some places, one half of the chil-
" dren born die before they are four years of
" age ; in many places before they are seven ;
" and in almost all places before they are 9 or
" 10. This great mortality, however, will
" everywhere be found chiefly among the
" children of the common people, who cannot
" afford to tend them with the same care as
" those of better station. Though their mar-
" riages are generally more fruitful than those
" of people of fashion, a smaller proportion
" of their children arrive at maturity. In
" foundling hospitals, and among the children
" brought up by parish charities, the mortality

" is still greater than among those of the com-
" mon people.

" Every species of animals naturally multi-
" plies in proportion to the means of their sub-
" sistence, and no species can ever multiply
" beyond it. But in civilized society, it is
" only among the inferior ranks of people that
" the scantiness of subsistence can set limits to
" the further multiplication of the human spe-
" cies; and it can do so in no other way than
" by destroying a great part of the children
" which their fruitful marriages produce."

When Dr Smith made this last remark, Mr
Malthus had not written. By thus proving
that improvident marriages are, in fact, nothing
less than premeditated infanticide, such consequences ought to induce mankind to think,
that prudence with respect to marriage, is as
necessary as with any other act of their lives;
and that it is even in the highest degree criminal to bring children into the world, for any
personal gratification whatever, with the chance
of starving them to death. The poor laws, as
they now stand, in as much as they promote
these dreadful effects, are little better than legal enactments for the encouragement of misery
and child murder.

In recommending restraint with respect to
marriage, Mr Malthus only recommends that
to be done a little longer from prudence, which

almost every one does more or less from necessity. It is not considered any hardship to exercise restraint in this respect, when a departure
from it would not only be considered want of
prudence but want of sanity. This restraint is
exercised for 6 or 7 years, or longer, perhaps,
upon the average, by every man, without its
being thought any thing more than natural. If
mankind would voluntarily add 6 or 7 years
more to it, they would probably remove a great
part of that misery produced by abject poverty
at present in the world. This effect the laws
ought surely rather to encourage than destroy.

It is at least obvious, that there is a sufficient tendency in mankind, to increase up to
the means of subsistence. This means, with
the mass of mankind, consists of the wages of
labour. " The liberal reward of labour" says
Smith, " by enabling them to provide better
" for their children, and consequently to bring
" up a greater number, naturally tends to
" widen and extend those limits," that is, the
limits to which population is confined.

Now, it is the scarcity of labour which increases the wages of it, the same as the price
of other commodities are enhanced by a diminished supply, or improved demand for them.
It is, likewise, the over supply by which its
wages are reduced. When, therefore, labour
is in demand, an additional supply is acquired,

in the only way in which an additional supply of men, or any other animals, can be obtained— by more being produced and reared, from the encouragement and support which the increased demand for labour gives. When, on the other hand, there is more labour than demand for it, the supply is diminished in the only way in which the supply of men can be diminished, by fewer being born, or brought to maturity; as well as from the ranks of mankind being thinned by the diseases incident to poverty. The supply of labour is therefore governed by the demand, upon the same principles as every other commodity except food; the supply of which, as it is our object to shew, creates the demand. In the present case, they cannot both be the cause, or both the effect.

" It deserves to be remarked," says Dr Smith, " that it necessarily does this," that is, the liberal reward of labour, enables the labourers to provide better for their children, and bring up a greater number, " as nearly as possible in " the proportion which the demand for labour " requires. If this demand is continually in- " creasing, the reward of labour must necessari- " ly encourage in such a manner the marriages " and multiplication of labourers, as may en- " able them to supply that continually increas- " ing demand by a continually increasing po- " pulation. If the reward should at any time

" be less than what was requisite for this pur-
" pose, the deficiency of hands would soon
" raise it; and if it should at any time be
" more, their excessive multiplication would
" soon restore it to this necessary rate. The
" market would be so much understocked with
" labour in the one case, and so much over-
" stocked in the other, as would soon force
" back its price to that proper rate which the
" circumstances of society required. It is in
" this manner that the demand for men, like
" that of any other commodity, necessarily re-
" gulates the production of men; quickens it
" when it goes on too slowly, and stops it when
" it advances too fast."

This of course does not refer to the money
price, but to the wages of labour in the necessaries of life. " The power of the labourer,"
says Mr Ricardo, " to support himself, and
" the family which may be necessary to keep
" up the number of labourers, does not depend
" upon the quantity of money which he may
" receive for wages; but on the quantity of
" food, necessaries, and conveniences, become
" essential to him from habit, which that mo-
" ney will purchase."

Consequently, a reduction in the price of
provisions, or of the necessaries and conveniences essential to him from habit, is as much

an increase of the wages of a labourer as the increase of his wages in money.

Any increase in the money price of labour, which is accompanied with a corresponding increase in the monied price of provisions, makes no alteration in the real recompence of labour ; nor does any reduction in the price of provisions, which is accompanied by an equal reduction in the wages of labour, in the least improve the situation of the working classes. It is only when the money price of labour rises, and the necessaries of life remain the same, or do not increase in the same proportion ; or when the necessaries of life are reduced, and wages either remain as before, or do not fall in a corresponding degree, that the wages of the labourer are improved. But they are just as much improved by the necessaries of life falling, and wages remaining the same, as by wages rising, while the necessaries of life continue unaltered. These effects, however, are produced by very different causes ; the one is the result of a diminished supply of labour ; the other of an increased demand for it.

Mr Malthus has shewn, that when the ranks of mankind are thinned by war, pestilence, or famine, it is followed by a rise in the price of labour. This must necessarily be the case. These causes, though they may reduce the population, do not decrease the quantity of money

in a country ; and the money price of commodities depends upon the quantity of it in circulation. Neither do they, except in extreme
cases, reduce the demand for provisions. They
only increase the consumption of the existing
inhabitants. The money in circulation, therefore, being the same, a greater quantity of it
is applied to the purchase of a smaller quantity
of labour ; and this enables the labourer to purchase a larger supply of the necessaries of
life. Thus the incomes of the proprietors of
the soil continue to be the same in money, but
become less in the produce of labour. The
first and immediate effect of a diminished supply of labour, therefore, is to increase the
price of it.

On the other hand, an increased demand for
labour is produced by an increased supply of
the means of subsistence. If the necessaries
of life, produced in any country, were to be
doubled,—if the soil was rendered twice as
productive as before, all experience points out
to us, that in time the population would double
itself also. Now this is always done through
the medium of a demand for labour, and it follows that such an increase of the produce of the
soil would produce this demand.

It would produce it, however, not by an increased demand for the quantity of labour.
The income from the soil would command no

more labour than before. But it would increase the recompence of labour in the necessaries of life, and thereby increase the supply; and as the supply increased, the power of commanding it by means of the income from the soil, would increase in proportion. Though the money in the country would not command more labour than before, the price of provisions would be reduced one half at least, if not more, by which the real recompence of labour would be increased in nearly, though not quite the same proportion.

Part of the necessaries required by every person, consists in the produce of labour, capital, &c. not immediately dependant upon the price of provisions. The wages of labour, therefore, must not only be equal to the purchase of provisions, but of other articles, formed of materials which every individual consumes. That part of those commodities, the value of which was determined by labour and profits, would continue at the same price as before. The recompence of labour would only be increased in proportion to the reduced price of provisions and commodities the produce of the soil.

As the supply of labour increased, the monied price of it would fall. By this means the monied income from the soil would command a larger quantity. In all cases, as we have shewn, the whole income of society is spent; and it will command labour, not in proportion to the supply of provisions, but in proportion to the price of labour; and this price is regulated by the supply. If the produce of the soil was doubled, and the quantity of labour in the first instance was the same, as it commanded all there was before, it could not command more by this increase; but there would be an increased natural demand for labour, the real wages of it would rise, and this would immediately have the effect of promoting an increase of supply.

Although in the event of a war, pestilence, or famine thinning the ranks of mankind, the first effect would be an increase in the monied price of labour, this effect would be only temporary. The causes which reduce the supply, and increase the demand for labour, in any particular nation, do not operate in the same manner with the other nations that trade with it. It is of no consequence to them what a change in the price of labour arises from. If the wages of labour are increased, the price of commodities will rise with it, and their demand will be diminished in proportion. The balance of trade will be determined against the country, and money will be abstracted from it, until the price of commodities fall so as to restore the balance of trade to its equilibrium. This reduced demand for commodities would reduce, in the first instance, the demand for labour; and this again would reduce the demand for provisions. The price of labour and of provisions would consequently both fall, but they would fall parallel with each other, and the real wages of labour, increased by the diminished supply of it, would remain the same. The same quantity of labour would still command the increased quantity of the necessaries of life, until an increase of population took place. As this, however, occurred, the money price of labour would fall, which would reduce the price of commodities, increase the foreign demand for them, produce an influx of money into the country, and gradually restore, with the increased supply of labour, the price of both in money to what they were previous to the loss of population which had been sustained.

An increased demand for labour by an increased supply of provisions would, on the other hand, have no immediate effect upon foreign trade. The price of labour, and the price of commodities, the produce of labour, would remain as before. The foreign demand for commodities, by which the national prices and money in circulation are determined, would not be altered. As, however, the supply of labour increased, and the wages of it and the price of commodities fell, the balance of trade would be determined in favour of the country, and an increased supply of money would be brought into it. This would continue until population had increased to its natural standard, when in the case supposed the monied income from the soil would be doubled, and its real income in the necessaries and luxuries of life would be doubled also.

Thus corn creates its own demand. Population is necessary to wealth. No country can be rich until it is populous. When population is thin, as in the back settlements of America, the land is in reality not worth any thing. The present price which it bears is a speculative one, in anticipation of an increase of inhabitants. On the contrary, countries which are thickly populated are always rich.

The advantage of increased fertility, however, is always immediately felt. Population keeps so close upon the means of subsistence, that an increased demand for labour is very soon supplied.

But individuals would, always immediately gain by any improvement which they might make in the fertility of their estates, even were this not the case; unless all improved alike, which never happens. Suppose two persons are each in the habit of bringing a bushel of wheat to market, and selling it for one pound per bushel. If one of them is enabled to double his quantity, and the three bushels

sell only for the same money that the two did
before, on the aggregate they are not richer,
but he who has the two bushels gains 6s. 8d.
out of his neighbour's income.   The wheat
sells for 13s. 4d. per bushel, and the one is 6s.
8d. richer, and the other 6s. 8d. poorer by the
increased supply.   The condition of the consumer is, however, improved fifty per cent. in
the quantity of provisions which his money will
command.

The present agricultural distress has been attributed to over production, while, at the same
time, in part of its progress at least, it has been
accompanied by a diminished demand for labour.   This circumstance alone proves it could
not have proceeded from that cause.   Although
the increased foreign demand for commodities
has of late partly relieved the labouring classes
from the depression under which they in the
first instance suffered, yet still a reduced demand for labour is the subject of complaint.
A general distress, in fact, such as the present,
from over production, could never happen.   In
the case just supposed, where one party loses,
another gains.   But now there is a universal
loss.   It began, not by increasing the comforts
of the poor, but by starving them in the midst
of plenty, and ends in the ruin of the agriculturists, with a consumption greater than the
annual supply.   That such are not the effects
of over production, may be very safely assumed.

# CHAPTER XIII.

*The Soil is the original Source of Wealth.*

If we admit the conclusions at which we attempted to arrive in the last two chapters, they will go far to establish the proposition which forms the title of this.

Experience of itself, however, establishes it. Where was there ever a rich country with a barren soil ? Gold is valuable, but only in fertile districts, where it will exchange for labour, or commodities more useful. It is worth nothing in a desolate country.

Labour and art are necessary to wealth ; and gold, the produce of labour and art, in general forms part of it. But it possesses no inherent value. Its value is entirely an exchangeable one ; an alteration of fashion or opinion might reduce it below that of iron.

The produce of the soil, on the contrary, possesses an inherent value—a value derived from itself. It produces men, and men produce gold. It creates its own demand, which gold does not. Gold, no doubt, possesses intrinsic value. As a commodity, it is actually worth the value it represents; which is not the case with Bank paper, though it answers the same purpose, and is, where it circulates, as valuable to those who possess it. But the value of gold is not self derived. It is an exchangeable value, and therefore, dependant upon a demand, the result, not of necessity, but of fashion and convenience. It will, perhaps, not be an inappropriate distinction to say, that gold possesses an intrinsic, but not an inherent value; whereas the produce of the soil possesses both. If the soil was a hundred times more productive, it would be a hundred times more valuable to the proprietors; it would support a hundred times the population, and command a hundred times the labour, and commodities, the produce of labour, which it did before. If gold mines were a hundred times more productive, gold would possess a hundred times less value in exchange; and, as it is not probable that the demand would increase in proportion, the mines would be probably much less profitable to the proprietors than they are at present.

Wealth may be said to resolve itself into the produce of the soil, labour, and commodities the produce of both.

Horses, dogs, and animals of every description, which contribute to the luxuries, and form part of the wealth of society, receive their sustenance exclusively from, and are in fact the produce of the soil. All persons who maintain them, must either possess land, or acquire sufficient of its produce for that purpose.

On the same principle, labour is also the produce of the soil, which furnishes the necessaries of life for its support. The necessaries of life consist not only of food, but of cloathing, and other articles which are composed of materials, or pre-existing materials and labour. Now, materials are the produce of the soil, and pre-existing materials are the produce of labour, which is derived from the soil, so that ultimately the wages of labour entirely resolve themselves into the produce of the soil. If you purchase the entire labour of one man, you must pay him in the produce of the soil, or in that which will command it, sufficient perhaps for the support of two. One half he consumes himself, and with the other half purchases such other necessaries, the produce of the labour of others, as he requires. The last half, though distributed in the purchase, in more or less minute proportions, of the labour of probably a hundred others, united, will perhaps, amount only to the labour of one ; and for the sake of illustration, we may suppose he employs only one individual. One man, therefore, by his labour, may acquire, as we have stated, possession of the produce of the soil, material, and victual, equal to the support of two, which he divides with another, who, by his labour, manufactures the cloathing, and furnishes the other necessaries required by both.

Besides labour, the cost of all commodities is more or less composed of profits of capital, taxes, &c. and with pre-existing materials, not only of profits of capital and taxes, but profits which are termed rents. The value, however, which they thus acquire, may be considered artificial, and only a mode, as we shall endeavour to explain in the next chapter, by which the original income derived from the soil is distributed amongst the class of persons who receive these profits, and paid to government, by whom the taxes are levied.

# CHAPTER XIV.

*Cost of Commodities in Profits of Capital.*

A GREAT part of the value of all manufactured commodities, consists in the profits of capital, employed in manufacturing, and transferring them from the original producer, into the hands of those who finally consume them. Though this cost, for the sake of distinction, may be called artificial; yet, by this employment of capital, the powers of labour are magnified, the facilities of transportation increased, and the price of such commodities reduced in a very extraordinary degree. Capitalists in consequence, however, acquire a very considerable share in the income derived from the soil. We shall take the article of corn for example. A capital is employed in its production by the farmer; by the individual attention of whom, and the skilful application of which, the soil is rendered much more productive than it would otherwise have been. His average profits we shall state at 10 per cent. upon his capital. He sells his corn, we shall say, direct to the miller, whose profit, for the capital he has em-

ployed in his mill and trade, we shall state at
7½ per cent. Next it is sold to the baker, who
charges, say, 10 per cent. From him it comes
into the hands of the manufacturing labourer,
and is consumed, and the value of his labour is
added to the material which he is employed in
manufacturing. By this operation it preserves
the same value, but changes its nature, and is
now represented by labour, added to some material which it is employed in manufacturing,
the value of which is increased by the labour
added to it. For the machinery and capital
employed in the various processes of manufacturing the commodity, of which the corn in
the shape of labour, now forms a part, we shall
say 25 per cent. The profit of the wholesale
dealer we shall state at 7½ per cent. ; of the retailer at 15 per cent. ; and it will stand thus :—

|  | £. | s. | D. |
|---|---|---|---|
| Capital    -    -    -    -    - | 100 | 0 | 0 |
| Farmer's profit,  10 per cent.    - | 10 | 0 | 0 |
|  | 110 | 0 | 0 |
| Miller's 7½ per cent.    -    - | 8 | 5 | 0 |
|  | 118 | 5 | 0 |
| Baker's 10 per cent. -    -    - | 11 | 16 | 6 |
|  | 130 | 1 | 6 |
| Manufacturer's 25 per cent.    - | 32 | 10 | 4 |
| Carried forward,    - | 162 | 11 | 10 |

|                               |   | £. | s. | D. |
|-------------------------------|---|----|----|----|
| Brought over,                 | - | 162 | 11 | 10 |
| Wholesale dealer 7½ per cent. | - | 12 | 3 | 10 |
|                               |   | 174 | 15 | 8 |
| Retailer 15 per cent. - - -   |   | 26 | 4 | 3 |
|                               |   | £200 | 19 | 11 |

By processes similar to this, some longer and
some shorter, all commodities come into the
hands of the original proprietors, or those who
in some way acquire a share of the income derived from the soil, surcharged with the profits
of capital employed in carrying them through
the different channels of trade, often times fully
equal to the value of the materials and labour
which the commodities contain, and when profits are high, sometimes far exceeding it.

In this country most commodities, in the
process of their manufacture, are subject to
taxation, which enhances their price, by increasing their cost in the same manner. To
the consumer, therefore, there is no difference
between taxes and the profits of trade. The
profits of trade are just as much a tax upon
them, as the imposts of government. They
equally enhance the cost of the commodity,
and are equally paid by the purchasers of it.

The great amount of government imposts in
this country, levied by taxing consumable com-

modities, sufficiently proves that they ultimately fall upon the only source of income which could bear them, the soil. This, in fact, as a general principle, is hardly disputed.

Those whose incomes are derived from trade, therefore, derive them from the soil also. In order to shew more clearly the manner in which this is done, we will suppose a case by way of example. We will imagine the soil to be represented by an income of £2000, the manufacturing labourers to be represented by 100 men, and the capitalists by ten, each of whom has ten of the hundred men under him. That the necessaries of life, independent of food, consist of ten different articles, the produce of labour alone, one of which each of these capitalists manufactures. We shall suppose one quarter of the income from the soil to be spent in victualling the families of the proprietors, supporting their establishments of horses, &c. or in that part of the hire of personal labour or services, which is consumed in provisions, and immediately returned to the proprietor in a demand for them ; and the other £1,500 to be spent either by the proprietors themselves, or by those who receive their wages, or by such as in some way come into possession of a share of this income, in consumption of those articles which these manufacturers produce. We shall suppose that £1000 represents the pro-

visions necessary for the support of the 100 labourers, and the profits of the capitalists to be
at least 100 per cent. That is, that their profits, or the artificial value of the commodities
manufactured to be equal, or more than equal,
to their value in the labour bestowed upon
them.

In addition to this, we shall suppose that one
third of these labourers were employed in administering to the wants of the other two-
thirds ; or in other words, that they consumed
one-third of the produce of their own labour
themselves. Each man would therefore receive
for his wages, besides a sum equal to the purchase of provisions for himself and family, a
sum sufficient to purchase that share in the ten
different commodities manufactured, which he
required. As this share would be charged to
him with the profits of capital upon it, we shall
suppose that it would take as much money to
purchase it as to buy provisions. Hence his
wages must be twice the sum his provisions
cost him. This would make the wages of the
whole in money £2000. Now we shall suppose that the commodities manufactured sold
in the gross for £4,500, with the profits of
capital upon them. The £1,500 income from
the soil applied to their purchase, would therefore only command three-ninths of them ; two-
ninths would be consumed by the labourers,

and the other five-ninths would be the profit of the capitalists. They would unitedly have an income of £2,500, five hundred of which would be made in the commodities sold to the manufacturing labourers. Whatever share of income the capitalists received, they would directly or indirectly have to spend. The other £2000 of profit, therefore, would be made upon the commodities sold to the proprietor of the soil and to each other. This £2,500 would go in supporting themselves and families ; in maintaining what is called unproductive labour, and in keeping horses, &c. Five hundred pounds of it would be spent in provisions, and the other two thousand in the consumption of the remaining produce of the manufacturing labourers. The consumption of the produce of the soil, and the labour of the 100 men would therefore stand as follows :—

### PRODUCE OF THE SOIL.

|  | £. | S. | D. |
|---|---|---|---|
| Consumed directly or indirectly by the proprietors themselves - - | 500 | 0 | 0 |
| By the manufacturing labourers - - | 1,000 | 0 | 0 |
| Direct or indirectly by the capitalists - | 500 | 0 | 0 |
|  | £2,000 | 0 | 0 |

PRODUCE OF MANUFACTURING LABOUR.

|  | £. | S. | D. |
|---|---|---|---|
| Consumed by the labourers themselves - | 1,000 | 0 | 0 |
| Directly or indirectly by the proprietors of the soil - - - - | 1,500 | 0 | 0 |
| Directly or indirectly by the capitalists | 2,000 | 0 | 0 |
|  | £4,500 | 0 | 0 |

Thus the proprietors of the soil would comparatively enjoy the consumption of but a small part of the produce of manufacturing labour to which it would give rise ; yet, nevertheless, its produce would be the foundation of the whole, and this accumulation of prices no more than the manner in which it and the labour it commanded were distributed by nature amongst the different orders of the community.

This case is a mere hypothesis for the sake of illustration. The produce of the soil consists of materials that are required to clothe and support labour, as well as food, of which every individual must either grow a portion himself, or if he does not, must, indirectly at least, exchange the produce of his estate, with either some home or foreign proprietor who does. This is generally effected through the medium of manufactured commodities. I have little doubt, however, that the proprietors of the soil get but a small part of its produce back,

in the labour which many of the commodities
they purchase contain. Labour is now so eco-
nomized, and machinery so much introduced
in every branch of manufacture, that a great
part of the cost of most commodities consists of
the profits of capital. That part of the income
of society which is gained by the capitalist in
trade, is spent in the luxuries of life, and gives
employment to what economists call unproductive labour, instead of manufacturing labour,
which this employment of capital has superseded. Hence the quantity of unproductive
labour in a country, is probably the best proof
of its improvement and prosperity.

# CHAPTER XV.

## *Rent.*

THE rent of land consists of that part of its produce which is received by the landlord, after paying the expence of labour, materials, and profits of capital employed in its cultivation. The produce of the soil, as we have shewn, creates population, which multiplies with the increase of it. As the value of labour becomes less, the surplus produce of the soil becomes greater.

Rent from mines is also their surplus produce, after paying for the labour, materials, and profits of capital employed in working them. The principles, however, which govern the demand, by which rent from mines is created, are different from those which regulate the rent of land.

There is always a given demand for every commodity of necessary, luxury, or convenience, in use. This demand is regulated by its price. If a carriage could be had for six-pence, beggars would ride. It is only the high price of the luxury which confines it to comparatively so few.

Beneath the cost of its production in labour, materials, profits of capital, &c. no commodity can, for any length of time, fall. If it could not be sold for what it cost, it would cease to be produced altogether. But if, on the contrary, the supply of any commodity is unlimited, except by the cost of production, as salt for instance from sea water, the price of it never can exceed that cost upon the average, as an increase of supply would always follow an increase of demand.

Should, however, the supply of any commodity be limited, and there is a demand for much more than can, by the application of labour and capital, be produced; this demand must be brought to an equality with the supply by an increase of price, which will reduce either the inclination, or confine the power of consuming it to a less number of persons. The difference between the cost of production, and this price, constitutes rent.

Thus there is no limit to the rent of mines, the quantity of whose produce is beneath the demand at its cost price, but the inclination and power of purchase by the consumers. On the other hand, they may leave no rent at all, if they are so extremely productive, as to yield upon the application of materials, capital, and labour, as great a supply of their produce at their cost price, as there is a demand for. But the rent of land, which derives its value from producing the necessaries of life, can never, in an old country, be any length of time, as we have shewn, below, nor yet above, its natural value in commodities.

The rent of mines is also a consequence of the rent of land. It is not until the soil will command considerably more labour than is necessary for its own cultivation, that a great demand arises for the luxuries of life; and it is probable there will be seldom much rent from mines until there is a considerable rent from land; unless it be for the purpose of exporting to richer countries, where rents are greater, and its inhabitants consequently more wealthy.

Though the causes of the demand which creates the rent of land and mines, be different, the principles upon which the increase of it takes place and is determined, are the same with both. These principles, however, are so very clearly explained by Mr Ricardo, that I shall claim his indulgence for the liberty of copying the principal part of his chapters on the subject.

" Rent* is that portion of the produce of the " earth, which is paid to the landlord for the " use of the original and indestructible powers " of the soil. It is often, however, confounded " with the interest and profit of capital, and in " popular language the term is applied to what-

* Principles of Political Economy, Chap. 2, on Rent.

" ever *is* annually paid by a farmer to his land-
" lord.  If, of two adjoining farms of the same
" extent, and of the same natural fertility, one
" had all the conveniences of farm buildings,
" were, besides, properly drained and manured,
" and advantageously divided by hedges, fences,
" and walls, while the other had none of these
" advantages, more remuneration would natu-
" rally be paid for the use of one, than for the
" use of the other; yet in both cases this re-
" muneration would be called rent.  But it
" is evident that a portion only of the mo-
" ney annually to be paid for the improved
" farm, would be given for the original and in-
" destructible powers of the soil; the other
" portion would be paid for the use of the capi-
" tal which had been employed in ameliorating
" the quality of the land, and in erecting such
" buildings as were necessary to secure and
" preserve the produce.  Adam Smith some-
" times speaks of rent, in the strict sense to
" which I am desirous of confining it, but more
" often in the popular sense, in which the term
" is usually employed.  He tells us, that the
" demand for timber, and its consequent high
" price, in the more southern countries of Eu-
" rope, caused a rent to be paid for forests in
" Norway, which could before afford no rent.
" Is it not however evident, that the person
" who paid, what he thus calls rent, paid it in

" consideration of the valuable commodity
" which was then standing on the land, and
" that he actually repaid himself with a profit,
" by the sale of the timber? If, indeed, after
" the timber was removed, any compensation
" were paid to the landlord for the use of the
" land, for the purpose of growing timber or
" any other produce, with a view to future de-
" mand, such compensation might justly be
" called rent, because it would be paid for the
" productive powers of the land ; but in the
" case stated by Adam Smith, the compensa-
" tion was paid for the liberty of removing and
" selling the timber, and not for the liberty of
" growing it. He speaks also of the rent of
" coal mines, and of stone quarries, to which
" the same observation applies—that the com-
" pensation given for the mine or quarry, is
" paid for the value of the coal or stone which
" can be removed from them, and has no con-
" nexion with the original and indestructible
" powers of the land. This is a distinction of
" great importance, in an inquiry concerning
" rent and profits ; for it is found, that the
" laws which regulate the progress of rent, are
" widely different from those which regulate
" the progress of profits, and seldom operate in
" the same direction. In all improved coun-
" tries, that which is annually paid to the land-
" lord, partaking of both characters, rent and

" profit, is sometimes kept stationary by the
" effects of opposing causes, at other times ad-
" vances or recedes, as one or other of these
" causes preponderates. In the future pages
" of this work, then, whenever I speak of the
" rent of land, I wish to be understood as
" speaking of that compensation, which is paid
" to the owner of land for the use of its origi-
" nal and indestructible powers.

   " On the first settling of a country, in which
" there is an abundance of rich and fertile land,
" a very small proportion of which is required
" to be cultivated for the support of the actual
" population, or indeed can be cultivated with
" the capital which the population can com-
" mand, there will be no rent; for no one
" would pay for the use of land, when there
" was an abundant quantity not yet appropri-
" ated, and therefore at the disposal of who-
" soever might choose to cultivate it.

   " On the common principles of supply and
" demand, no rent could be paid for such land,
" for the reason stated why nothing is given
" for the use of air and water, or for any other
" of the gifts of nature which exist in boundless
" quantity. With a given quantity of mate-
" rials, and with the assistance of the pressure
" of the asmosphere, and the elasticity of steam,
" engines may perform work, and abridge hu-
" man labour to a very great extent; but no

" charge is made for the use of these natural
" aids, because they are inexhaustible, and at
" every man's disposal. In the same manner
" the brewer, the distiller, the dyer, make in-
" cessant use of the air and water for the pro-
" duction of their commodities ; but as the
" supply is boundless, it bears no price. If
" all land had the same properties, if it were
" boundless in quantity, and uniform in qua-
" lity, no charge could be made for its use,
" unless where it possessed peculiar advantages
" of situation. It is only then because land is
" of different qualities with respect to its pro-
" ductive powers, and because in the progress
" of population, land of an inferior quality, or
" less advantageously situated, is called into
" cultivation, that rent is ever paid for the use
" of it. When, in the progress of society, land
" of the second degree of fertility is taken into
" cultivation, rent immediately commences on
" that of the first quality, and the amount of
" that rent will depend on the difference in the
" quality of these two portions of land.

" When land of the third quality is taken in-
" to cultivation, rent immediately commences
" on the second, and it is regulated as before,
" by the difference in their productive powers.
" At the same time, the rent of the first quality
" will rise, for that must always be above the
" rent of the second, by the difference between

" the produce which they yield with a given
" quantity of capital and labour. With every
" step in the progress of population, which
" shall oblige a country to have recourse to
" land of a worse quality, to enable it to raise
" its supply of food, rent, on all the more fer-
" tile land, will rise.

" Thus suppose land—No. 1, 2, 3,—to yield,
" with an equal employment of capital and la-
" bour, a net produce of 100, 90, and 80 quar-
" ters of corn. In a new country, where there
" is an abundance of fertile land compared with
" the population, and where therefore it is only
" necessary to cultivate No. 1, the whole net
" produce will belong to the cultivator, and
" will be the profits of the stock which he ad-
" vances. As soon as population had so far
" increased as to make it necessary to cultivate
" No. 2, from which ninety quarters only can
" be obtained after supporting the labourers,
" rent would commence on No. 1; for either
" there must be two rates of profit on agricul-
" tural capital, or ten quarters, or the value of
" ten quarters must be withdrawn from the
" produce of No. 1, for some other purpose.
" Whether the proprietor of the land, or any
" other person, cultivated No. 1, these ten
" quarters would equally constitute rent; for
" the cultivator of No. 2 would get the same
" result with his capital, whether he cultivated

" No 1, paying ten quarters for rent, or conti-
" nued to cultivate No. 2, paying no rent. In
" the same manner it might be shewn, that
" when No. 3 is brought into cultivation, the
" rent of No. 2 must be ten quarters, or the
" value of ten quarters, whilst the rent of No.
" 1 would rise to twenty quarters; for the cul-
" tivator of No. 3 would have the same profits
" whether he paid twenty quarters for the rent
" of No. 1, ten quarters for the rent of No. 2,
" or cultivated No. 3 free of all rent.

" It often, and indeed commonly happens,
" that before No. 2, 3, 4, or 5, or the inferior
" lands are cultivated, capital can be employed
" more productively on those lands which are
" already in cultivation. It may perhaps be
" found, that by doubling the original capital
" employed on No. 1, though the produce will
" not be doubled, will not be increased by 100
" quarters, it may be increased by 85 quarters,
" and that this quantity exceeds what could be
" obtained by employing the same capital on
" land, No. 3.

" In such case, capital will be preferably em-
" ployed on the old land, and will equally cre-
" ate a rent; for rent is always the difference
" between the produce obtained by the em-
" ployment of two equal quantities of capital
" and labour. If with a capital of 1,000*l.* a
" tenant obtain 100 quarters of wheat from his

" land, and by the employment of a second
" capital of 1,000*l.*, he obtain a further return
" of eighty-five, his landlord would have the
" power at the expiration of his lease, of oblig-
" ing him to pay fifteen quarters, or an equiva-
" lent value, for additional rent; for there
" cannot be two rates of profit. If he is satis-
" fied with a diminution of fifteen quarters in
" the return for his second 1,000*l.*, it is be-
" cause no employment more profitable can be
" found for it. The common rate of profit
" would be in that proportion, and if the ori-
" ginal tenant refused, some other person would
" be found willing to give all which exceeded
" that rate of profit to the owner of the land
" from which he derived it.

" In this case, as well as in the other, the
" capital last employed pays no rent. For the
" greater productive powers of the first 1,000*l.*,
" fifteen quarters is paid for rent, for the em-
" ployment of the second 1,000*l.* no rent what-
" ever is paid. If a third 1,000*l.* be employed
" on the same land, with a return of seventy-
" five quarters, rent will then be paid for the
" second 1,000*l.* and will be equal to the dif-
" ference between the produce of these two,
" or ten quarters; and at the same time the
" rent of the first 1,000*l.* will rise from fifteen
" to twenty-five quarters; while the last 1,000*l.*
" will pay no rent whatever.

" If then good land existed in a quantity
" much more abundant than the production of
" food for an increasing population required,
" or if capital could be indefinitely employed
" without a diminished return on the old land,
" there could be no rise of rent ; for rent in-
" variably proceeds from the employment of
" an additional quantity of labour with a pro-
" portionally less return.

" The most fertile, and most favourably si-
" tuated land will be first cultivated, and the
" exchangeable value of its produce will be ad-
" justed in the same manner as the exchange-
" able value of all other commodities, by the
" total quantity of labour necessary in various
" forms, from first to last, to produce it, and
" bring it to market. When land of an infe-
" rior quality is taken into cultivation, the
" exchangeable value of raw produce will rise,
" because more labour is required to produce
" it.

" The exchangeable value of all commodi-
" ties, whether they be manufactured, or the
" produce of the mines, or the produce of land,
" is always regulated, not by the less quantity
" of labour that will suffice for their produc-
" tion under circumstances highly favourable,
" and exclusively enjoyed by those who have
" peculiar facilities of production ; but by the
" greater quantity of labour necessarily bestow-

" ed on their production by those who have no
" such facilities; by those who continue to
" produce them under the most unfavourable
" circumstances; meaning—by the most un-
" favourable circumstances, the most unfavour-
" able under which the quantity of produce re-
" quired renders it necessary to carry on the
" production.

" Thus, in a charitable institution, where the
" poor are set to work with the funds of bene-
" factors, the general prices of the commodi-
" ties, which are the produce of such work,
" will not be governed by the peculiar facilities
" afforded to these workmen, but by the com-
" mon, usual, and natural difficulties, which
" every other manufacturer will have to en-
" counter. The manufacturer enjoying none
" of these facilities might indeed be driven al-
" together from the market, if the supply af-
" forded by these favoured workmen were
" equal to all the wants of the community;
" but if he continued the trade, it would be
" only on condition that he should derive from
" it the usual and general rate of profits on
" stock; and that could only happen when his
" commodity sold for a price proportioned to
" the quantity of labour bestowed on its pro-
" duction.

" It is true, that on the best land, the same
" produce would still be obtained with the

" same labour as before, but its value would
" be enhanced in consequence of the diminish-
" ed returns obtained by those who employed
" fresh labour and stock on the less fertile land.
" Notwithstanding then, that the advantages of
" fertile over inferior lands are in no case lost,
" but only transferred from the cultivator, or
" consumer, to the landlord, yet since more
" labour is required on the inferior lands, and
" since it is from such land only that we are
" enabled to furnish ourselves with the addi-
" tional supply of raw produce, the compara-
" tive value of that produce will continue per-
" manently above its former level, and make
" it exchange for more hats, cloth, shoes, &c.
" &c. in the production of which no such addi-
" tional quantity of labour is required.

" The reason then, why raw produce rises
" in comparative value, is because more labour
" is employed in the production of the last
" portion obtained, and not because a rent is
" paid to the landlord. The value of corn is
" regulated by the quantity of labour bestowed
" on its production on that quality of land, or
" with that portion of capital, which pays no
" rent. Corn is not high because a rent is
" paid, but a rent is paid because corn is high;
" and it has been justly observed, that no re-
" duction would take place in the price of corn,
" although landlords should forego the whole

" of their rent. Such a measure would only
" enable some farmers to live like gentlemen,
" but would not diminish the quantity of la-
" bour necessary to raise raw produce on the
" least productive land in cultivation."

" The metals,* like other things, are obtain-
" ed by labour. Nature, indeed, produces
" them; but it is the labour of man which ex-
" tracts them from the bowels of the earth, and
" prepares them for our service.

" Mines, as well as land, generally pay a
" rent to their owner; and this rent, as well as
" the rent of land, is the effect, and never the
" cause of the high value of their produce.

" If there were abundance of equally fertile
" mines, which any one might appropriate,
" they could yield no rent; the value of their
" produce would depend on the quantity of
" labour necessary to extract the metal from
" the mine and bring it to market.

" But there are mines of various qualities,
" affording very different results, with equal
" quantities of labour. The metal produced
" from the poorest mine that is worked, must
" at least have an exchangeable value, not on-
" ly sufficient to procure all the clothes, food,
" and other necessaries consumed by those em-
" ployed in working it, and bringing the pro-

* On the Rent of Mines, Chap. iii.

" duce to market, but also to afford the com-
" mon and ordinary profits to him who ad-
" vances the stock necessary to carry on the
" undertaking. The return for capital from
" the poorest mine paying no rent, would regu-
" late the rent of all the other more productive
" mines. This mine is supposed to yield the
" usual profits of stock. All that the other
" mines produce more than this, will necessa-
" rily be paid to the owners for rent. Since
" this principle is precisely the same as that
" which we have already laid down respecting
" land, it will not be necessary further to en-
" large on it.

" It will be sufficient to remark, that the
" same general rule which regulates the value
" of raw produce and manufactured commodi-
" ties, is applicable also to the metals; their
" value depending not on the rate of profits,
" nor on the rate of wages, nor on the rent
" paid for mines, but on the total quantity of
" labour necessary to obtain the metal, and to
" bring it to market.

" Like every other commodity, the value of
" the metals is subject to variation. Improve-
" ments may be made in the implements and
" machinery used in mining, which may con-
" siderably abridge labour; new and more pro-
" ductive mines may be discovered, in which,
" with the same labour, more metal may be ob-

" tained ; or the facilities of bringing it to
" market may be increased. In either of these
" cases the metals would fall in value, and
" would therefore exchange for a less quantity
" of other things. On the other hand, from
" the increasing difficulty of obtaining the me-
" tal, occasioned by the greater depth at which
" the mine must be worked, and the accumu-
" lation of water, or any other contingency, its
" value, compared with that of other things,
" might be considerably increased.

" It has, therefore, been justly observed, that
" however honestly the coin of a country may
" conform to its standard, money made of gold
" and silver is still liable to fluctuations in va-
" lue, not only to accidental and temporary,
" but to permanent and natural variations, in
" the same manner as other commodities."

# CHAPTER XVI.

## *Taxes.*

As the whole income of society must be spent, taxes can be no evil to a nation, in a commercial point of view. Those who supply the consumption of the country, or the goods that are exported in payment of those foreign commodities which the nation consumes, can do no more than supply it; and it has never been contended that the receivers of the taxes were in a different situation with respect to the expenditure of them, than those who derived their incomes from any other source. Both must spend them in one way or other, and neither can do more.

It may be a very annoying circumstance to the ultimate payers of the taxes, to have their property, when there is no danger at hand, encumbered with the support of a great many persons who are of no present use to them ; even though these individuals may have spent the prime of their days in their service, or may have hazarded their lives in order to protect them, their families, and those properties out of which the taxes are paid, from oppression, spoliation, and plunder. It may be very provoking also to pay the interest of the debts, which they may have contracted, as without these incumbrances they would have so much more to spend in their own personal gratifications. But, to those who supply the articles which are consumed, by means of the expenditure of the collective income of the nation, it is quite immaterial whether it is consumed by the pensioners and national mortgagees, or by the ultimate payers of the taxes, in administering to their own gratifications.

To those who have the taxes ultimately to pay, they are of course an evil; as much as an encumbered estate is worse than one which is not so. But the labouring classes, who are often the most clamorous against taxes, have in fact the least to do with them. The wages of labour are proportioned to the supply and demand for it, and are not at all affected by the average monied cost of commodities, whether high or low, or whether it proceeds from taxes, the balance of trade, profits of capital, or whatever cause. If taxes are an evil to the lower classes, so are profits of trade. A certain demand for labour must be requited by a certain payment in commodities, by which it is supported; and though changes of price, by good or bad harvests, or other causes which often temporarily affect the price of every different commodity, have the effect of injuring or improving for the moment the situation of the labourer; yet all permanent changes in the general price of commodities, whether they proceed from taxes or any other cause, are ultimately followed by a corresponding change in the wages of labour, as, we trust, has been already established.

Taxes, in whatever manner they may be levied, fall ultimately upon real property; and when they are laid on gradually, in the manner in which they are generally imposed, they fall so imperceptibly and equally upon every one, that probably no ill effects are experienced from them. After absolute necessaries, the gratification derived from expenditure is the result of habit and ambition. The former may gradually be changed without much violence, when the latter is not affected. There is no great difficulty in laying down a carriage, dispensing with a servant, &c. if every person in similar circumstances does the same. It is the rank which fortune gives that constitutes a great part of its value; and as the imposts of government fall equally upon all, according to their incomes, though they may be the means of curtailing the gratification of some artificial wants, they leave the gradations of rank and fortune undisturbed.

With respect to taxation on articles of foreign trade. The first effect of a tax upon a commodity, is to increase the price of it; and the next, to reduce the consumption in a proportionate degree, of both the home and foreign consumer. This is intended by it; it is an indirect way of taxing income, which thereby cannot command the same quantity of consumable commodities as before. But it does not in the least diminish the general demand for labour and commodities. The object of the tax is to acquire income with a view to expenditure; and if the foreign consumer, from having to pay more in price, consumes less in quantity, the power of consuming the difference is acquired by government, and the foreign consumer thus contributes his share to the expences of the state.

# CHAPTER XVII.

*Tax upon Foreign Corn.*

WHEN the foreign demand, for the commodities of this, or any other country, determines the balance of payments in its favour, there are two ways in which the trade may be brought to a balance : either by a general elevation of prices sufficient to curtail the demand ; or by an elevation sufficient to create an importation of the produce of the soil that will command labour and commodities enough to supply it.

In the latter case, no great rise of the national prices beyond those of the neighbouring countries trading with it would take place. Instead of the increased demand for commodities being paid for in money, it would be paid for with food and materials, by which an additional quantity of commodities, corresponding to the increased demand, would be produced. It is of no importance to a British manufacturer, for instance, from whence the demand comes which he supplies ; or where the food is grown which he eats. If his bread be good, it is immaterial to him, whether it is the produce of Yorkshire, or of Poland.

The advantages which Great Britain would gain by such an additional trade, would consist in the increased manufacturing population it would support, and the profits of capital which its merchants and manufacturers would gain. Not half, it is probable, of the food and materials would be embodied in, and represented by the materials and labour which the commodities that were returned in payment for them contained. The rest would be retained as profits of capital, &c. and be consumed by the merchant, manufacturer, and capitalist, in the necessaries, conveniences, and luxuries of life.

In this case, however, no great advantage would be gained by the proprietors of British soil. The incomes from their estates would not, as with an elevated standard of prices, command a greater quantity of foreign commodities than before. The trade would be little more than a commercial extension of territory. A greater surface of soil would, in the support of labour and profits of capital, pay tribute to our manufacturing superiority. If another county was added to Great Britain, it would confer no particular advantage on the rest of the kingdom, so far as the interest of the landed proprietors were concerned; neither by the same rule, does bringing the general produce of other soils to this country do so. Geographical situation is nothing in the eye of commerce. J. Conolly,

Esq. one of the witnesses before the agricultural committee of 1821, stated, that flour could be sent cheaper to Liverpool from America, than he could send it from his mills to Dublin, by only 44 miles of canal navigation. The American proprietor in the neighbourhood of a convenient place of shipment, is of course in that case as well situated for the trade of this country as the Irish proprietors in the neighbourhood of Mr Conolly's mills; nor could the Irish proprietors gain any advantage by such trade.*"

Very different, however, would be the case, were the importation of victual produce not allowed. Our demand for materials would then

* " James Conolly, Esq. again called in and examined."
" You were asked on your examination, respecting the
" power of this country to compete with America in the
" article of flour, in the general markets of the world; have
" you any thing to add to your answer upon that subject?
" My object is to shew the effect of the importations of
" American flour upon these countries; America possesses
" a prodigious advantage over us in respect of freight, so
" much so, that at my mills, 44 miles from Dublin, which
" are very extensive, and from which there is a water car-
" riage the whole of the way from the mill door to Dublin,
" and which water carriage, has cost at least 400,000l. (the
" grand canal goes about 33 miles, and there is a barrow
" navigation which takes up the remainder of it) notwith-
" standing that, flour comes from America to Liverpool, at
" a lower freight than it can be put on board ship (from
" that mill) in Dublin."—*Report, page* 319.

be necessarily confined to the consumption of that population which our own soil would support ; the balance of trade in our favour would elevate the national prices ; a less quantity, though an equal value of, British goods would be exported, and the rest would be consumed at home ; foreign commodities would become comparatively cheap, and the incomes of proprietors would go further, in commanding all the luxuries of life. The higher the national prices, the richer of course a nation becomes ; its income will command a greater quantity of foreign commodities. . Almost all our luxuries are of foreign production, and would rather be reduced than increased in price, by any balance of payments which raised the general prices of the country.

The situation of the labourer, with a high state of national prices, would also be improved. Dearness and cheapness are relative terms, and only applicable to prices, which are raised above the national level, by scarcity, or reduced below it by abundance. When the average wages of labour, and prices of the necessaries of life, are rightly apportioned to each other, according to the existing supply of labour, the labourer is enabled to say when necessaries are dear and when they are cheap. But it is by comparison with a standard, determined by the quantity of money in circulation, that he is enabled to make this deduction. This standard is of course quite arbitrary, so far as the supply and demand for necessaries are concerned, and his wages, according to the supply of labour, are always accommodated to it. A labourer considers only those prices dear, and those cheap, which are above or below the national level, whatever that level may be. A state of prices which may mark scarcity in one country, may denominate plenty in another. If the inhabitant of a country with a low standard of prices, comes to spend his income in a country with the reverse, he considers all the necessaries of life dear, because they are at prices which would betoken scarcity at home. On the other hand the inhabitant of a rich country, spending his income in a poor one, considers the necessaries of life cheap, because they are what he would consider cheap at home ; on the same principles that Gulliver found himself a giant in Lilliput and a dwarf in Brobdingnag. In neither case, however, would they be either dear or cheap, but only in both cases be measured by a wrong scale. Gulliver was neither a dwarf nor a giant in his own country ; and it would have been absurd to have considered him either the one or the other, because he was thought so in countries to which his natural standard of admeasurement did not apply.

In countries with high national prices, it is found, in general, by experience, that the lower classes are in better circumstances than in countries where the national prices are low. Now the necessaries of life must always be the first and principal object with every labourer, and luxuries and conveniences only a matter of secondary consideration. When, however, the latter are easily acquired, and it takes no great quantity of labour, or sacrifice of articles of more absolute necessity, to purchase them, it is natural to suppose that more will be consumed than if they were of more difficult attainment. In a high state of national prices, therefore, to which wages are accommodated : when money will command a much greater proportion of luxuries than of food ; or where luxuries are comparatively low, while the money price of food is high,—the lower classes will be able to increase their comforts by the comparative ease with which they can be procured.

In countries, on the other hand, with a low state of national prices : where foreign luxuries are comparatively dear ; to acquire them will take a greater sacrifice of labour and the more absolute necessaries of life, than the working classes probably would make if they could, or could make if they would. They, therefore, learn to dispense with those articles of comfort which are common to the poor in richer countries, or rather never acquire a taste for them, and often live in a miserable and degraded state of abject poverty.

A high state of national prices, so far, in fact, from denominating dearness or scarcity, is the means and proof of abundance. A mere extension of trade, by the importation of corn, may increase the numbers, but high national prices increase the comforts of the poor, and are as much to be desired by them as by any class of the community.

If, however, a great manufacturing country were entirely to prevent the importation of corn, prices would probably rise so high as to foster a competition by other countries, which, in the end, might rival and reduce its manufacturing superiority beneath what, by the exercise of better policy, it might continue to uninterruptedly maintain. By a total exclusion of victual produce it might have a greater advantage for a time, but in the end gain less than by preserving its national prices at a more moderate standard.

That a country, however, should throw away its manufacturing superiority altogether, and by unlimitedly permitting the importation of corn, render itself dependant upon other nations for this principal necessary of life, merely for the sake of increasing its manufacturing population, will never, I should think, be contended. That it is entitled to make a fair advantage of its manufacturing superiority, is too reasonable a proposition to be denied.

This may be done in a most advantageous manner, without going to either extremes, of a free importation, or an entire exclusion. A tax upon foreign corn, and other victual produce, would have the effect of maintaining the national prices at any level that might be desired, beneath what would be attained by complete prohibition. If a tax were laid upon foreign corn in this country, our national prices must attain an elevation above those of the country from whence the corn came, sufficient to cover the tax upon it, before it could be imported. The tax would amount to prohibition until this were the case. But this level we should be certain to attain ultimately, if our manufacturing superiority would command a favourable balance of trade at the elevation ; while at the same time the tax would possess the advantage of being no burden on this country, but exclusively a tax upon foreign nations :—To illustrate this principle.

If, for instance, corn imported from the Baltic, the prime cost of which, to the importer, was one million, were subject to a tax of another, its selling price in this country must, at least, be two millions. The price of British labour and commodities would consequently have to bear a price in proportion.

It is unnecessary, perhaps, to remark, after what we have before said, that the price of corn governs the price of labour, and *vice versa*; and that the prices of corn and labour govern the price of every thing else. If they are doubled, the amount of capital in trade is doubled, and the profits expressed in money are necessarily twice as great as before, &c.; although the merchants and manufacturers may be no richer, except in the additional command of foreign luxuries, which, by the altered state of the national prices, they acquire; and that consequently doubling the price of corn, doubles the price of all commodities so far as they represent British labour and British produce.

The prime cost, therefore, of this corn, would only command half the quantity of British labour and produce in return, that it would have done without the tax; while the million levied by government would command the other half, which would, either directly or indirectly, be consumed by those to whom the money thus levied was paid.

Neither is it probable that the tax would fall in any great degree upon the nation from whence the corn came. The returns which are usually made to the Baltic for goods imported from thence, consist principally of tea, coffee,

sugar, cotton, and generally the produce of the
East or West Indies, and of wines, gold, silver,
&c. in the price of which there is but little British labour or produce represented. The value
of these commodities is only affected by the
state of national prices in the countries from
whence they come; they are as cheap as they
would be with any state of prices in England.
The national prices in England, however high,
have no other effect than to lower those of
every other country. In the purchase of these
commodities, British labour or produce, however, has been exchanged; and it is the consumers in those countries, or deriving their incomes from those countries where these commodities are produced, who pay the tax levied
upon the corn, in the payment of which they
are returned.

By brandies imported into the Baltic direct
from France, or tobacco from America, or tea
from China, corn imported into England may
also be paid for, the same as if they came
through England. Goods, we shall say, are
imported into France or America from Britain ;
and France and America having exported goods
to the Baltic, for which we shall suppose they
do not import an equal value in return, draw
bills upon the Baltic for the balance. In England, in consequence of the importation of
corn, there is a demand for bills upon the Bal-

tic. America and France, therefore, pay their debts to Great Britain with the bills they have drawn upon the Baltic, and these again are remitted to the Baltic in payment of the corn. The result consequently is, that the tax upon the corn is paid in the increased price of the goods sent to France and America, while the corn sent to England is paid for by the brandies and tobacco imported into the Baltic direct from those countries.

Teas imported into the Baltic from China, are often paid for in gold and silver, to purchase which England ships goods to South America. The gold and silver thus received, may be sent to the Baltic in payment of the corn, and from thence to China, or be shipped to the order of Baltic merchants direct for China. By these means the South American consumer of British labour and produce pays the tax upon the corn; while the corn itself is paid for by the teas imported into the Baltic direct from China. If imported by way of America, or any other channel not British, the American merchant who imports the teas from China, and ships them to the Baltic, draws upon the Baltic for them, and sells his bills in England for gold and silver brought from South America. Thus British goods are sent to pay for the gold and silver, it is remitted to pay for the tea, and the bills are sent to pay for the corn.

The amount of the tax proper to be imposed upon corn, is altogether a question of mercantile superiority, and ought to be determined on precisely the same principles as would govern a prudent manufacturer in similar circumstances. It can never be correctly determined by enquiries addressed to agriculturists. If it was too heavy, it would defeat its object as a tax by which to raise money. Were it to elevate the national prices so high as to enable other nations to undersell us, it would drive off into other channels that demand for commodities by which the demand for foreign corn was created. It must always be sufficiently low to preserve the demand for our labour and produce beyond what our own soil can support and furnish. Were the duty too high, as we have before stated, it would merely operate as a prohibition.

If a manufacturer could make so good and cheap a commodity as to prevent all competition, he would be anxious to make as much of his manufacturing skill as possible, and yet not raise his prices so high as to foster competition. In determining the price which he would set upon his commodity, his first point would be to ascertain the extent in lowness of price, and goodness of quality, in which he could exceed his neighbours, in any attempt which they might make to rival him. Having done this, he would next ascertain how much of this arose from local circumstances, in which they could not compete with him, such as in cheapness of coal, facilities of carriage, &c. A price adequate to this he would lay on without any hesitation, as he never could be rivalled in these advantages. That superiority, however, which merely depended upon skill and capital, he would perhaps not be disposed to build upon too far ; as if he did encourage his neighbours, by his high prices, to establish similar manufactures, practice might give them skill, and success might give them capital.

Upon principles similar to these, ought a nation to determine the amount of the tax it imposes upon foreign corn, if it be desirous to make the most of its manufacturing superiority ; and that this or any other country should not be so desirous, it is impossible to conceive.

Although the parliamentary enquiries upon this subject have been upon the whole unsatisfactory, so far as they have gone they are extremely useful. It is evident that with a high state of national prices, land can be cultivated which would have to be thrown into pasture were those prices not maintained ; and it is important to ascertain the prices at which inferior land can be preserved in tillage. As nature has made us equally carnivorous as well as herbivorous animals, it is perhaps intended that a great part of the soil should be devoted to the rearing of cattle, in order to keep down its price to a level with that of grain, so that the labouring classes might be able to command a proportion of both. It is probably designed, therefore, that a considerable part of the soil should not pay for cultivation, in order to secure this. We might at the same time remark, that as the improved system of farming consists in rearing turnips and green crops for cattle, where they had not been reared before, the proportion of each, which it is the design of nature to preserve between animal and vegetable produce, is probably not at all altered by these improvements.

There can perhaps be little doubt, that in order to maintain all that land in cultivation which had been brought into tillage during the war, 80s. per quarter would be necessary. But, in order more clearly to show how this effect is produced, let us, for example, assume that the price of one half of the materials employed in working the land, and one half the wages of the labouring population of this country are determined by the price of foreign commodities. Let us also, in the first place, suppose, that foreign commodities are in all respects on a par with our own ; that in our trade with foreign countries, the exchanges are equal in quantity as well as price ; so that an acre of produce in Great Britain is only of equal value with an acre of foreign produce. We should then have no manufacturing superiority. In this state of prices, there would of course be land which would just clear the expence of its cultivation, and nothing more. We shall suppose the produce of 50 acres of this to sell for £125, and the account of its produce and expence of cultivation to stand thus :—

| | | | | |
|---|---|---|---|---|
| Rent, by rearing cattle | £25 0 0 | By produce sold for | £125 0 0 |
| To the expence of its cultivation, determined by the price of British produce | - 50 0 | | |
| To ditto by the prices of foreign produce | - 50 0 0 | | |
| | £125 0 0 | | £125 0 0 |

Gain for the trouble of tillage, nothing.

But were our prices to rise to double those of our neighbours, the produce of an acre of land, would through the medium of our manufacturing labour, by this means, command the produce of two acres of any other nation, and that land which would pay no additional rent in tillage before, would now leave a rent of £50. The account would stand thus :—

| | | | | |
|---|---|---|---|---|
| To rent by rearing cattle, which would be doubled with the value of cattle and other things | £50 0 0 | By value of produce doubled | £250 0 0 |
| To expence of cultivation determined by the price of British produce doubled also - | 100 0 0 | | |
| To ditto by the prices of foreign produce, reduced if any thing, but supposed to be the same | 50 0 0 | | |
| To additional rent cleared - | 50 0 0 | | |
| | £250 0 0 | | £250 0 0 |

Gained for the trouble of tillage, £50.

It is upon this principle that land must be thrown out of cultivation, with a low state of national prices, which would leave a rent when prices were high. Our national prices were very much elevated during the late war, and land was brought into tillage which will not now pay for cultivation. The prices, however, at which the land in tillage would pay for cultivation, it was important to ascertain. This has been done by the agricultural committee, and fixed at 80s. per quarter, and I have no doubt with great truth. But how far it may be proper to maintain the national prices at that standard, is another branch of inquiry. The particular cause of the high prices during the war, and the present low prices, we shall hereafter consider.

Although we should thus gain such considerable advantages by our foreign trade, it would still be the interest of foreign nations to trade with us. The cold regions of the north of Europe, and British America, can never become manufacturing countries. The extreme of cold, and even of heat, to which they are subject, forbid it; while their climate is very favorable to the growth of corn. On the other hand, the excessive heat of the tropical climates equally renders them unfavorable to manufacturing industry, but superabundantly fertile in all the vegetable luxuries of life. The temperate regions less favoured with natural fertility, but infinitely more so in the manual energy of their inhabitants, seem destined by nature to supply the rest of the world with the produce of art and labour, and be the connecting link by which the extremes of climate administer to the comforts of the population of each other.

The other nations of Europe, with climates equally temperate, and circumstances equally favourable for manufacturing industry, may perhaps object to take our manufactures were a tax thus to be levied upon them, and endeavour to improve their own; at least to the extent of supplying their own consumption. Any laws to this effect, however, it is extremely probable, if not certain, would be laws which would rather retard than promote this object. The first thing to stimulate a nation to industry, is to create a demand for its labour. The only way to do this is to provoke expenditure by the introduction of foreign luxuries. By this means a demand for commodities in order to pay for them is produced. The money made by the trade, and the knowledge gained of the demand, cost, and quality, of the foreign articles consumed, foster attempts to produce them; to which attempts, however, an existing demand is necessary. Manufactures will seldom to any great extent, be set on foot, if the parties have not only to make the commodity, but create a market for it; and this would have to be done if the habit of consumption be prevented by restrictions upon import. All experience has in fact shewn that foreign trade has proved the best mode of giving a taste for, and introducing domestic manufactures. It introduces both knowledge and enterprise.

When an individual has made money by the importation of any commodities, he is apt to acquire some knowledge respecting its manufacture ; from this he is induced to attempt to manufacture it, and if the country is in that state to render the attempt practicable, he succeeds. In the mean time there is a demand for produce in order to pay for these manufactures, until the nation is fit for producing them itself, which would otherwise not exist.

All decrees to prevent the importation of foreign manufactures may be considered decrees of present poverty by the nation which enforces them. They destroy the existing demand for those commodities that have been sent in exchange for the prohibited manufactures, as well as deprive the country of the power of consuming the manufactures thus prohibited. They thus begin by paralizing the whole system ; and it is extremely probable that they retard rather than encourage the growth of that domestic industry which they are intended to promote. If a nation possesses natural facilities for manufacturing, with good laws and a free constitution, by which a stimulus is given to industry and enterprise, it will become a manufacturing country in time. It seems, however, most probable, that prohibitory laws will not accelerate that time, while they are certain to involve the nation in poverty, if not distress.

No judicious government would therefore hastily pass any laws of this kind.  This, however,
ought, I think, to be a matter of perfect indifference to the British nation.  By properly en-
couraging a trade with her own colonies, and
those countries and nations who are her natural
customers, and will at all times be glad to
trade with her, she may be sufficiently independent to be entirely indifferent to the policy by which those nations may govern themselves, who wish to be rich before their time.

# CHAPTER XVIII.

## *Money.*

THERE are two things necessary to the price of commodities, viz. money, and the commodities the value of which it expresses. Price knows no distinction of persons, but is formed by their conjunction alone. In the market, the demand is represented by money, the supply by commodities. If there is a smaller quantity of any particular commodity brought into the market for sale, but the same quantity of money brought to purchase it, its price rises; the demand is greater than the supply. On the other hand, if with the same supply of the commodity, a greater quantity of money is brought in demand for it, a rise in price takes place precisely on the same principles; except that in the one case, it is produced by a reduced quantity of commodities, in the other by an increased quantity of money. Just, the reverse is the case when the supply of commodities is enlarged, or the quantity of money in the market diminished; in both instances, a declension of price is the consequence.

What is the case with any particular commodity, is also the case with commodities generally. Any alteration of prices that is universal, must be the result either of an alteration of the supply of commodities, or an alteration in the supply of money; but it may equally result from either.

Now, the supply of money may be perfectly arbitrary, and is at least as much determined by chance as rule; whereas the supply of commodities is not. Paper money may be created to any extent; and the value of gold is accidental. Had the mines been twenty times more productive, the supply would have been twenty times greater; and that commodity which is now worth a shilling would then have been worth a pound. The supply of commodities, however, is less arbitrary. The soil will yield, upon the average, a given produce, and support a given quantity of labour, and united they will supply a given quantity of consumable commodities. But as neither population nor the produce of the soil can be created like paper money, nor yet depend upon the accidental productiveness of mines, general variations of price, resulting from variations in the supply of commodities are not so likely to happen.

Sudden general alterations in prices are therefore more likely to proceed from an alteration in the supply of money, at least when that money is paper, than by an alteration in the supply of commodities. But at the same time, if a nation is commercial, and in the habit of supplying its consumption by exchanging its commodities with those of other nations, great alterations in the supply of commodities may be suddenly caused by political events.

A great and general reduction of prices has of late taken place in this country, which must either be the consequence of an increased supply of commodities, or a reduced supply of money. That this reduction is not a fall in our national prices resulting from a diminished foreign demand for our manufactures, is proved by the fact, that the foreign demand for our manufactures has and is continually increasing, and at this moment the balance of trade and payments in our favour, and the influx of money into the country, are greater than perhaps were ever known. Nevertheless, prices, instead of rising above, have fallen below the national level, determined by the present corn law, and are not now more than half the amount at which that law has fixed them.

That this reduction does not proceed from the supply of foreign corn, is also evident from the simple fact, that though the prices are now lower than ever, there is no foreign corn in the market. Foreign corn might affect the market while it was in it, but after it was consumed, unless there was a reduced quantity of money in the market, as well as corn, the price of it must rise again.

The present prices might also proceed, as some have supposed, from over-production; but as we have already seen, it would in that case reduce the price of corn, but not the price of labour; whereas the price of labour has been reduced as well as the price of corn. Hence we are brought to the inference that it must be a question of currency.

This again presents considerable difficulties. Great fluctuations in prices have been known to take place without any, at least, apparently adequate alteration either in the quantity of money in circulation, or in the supply of corn by which to account for it; and at present there does not seem a reduction in the circulation of London at least, that will at all explain the low prices to which agricultural produce has fallen. A proper acquaintance, therefore, with the principles which govern the connection of money with commodities, and the laws which regulate its motions, and determine and restrain the issues of bank paper, become absolutely necessary to any sound conclusions on the subject; and this and the following chapter contain what I am afraid is but a very imperfect attempt to develope those laws and principles.

The money in circulation may be divided into two descriptions; that which is employed in exchanges of consumable articles, and that which is employed in making transfers of capital and property. The first may be termed its consumptive, the last its abstract circulation.

## Money in Consumptive Circulation composed of Individual Currents.

From that great lake, if it may be so termed, or mass of money in consumptive circulation, each individual has a stream of his own, that continually flows in to him, and from him. The magnitude of this stream is proportioned to his income and expenditure, which it forms. The stream that flows in is his income, the stream which flows out his expenditure ; or if he does not expend it himself, he lends it, which is the same, to others who do.

This mass, or lake, is entirely formed of these streams, which are in continual motion. It is not all the money that passes through the hands of a merchant or trader, however, which forms his own particular stream of circulation. In general, only a very small part of it does so. That part alone which becomes his, in the shape of profit, belongs to his own current. With the rest, he is only an agent, by which it is advanced forward in the respective streams to which it belongs. Thus, a manufacturer, who employs workmen, is the approximate medium between the ultimate consumer of the manufactured commodity, and his men, by which the money that composes their income comes into their hands. The manufacturer again receives the money from the wholesale dealer, who is also his agent, as well as those of his men, to the amount of the profits that the goods sold contain, and which form part of his income. They are again sold to the retailer, who, in his turn, becomes an agent in transmitting the money forward that forms the profits and income of both wholesale dealer and manufacturer, as well as the workmen ; and he again sells them to the consumer, from whom he receives the profits which form his own stream of circulation as well as the rest.

The streams of circulation may also be divided into superior and subordinate. A person of large property expends a great part of his income, not only in purchasing necessaries, but in commanding a higher description of labour, such as that of stewards, teachers, painters, musicians, and in those innumerable modes of enjoying the superior elegancies of life, in which large fortunes are generally spent. This, which forms the out-lay of one party, forms the income of another; is again spent, and again forms part at least of the income of a third, who administers to those superior luxuries, &c. Thus it descends down, step by step, in the great channel of consumption, forming numerous subordinate currents, until it perhaps returns to the original proprietor at last, in the purchase of that produce from whence it was first derived.

## Money in consumptive Circulation the actual Representative of Commodities.

Now the great and important feature of money in the channel of consumptive circulation is, that it must necessarily, and always does, represent an equal value with itself of unconsumed commodities in the market. Every guinea or pound note which a person receives in the channel of consumptive circulation, may be said to be the shadow of an actual substance, or the representative of a constituent value, at the moment remaining in some shop or warehouse unconsumed. It is a check upon the storehouse of society for a particular value of goods, the possessor of which is virtually the owner of the goods it represents.

" When the division of labour," says Smith,

as we have before quoted, " has been once " thoroughly established, it is but a very small " part of a man's wants which the produce of " his own labour can supply. He supplies the " far greater part of them by exchanging that " surplus produce of his own labour, which is " over and above his own consumption, for " such parts of the produce of other men's la- " bour as he has occasion for. Every man " thus lives by exchanging, or becomes in some " measure a merchant, and the society itself " grows to be what is properly termed a com- " mercial society."

That part, we have also stated, of the aggre- gate wealth of a nation, which forms the wealth or income of each individual, consists of some particular description of labour or pro- duce of which the whole is composed. The income of one person is derived from land which produces corn, another from land which produces cattle; one has a tin mine, another a mine of coal; one man makes nails, ano- ther shoes, &c. Thus the income of each individual is generally derived from contribu- ting to some particular want of a great many different persons. On the other hand, the necessaries and luxuries which each individual requires, take some portion of the labour and produce of as great a variety of persons to sup- ply; and it is necessary for him to exchange that in which his income consists, with all those who may desire a part of it, in order that he may procure from them that portion of each of their labour or produce, which he requires for himself. In order to facilitate these exchanges money is necessary, &c.

Now, it is evident, that a person must actually, before he can acquire the money necessary to enable him to command that portion of the produce or labour of others which he requires, dispose of his own labour or commodities for it. As every individual must do this before he can gain possession of money in the channel of consumptive circulation, it equally follows that every pound so acquired, represents the value which was given for it. This value is placed in the hands cf the merchants, traders, &c. of society, who have furnished this money; and, as this must have been done with every commodity in the market, they cannot be consumed until the money returns in purchase of them. The original intention in selling them for money is merely to facilitate the exchange of one commodity for another; the money, therefore, naturally must represent the commodities to be thus exchanged; nor will the dealer, who conducts these exchanges, dispose of them again without such money. Whenever that consumptive demand comes round, however, which places the money again in the hands of the dealer, his stock being reduced, he purchases more to supply its place. The money, therefore, goes again into the hands of the original producer, to replace the commodity consumed. It again becomes income; again represents the commodity purchased by the dealer; and is again returned in promoting a consumptive demand for those which are in the market. The money may not, perhaps seldom does, return in demand for the particular commodity it represents; that is not the original intention. It goes in purchase of other commodities of equal value, and the money which represents them, comes in purchase of the commodity which is represented by it. Thus, there must necessarily be, at all times, a stock on hand, of goods, equal to the value of the money in consumptive circulation. It never is spent in a consumptive demand, without reproducing in the market a commodity of equal value to what has been consumed.

To make the explanation more clear, we shall suppose society to consist of ten persons, besides merchants and dealers; that the money in consumptive circulation be represented by £1,000; that each of these persons furnish one hundred pounds worth of different commodities for general consumption, and that the wants of society are confined to the commodities thus furnished. The object of each individual, of course, is to exchange his commodities for those of his neighbours. In order to effect this, he first sells them to the dealer for a hundred pounds, and each individual does the same; this absorbs the £1,000 in circulation. The money thus received, therefore, represents the commodities sold to the dealer; and as the wants of each individual, or those to whom he pays or lends the money, arise, they come to the dealer with it, and receive for it that portion of the commodities originally sold to him, which it will command.

When the dealer receives the money in purchase of any particular commodity for consumption, he of course returns with it to the original producer of that commodity, purchases an equal quantity in order to replace it; and the producer again puts forth the money into the market, either by lending or paying it to others, or in order to supply his own consumption. By these means, the supply in the market is always equal at least to the value of the money in consumptive circulation, and the money is an order upon this stock for the value it expresses.

It is of no consequence what description of money it is; its intrinsic value is totally unimportant; its value to those who receive it consists in its being the actual representative of a given quantity of consumable commodities.

## *Merchant Stock.*

If the whole income of society had always been spent in actual consumption, the stock of goods in the market could never have exceeded in amount the value of money in circulation, though it never could have been less. But shopkeepers, manufacturers, and others, find it convenient to keep larger stocks on hand than this would amount to. In order to increase them, therefore, instead of spending their profits in actual, they usually spend a part of them in commercial consumption. They purchase the particular commodities in which they deal, with their profits or income, instead of purchasing commodities for their own consumption. By this, production is equally promoted, though consumption does not actually take place. The commodities thus laid up, however, cease to be represented by the money in consumptive circulation : so far as regards it, they appear to have been consumed ; the producer has placed a commodity in the market, and though that may not be consumed, money has been returned upon him for a fresh supply, to be placed there the same as if it had.

For the sake of distinction, we have termed that stock which is represented    the money in actual circulation, *market stock ;* and the stock which exceeds this, we have termed *merchant stock.* Commercial stock might at first, as it is an old term, appear the most proper to mark this distinction ; but, correctly speaking, commercial applies as much to one stock as the other.

The object of the dealer in thus accumulating a merchant stock, is to provide against any falling off in the regular supply, or market stock of the commodity in which he deals. The production of all commodities, except victual produce, is regulated by the supply and the demand. When the original producer brings to market more goods than the community wants, the dealer will not give him the money for them which they are actually worth, and he ceases to produce so much as before. One extreme begets the other, and the supply then falls beneath the regular demand. When this occurs, the dealer brings into the market his merchant stock, puts himself in the situation of the producer for the time being, and provides for the regular consumption, without any inconvenience having been suffered by society from the want of supply, which would otherwise have been felt.

This is the legitimate object of all stocks of commodities which are held by dealers. Beyond what is sufficient for the attainment of this purpose, they can never accumulate to any amount. In those commodities, the supply of which is certain and regular, and easily attained, the stocks held are comparatively small. In foreign commodities, the supply of which is received from distant countries, or cannot be calculated upon with certainty, the stocks are generally large. With all foreign trade this must necessarily be the case. The foreign commodities consumed, as we have before shewn, merely represent home commodities exchanged for them. When brought into the market, therefore, they are sold for money, which represents home commodities. As a foreign commodity is placed in the market, a home commodity of equal value is taken out of it. The market stock is not increased in value by the exchange. The foreign commodity only represents the home commodity purchased for exportation with the money, or with an equal sum with that for which it sold. Both the foreign and the home market, however, must be regularly supplied with the respective commodities exchanged. In order to this, a very large merchant stock both in ships conveying the commodities between the two countries, and in warehouses and shops, at both ends, must be at all times on hand.

The consumers know nothing of the commercial operations by which they are supplied;

but in the price of the commodity, pay a profit to the dealers for their trouble, and the stocks which they thus continually hold.

## Effects of an increased Supply of Commodities.

Should a producer bring an additional supply of his particular commodity to market, when both the market stocks and merchant stocks, which the dealers think proper to hold, are full, if he is determined to sell, he must reduce the price of the commodity in order to procure a demand for it. In this way, he brings it within the reach or attraction of the money in consumptive circulation, which has one of two effects, or perhaps both : it either increases the consumption of the commodity, or diminishes the supply of it by others. If it is an article of first necessity, such as food, it increases the consumption ; if an article of less, but still of great necessity, such as cloathing, it may do so, but in a less degree. With most articles, however, except food, its principal effect is to diminish the supply by others ; and, at the same time, induce the dealers, if they can command money, to increase their merchant stocks. They buy up the commodity sold beneath the cost price. Their stocks, however, being much larger than usual, they will not purchase more, except upon the same or lower terms. The richer producers, in consequence, being unable to get the market price, or what they can sell their commodities at with a profit, hold back their supplies until the additional quantity is carried off by the regular demand, and the usual supply is again required. The same is the case when any particular dealer brings his merchant stock into the market, by selling it off beneath its value; other dealers cannot effect sales, and therefore will not purchase of the producer until the stock thus sold is consumed. By this diminished market price of any particular commodity, the money in consumptive circulation will go further in the purchase of commodities generally, and the consumption will of course be increased; but it is probable, that a principal share of the increased consumption will fall upon other commodities, and not altogether, as has been supposed, upon the particular commodity whose price is diminished.

### Quantity of Commodities of which the Market Stock is composed.

Now, the market stock of commodities must always be equal in quantity to supply consumption, during one revolution of the currency in consumptive circulation. The ten persons, in the imaginary case stated, would furnish a stock sufficient to supply the consumption, until the money they received and expended came round to them again, in a demand for more. Had the £100 of each individual been the representative of double the quantity of goods, there would have been double the consumption, before this revolution was performed; or had it represented half the commodities, the consumption of them could not have exceeded that amount.

The annual produce of a nation, however, and the annual consumption are equal. A person does not take his commodities to market before they are wanted; and as soon as he does so, his demand, directly or indirectly, for the commodities of others, becomes equal to their demand for his. Upon receiving the money for his goods, he sends it forth in a consumptive demand, by himself or those to whom he pays or lends it, to the extent of its value.

Consumption is also regular. The consumption of one month is, on the average, equal to the consumption of another. A spendthrift may get rid of his fortune in a very short time, but he can only do so by purchasing the savings of others. He may waste his property by losing it at play, or by squandering it in different ways. But, in this manner, it only changes

hands ; he cannot force consumption much beyond its ordinary pace ; what he himself eats
and drinks, forms but a small part of his expenditure. Other people, though they may acquire
his money, will not forget, if he has done it,
that they have to live through the year, as well
as at present ; or should they, they can only
throw it away as he has done : it will come into the hands of more prudent people at last.

The consumption being regular, the revolutions of the currency, on the average, must be
equally so : thus if we take the income of the
society, for the sake of example, at 432 millions, and the currency at 72, it must necessarily perform six revolutions in the year, or one
every two months ; and the market stock of
commodities would in that case always be equal
to two months consumption.

*The Money in consumptive Circulation must al-
ways be equal to the Value of the Market Stock
of Commodities.*

Whatever be the quantity of money in consumptive circulation, it must always be equal
to the value of the market stock of commodities, let that stock be great or small. The ten
persons in the supposed case, who sold their
commodities, would acquire in the money they
received, the power of consumption equal to

the commodities placed in the market; and by the expenditure of this money, the whole in the regular time would be consumed : and this is the case with society at large. But when money comes into a country by the balance of trade, it comes in a demand for commodities which their cheapness has caused, while the money previously in circulation, furnishes a demand equal to the supply. The foreign money thus introduced is not the representative of any commodities in the market. Hence a demand is created greater than the supply. This being the case, commodities must rise in price equivalent to this increased demand. The foreign money introduced has the same affinity for the commodities in the market, as that which was in previous circulation. But the supply of commodities being less than the demand, an elevation of prices must take place in order to bring them to a parallel ; and the consumption of the producers, or those who possess the money in previous circulation, is of course proportionately reduced. Every rise in price is the consequence of increased demand by those who are willing to pay more, and the immediate effect is a reduced consumption on the part of those who are unable or unwilling to give the increased price. When, however, the money makes one revolution, the producers are placed on the same footing as before. The increased price of commodities has increased their incomes; and the power of consumption derived from their income becomes equal to what it was previous to the foreign money coming into the market. A general rise in prices has taken place, by which room is made for the additional money introduced into the country, to circulate. It still therefore represents the market stock of commodities, or two months consumptionn; an alteration in the value of money alone has taken place. Just the reverse is the case when money is exported. It is originally acquired by a quantity of commodities for consumption being placed in the market, which waits the return of it, or an equivalent value, in order to be consumed. The possessor of the money, however, either from inclination or cheapness, increases his consumption of foreign commodities; and this determines the balance of trade against the country: by which means the money instead of producing the consumption of an equivalent value of commodities in that market where its constituent value is deposited, is transported to a foreign market, in order to replace those foreign commodities, the increased consumption of which has taken place; or, which is, in effect, the same, the dealer in consequence of a diminished foreign consumption, instead of purchasing as usual, home produce with the money he receives, with which to pay for the foreign commodities imported, sends the money out of the country for that purpose. In this case, the demand for home commodities is reduced; the dealers are under the necessity of selling them at a lower rate; and the consumption of those who possess the money left in circulation is increased. But after one revolution, the income of the producers begins to fall in equal proportion, and a general reduction puts income and expenditure upon a par again; and the chasm thus caused by the money exported is filled up. Hence the money in the world, or any particular nation, is always rendered sufficient for the use of it.

Precisely the same are the effects produced by money which is issued by banks. It is advanced upon the security of property or personal sureties, and represents property or capital, but possesses, in the first instance, no constituent value of commodities in the market. Those who borrow it, however, for consumptive circulation, expend it in consumption, and by a consequent increase of prices it makes way for itself. A contraction of currency produces the opposite effect: it leaves in the market commodities of equal value to itself, without the means of consumption at existing prices; and it is only by a reduction of prices adequate to the de-

mand thus reduced, that the market stock can
be carried off.

## Abstract Circulation.

The abstract circulation of a country is that
part of its money which is employed in making
transfers of merchant stock, capital, and property. In every country the sales of property,
transfers of capital, and transactions in merchant
stock, must bear some proportion to the quantity of its consumable produce, in the power of
commanding which their value consists ; and
money is equally required to conduct them.
In this use of it, however, it is an abstract measure of value ; it represents no constituent commodities in the market. Upon the average, a
given quantity of the money in circulation must
be thus required, and it must have been first
taken out of consumptive circulation, in order
to be so employed ; a reduction of prices must
have consequently taken place. This, however,
would only have the effect of determining the
balance of trade in favour of the country ; and
the money thus absorbed, would be replaced by
a foreign importation. If at any time the average transactions in capital should be diminished, or an economy in the use of money thus
employed be introduced, it would again descend

into consumptive circulation, increase prices, and determine the balance of trade the other way.

Any variation in the quantity of money in consumptive circulation, must also vary the quantity in abstract circulation. It must draw it down as it diminishes, raise it up as it increases. As the value of money increases by the quantity in circulation being reduced, the value of property must sooner or later fall likewise; and less money be required to conduct the exchanges of it; it is the quantity of consumable commodities it will command that ultimately determines the value of all property. On the other hand, as the quantity of money in consumptive circulation increases, the value of property in money, for the same reason, must re-increase with it.

With bank notes the difference is, that the money in abstract does not descend down into consumptive circulation, whereas with metallic money it is taken up from it.

*With the same State of Prices, the Quantity of Money required varies.*

The quantity of money required to conduct the circulation of a country, even with the same level of national prices, is not always equal.

When there is a demand for money, and it becomes scarce, or when the interest of money and profits of trade rise, an economy in the use of it begins to take place. If a person cannot raise money, he will purchase goods upon credit; by which they are taken out, as it were, from under the money which represents them. This has the effect of raising prices, the same as if an additional quantity of money had been brought into circulation. The diminished quantity of commodities which the money in circulation will command, raises the price of them, determines the balance of trade against the country, and part of it is remitted abroad, until the prices resume their usual level. Tradesmen, under these circumstances, often make large profits, and, instead of receiving payment in cash, not unfrequently take a mortgage, or other securities, for their debts. Being also in the habit of selling for credit, they are obliged, on the other hand, to require it. This leads to bill transactions, by which, knowing the day that their payments are to be made, they are satisfied if they can acquire the money necessary for the purpose, by the time it is wanted, and keep none idly by them. As money becomes scarce and valuable, people are thus more economical in the use of it. If a profit is sure to be made, by turning it over, none of it is allowed to be unemployed. It, consequently,

performs its revolutions quicker, and a less
quantity is necessary. Instead of performing
six revolutions in the year, it may perform seven. In order, therefore, to represent a value
of 432 millions, it would require, in that case,
not quite 62 millions, instead of 72, which with
only six revolutions, would be necessary.

Whether the currency moves quickly or slowly, however, is of no importance to the foreign
consumer; therefore as soon as prices, by an accelerated motion, began to rise, the foreign demand would diminish, if prices were previously
at the national level, until by an unfavourable
balance of payments, the quantity of money in
circulation was reduced, and prices resumed
their former state. The only difference in this
case would be, that the market stock on hand
would be reduced in proportion as the motion
increased : if it was increased one seventh, the
market stock would be reduced in that amount :
a greater market stock would not be necessary
than what was equal to the consumption of between six and seven weeks. A still greater difference, however, would perhaps take place in the
amount of money in abstract circulation. Bills
of exchange, in the transactions of merchant
stock, are very much substituted for money when
it is scarce. I have heard that in Lancashire,
during the war, there were five bills for one in

circulation at present; and I have no doubt this was also very much the case in other places.

On the other hand, property is also much more valuable, and there is a greater quantity of capital, when the interest of money is low; and more exchanges of it are made, at least in this country : for when government securities pay the legal rate of interest, there is comparatively very little borrowing and lending by individuals : government itself borrows the bulk of what there is to lend. Thus both the number and value of such transactions being greater, a larger quantity of money in abstract circulation is required.

When there is a difficulty of finding employment for money, profits of trade also fall, and credits are neither given nor received as before; the market stock becomes larger, and more money is required to represent it at the national standard ; there are not so many bills in circulation, and generally there is less economy in the use of money, for which it is difficult to find a profitable employment. Thus in times of peace, when the interest of money is low, much more money is required than in times of war, when the demands of government increase its value.

With the increase of machinery and capital, a greater quantity of money in circulation will also become necessary. Suppose for instance, that by the aid of capital and machinery, labour is ten times more productive than it used to be, and that for the use of this machinery and capital 100 per cent. profit is charged; the produce of labour will be now one-fifth as cheap as it was before, but upon the aggregate, it will be worth twice the money, and will take twice the money to represent it in the market. The same with commodities which are taxed; taxes increase their monied price, and render a greater quantity necessary to promote their consumption.

When the foreign trade of a country is extended or curtailed, a larger or a less supply of money also becomes necessary. At the time that we were shut out from all legitimate trade with Europe and the United States, and our supplies of foreign commodities were comparatively small, less money must have been required, and, a smaller amount would then of course, express a higher state of prices than at present.

### The effect of good and bad Seasons upon the Circulation of Money.

" A French author," says Dr Smith, " of " great knowledge and ingenuity, Mr Mess-

180

" ance, receiver of the taillies in the election
" of St Etienne, endeavours to shew that the
" poor do more work in cheap than in dear
" years, by comparing the quantity and value
" of the goods made upon those different occa-
" sions, in three different manufactures ; one
" of coarse woollens, carried on at Elbeuf;
" one of linen, and another of silk, both of
" which extend through the whole generality
" of Rouen.  It appears from his account,
" which is copied from the registers of the
" public offices, that the quantity and value of
" the goods made in those three manufactures,
" has generally been greater in cheap than in
" dear years; and that it has always been
" greatest in the cheapest, and least in the
" dearest years.  All the three seem to be sta-
" tionary manufactures, or which, though their
" produce may vary somewhat from year to
" year, are upon the whole neither going back-
" wards nor forwards.

" It is because," observes Dr Smith, " the
" demand for labour increases in years of sud-
" den and extraordinary plenty, and diminishes
" in those of sudden and extraordinary scarci-
" ty, that the money price of labour sometimes
" rises in the one and sinks in the other.

" In a year of sudden and extraordinary plen-
" ty, there are funds in the hands of many of the
" employers of industry, sufficient to employ

" and maintain a greater number of industrious
" people then had been employed the year be-
" fore ; and this extraordinary number cannot
" always be had. Those masters, therefore,
" who want more workmen, bid against one
" another in order to get them, which some-
" times raises both the real and the money
" price of their labour.

" The contrary of this happens in a year of
" sudden and extraordinary scarcity. The
" funds destined for employing industry are
" less than they had been the year before. A
" considerable number of people are thrown out
" of employment, who bid one against another
" in order to get it, which sometimes lowers
" both the real and the money price of labour.
" In 1740, a year of extraordinary scarcity,
" many people were willing to work for bare
" subsistence. In the succeeding years of
" plenty, it was more difficult to get labourers
" and servants."

Men may and will no doubt be excited to
additional labour with the hope of making more
money ; but not by the mere effect of cheap
provisions. If at their ordinary rate of wages
they can live better, and do not work less, they
will not be induced, for the same money, to
work more. They might be induced to work
more, did wages fall with the price of provisions ; but it appears on the contrary that they

rise—that the fund for the employment of labour or the monied demand for it increases. A fall in the wages of labour, however, is the result of an additional supply of labour itself, and though it may be the ultimate, is never the immediate effect of abundance. The difficulty of procuring provisions, as Dr Smith states, may induce men to bid against each other, and lower their wages for the sake of additional employment, but abundance never produces that effect.

At the time that Mr Messance wrote, as well as now, the currency of France was metallic, and as a good harvest does not grow money as well as provisions, the increased monied demand for labour must have been the result of an alteration in the movements of the currency. Were this not the case—did there not exist a greater monied demand for labour, there could only be the same monied demand for provisions : the increased supply would consequently have to be sold at a proportionably less price, and the farmer would gain nothing by the quantity exceeding the average supply which he brought into market ; while it is not improbable that the low prices of the necessaries of life would induce men to work less instead of more. This would probably convert a year of abundance, which is considered a blessing, into a curse : it would become a year of riot to the poor, and of loss to the farmer : instead of being an advantage to both, it might prove a moral evil to the one, and a pecuniary disadvantage to the other.

Money, as we have already stated, in its progress to consumption, has in general to pass through many hands. The proprietor, we shall say for example, pays it to his mortgagee ; his mortgagee to his bookseller ; his bookseller to his shopman ; his shopman to his landlord ; his landlord to his house-painter ; his house-painter to his colour-man ; his colour-man to a foreign merchant ; the foreign merchant to a British manufacturer ; the British manufacturer to his workmen ; from the workmen, through the miller, baker, &c. it will come into the hands of the farmer ; and from him again be paid to the proprietor. It may also be observed, that it would move much more quickly after it came into the hands of men of business ; and while it would not stop a day with the labourer, it would, from the quick nature of their returns, probably rest a shorter time with the baker and miller, than in any part of its progress previous to its coming into the labourer's hands. Had this money, however, been lodged in a bank, instead of making the circuit through which we have traced it, it would have most likely been at once lent out to the manufacturer, and would have returned in demand for the commodities placed in the market, in a tenth of the time. Now in a year of extraordinary abundance, this is the progress of that part which exceeds the farmer's average gains :—The price of corn does not fall in proportion to the increased supply; and the surplus above what is necessary for his rent is placed in banks, or lent to those who immediately expend it in the employment of labour; by which means it makes shorter circuits, more labour is employed, and a greater consumption is created. The poor thus enjoy all the advantages of the abundant season ; but it is in that way best suited to them, in a moral as well as in a physical point of view. Money being more abundant, creates itself employment, either by the increased facilities with which it is lent out, or by the reduced interest which is charged for it ; by which means traders are induced to increase their merchant stocks, and people in general to enter into undertakings in which the employment of labour is involved ; but which, with a greater scarcity of money, they would not have attempted.

In years of scarcity, on the other hand, the very opposite effects are produced. As with an increased supply of food, nature thus provides an increased demand for labour, so with a scarcity of food, the demand for labour is reduced. By these means, when there is less food, less is required. A man with little work can be supported upon a smaller quantity of provisions than with full employment. If there was the same employment for labour, and the same money brought into the market in demand for provisions, the consumption would have to be kept down to the supply by their excessive price, while the farmer would hardly be a sufferer; his loss in quantity would be made up in price.

In bad years, however, the farmer cannot get a price at all proportioned to the deficiency of his crop, and is unable to pay his rent in consequence. He is under the necessity, therefore, of withdrawing money from bankers or others, which he has saved in better seasons, or his landlord is obliged to give him credit to another year, and borrow money to meet his expenditure until his rents can be paid him. Thus a demand for money is created, and bankers are obliged to reduce their accommodations to trade, in order to meet it. It can only, however, be acquired by placing commodities in the market. This renders it necessary for traders to reduce their merchant stocks, in order to be able to meet their engagements. The money, therefore, called in by the banks, and paid to the farmers, or lent on better terms to their landlords, now represents not the immediate productions of labour, but the merchant stocks of tradesmen, the production of previous years. This necessity of reducing their stocks prevents them from purchasing their usual supplies, and labour is thrown out of employment adequate to the demand for money thus created and supplied. That money which represents previous labour will not create a fresh demand. It is only the money in circulation which represents food that can ever do so; and there would only be a demand for labour in proportion to the food in the market for its support. Should the cheapness of labour in any particular trade induce wealthy individuals to increase their stocks rather than diminish them, they can only do so by acquiring possession of that money which represents the market stock of provisions. Hence their demand for labour must reduce the demand for some other description, the employment of which does not hold out equal temptations. Individuals may alter the channel, but cannot increase that general demand for provisions which the failing crop has curtailed. Were this principle perfect in practice, there would be no rise in the price of provisions whatever. A portion of the wages of labour, however, and of income generally, which had hitherto been spent in other commodities, is in a scarcity exclusively appropriated to the purchase of food. Provisions consequently rise, and other commodities, the produce of previous labour, fall ; but more present labour is in consequence turned out of employment.

A failing crop, it is thus probable, has not so much the effect of raising prices, as of reducing employment; and this seems a wise disposition of Providence. If men are to have little food, it is evidently better that they should also have little work. Had they the same employment, it would not increase the supply of provisions, while it would increase the necessity for them, and add to the evils of scarcity. That the demand for provisions is thus curtailed with the supply, and prices prevented from rising, is consistent with experience. In 1740, which Dr Smith speaks of as a year of great scarcity, there was very little demand for labour, but the price of wheat does not appear to have risen above 30 per cent. : viz. from 34s. to 45s. per quarter; and as it was then much more exclusively the food of the rich than now, other grain perhaps might not have risen in equal proportion.

At that time the circulation of the country was principally metallic. With the power which the banks possess of making money or destroying it at pleasure, very different effects might be produced; but this falls more properly to be considered in the next chapter.

*A small Addition to the Currency may produce a great Effect upon Prices.*

If the currency makes six revolutions in the year, it is evident that the addition of one million must make six in the annual income. But should it make on the average twelve, which I think is at least as probable, then an addition of one million would make a difference of twelve. The very great difference in prices which occasionally does take place, without any comparatively great alteration in the amount of money in circulation, seems to warrant the inference, that the proportion of money in consumptive circulation is less, and the number of revolutions which it performs in the year greater, than might be at first supposed. But I am not aware of any correct data by which to come at certain conclusions on this subject.

## CHAPTER XIX.

*Paper Currency.*

THE principal circulation of this country is composed of the promissory notes, payable in metallic money on demand, of public and private banks. In England, this money is issued by one public bank, the Bank of England, and by several hundred private banks. In Ireland, it is also issued by one public bank, the Bank of Ireland, and a number of private banks; and in Scotland, it is almost totally issued by public banks, or joint stock companies, constituted on the same principles, though not equal in magnitude to the public banks of Ireland and England.

For a more particular inquiry with respect to the advantage which joint stock companies possess over private banks, we must refer the reader to the Essay which he will find at the end of this treatise; and as a proper understanding of the present system of banking seems connected with, if not necessary to, the consideration of the branch of the subject at which we have arrived, we shall recommend the attention of the reader to that Essay, before he proceeds further.

It may not be improper, however, as an additional argument, to remark that the charters of the Banks of England and Ireland, by preventing more than six partners from entering into any banking concern, have the effect of still further contracting the number even below that amount. The business of banks, as we have shewn, is to deal in money, and they do not require capital for that purpose, but credit; though capital is necessary, in order to give credit. The capital of private banks, however, not being known to the public, does not confer credit, and private bankers have no inducement to advance money. Private banks are in general, therefore, set up by men of property or credit, who join their respective credits to establish the concern, without any advance of capital. If we suppose, therefore, a private bank to commence with six partners, the full number allowed, it must either do well or ill, or neither well nor ill. If it is not doing well, however, it may be said to be doing ill; for in that case it leaves no adequate compensation for the risk which a private banker runs. If it is doing well, it has probably got into good business and credit. In this case, should a partner die, the credit of the bank would be such as to render one to supply his place unnecessary; and

another would not be taken in, merely for the
sake of receiving one-sixth of the profits of a
flourishing business. The remaining partners
would divide the share amongst them ; and this
they would continue to do as the partners drop-
ped off, until the number was as few as the
credit of the bank (considered to be firmly
established) could be supported with. If the
bank was a bad concern, no new partner would
join it. If it was neither good nor bad, there
would be no temptation to do so. Hence with
private banks, the number of partners under the
present law gravitates downwards, until each
bank presents the least security to the public
with which it can possibly exist. Consequently,
though six is allowed, there are not more than
three partners to each bank on the average of
the kingdom ; and as at least one of these is an
acting partner, there does not appear to be
more than two persons of property to support
the credit of each concern, even presuming
every partner in a bank but the acting partner
to possess the fortune requisite for such an
establishment. The effect of the present law,
therefore, is to give each bank as little credit,
instead of as much, as possible.


*Paper, as Money, of the same Value as Gold.*

The notes of these banks are issued in discount of commercial bills, in loans upon personal and other securities to individuals, and by the Bank of England, partly in discount of commercial bills, but principally upon bullion, and in advances to government.

This paper, in its character of money, is of the same value as gold. Gold, as a commodity, possesses intrinsic value, which bank-notes do not; it represents a value in materials, labour, and capital, which has been expended in procuring it; but as money, it is only worth the commodities in the market that it represents, whatever it may have cost; and paper money is the same. Each individual who originally acquires paper in consumptive circulation, does so by placing commodities in the market.

*Paper and Metallic Money are introduced into Circulation in the first Instance upon different Principles, but the Effect upon Prices is the same.*

Metallic money is introduced into circulation by a foreign demand for commodities, in consequence of their cheapness ; whereas paper money is introduced by the demand of individuals for money itself. The metallic money which comes into a country, has been the representative of income in the country from whence it came; whereas paper money is made for the purpose of the demand which it supplies.

Paper money, therefore, when first issued, represents no constituent value in the market: property, or personal sureties which are indirectly the same, have been pledged for its repayment: the person who receives it, has deposited with the bank of which it is borrowed, a value of inconsumable property, equal to what he has received; but he has placed no commodity which it represents, in the market, and a demand in the market is, therefore, created beyond the supply. By this means, an elevation of prices takes place; and the paper makes way for itself, in the same manner as metallic money introduced by a foreign demand, as previously described. Precisely the reverse is the case when notes are taken out of circulation. A certain value of commodities is left in the market, without the money which represents them, and prices, consequently, fall to a parallel with the quantity of money which remains.

*The Effect upon Prices produced by an Altera-
tion in the Issues of Bank Notes, sufficiently
proved by Experience.*

The effect in elevating and depressing prices,
produced by any alteration in the circulation of
banks, is a fact now perfectly notorious, and to
prove it, by a reference to particular instances,
unnecessary. I shall, however, mention one,
which occurred with the Bank of France. Mr
Haldiman, in his evidence before the committee of the House of Commons, appointed in
1819, to consider the expediency of the Bank
of England resuming cash payments, gives the
following particulars :—

" I think there would be great distress occa-
" sioned in the commercial world by the forced
" reduction to which I have alluded. Prices
" cannot be forcibly lowered without producing
" very great mischief in trade ; we should all
" feel the effects of it, some directly and some
" indirectly. I express myself rather strongly
" upon this point, because I happened to be in
" Paris, in October last, when the bank reduced
" its issues upon discounts very considerably
" and suddenly ; the distress and failures which
" took place, in consequence of this measure,
" went much beyond what any merchant could

" have anticipated. The issues of the Bank of
" France upon discounts, at that period, were
" 130 millions of francs, which was more than
" double the highest amount that was ever
" previously known. I believe the discounts
" usually were from 25 to 35 and 40 millions."

It must be observed, that a contraction of issues, by curtailing advances to trade, has a double effect; it not only reduces the demand for
commodities, but it increases the supply of them.
The merchants, by the liberal accommodations
of the bank, had no doubt been induced to increase their merchant stocks, and extend their
transactions; and when suddenly called upon to
repay the money borrowed, their only mode of
doing so would be, to force their stocks into the
market. This, at any time, would be a great loss;
but as the money was not lent out again by the
bank in promoting consumption, and did not
return into the market, the demand would be
reduced in equal proportion. Thus, therefore,
in the same degree that the commodities in the
market exceeded the average supply, the money
in the market would present less than the average demand.

" This step on the part of the directors of
" the Bank of France, was occasioned by the
" following circumstances:—The metallic cur-
" rency was leaving the country in every direc-
" tion, owing, in all probability, in some trifling

" degree, to the over issue of paper ; partly to
" some large financial operations in Russia, and
" partly to the enormous payments that France
" had engaged to make to foreign powers,
" which amounted nearly to 20 millions ster-
" ling. The Paris bankers, therefore, antici-
" pating a great demand for bills upon all fo-
" reign countries, were remitting specie to meet
" the drafts, which they intended to negociate
" to the agents of all those foreign powers, with
" a small advance upon their remittance. The
" sudden diminution, however, of the discounts
" of the bank, caused the exchange to turn in
" favor of France, and immediately paralized all
" their operations ; the metallic currency made
" a retrograde movement, and was restored
" to Paris and to those parts where the greatest
" distress had been felt. I have stated these
" circumstances thus minutely, because I think
" them perfectly applicable in reasoning, though
" not in extent, to the case of the Bank of
" England."

It appears also that the extension of issues
was sudden as well as the contraction. Mr
Haldiman states, that the great increase took
place he believed in June, July, August, and
September ; while the reduction took place in
October. There is little doubt that the effect
of the payments made by France to foreign
powers, would have been to have determined

the balance of trade against the nation ; but as these payments were made gradually, and principally by loans contracted in other countries, we should hardly think that they were the cause. It is much more probable that the extent and suddenness of the issues made by the bank, had produced that effect which was so immediately counteracted, but with such ruinous consequence to individuals, by its retracing the steps that had caused it.

## With a Metallic Currency, sudden Fluctuations in Prices could not happen.

As the philosopher's stone has not yet been discovered, neither individuals nor bodies have the power of making gold at pleasure, and we are pretty well assured that it is never their pleasure to destroy it. The directors of the Bank of France might desire to circulate its notes, but it is quite clear that they wished to keep the gold in the country also. No increase or reduction therefore in the amount of money in circulation could be made with a metallic currency, except through the medium of trade : there would be no acquiring it except in the regular channel of circulation. If a person saved money, he would lend it out at one rate of interest or other ; and if he placed it in the hands of bankers, they would do the same. A banker does not receive deposits to let them lie idle : whether he pays interest for them or not, he lends them out on the best terms he can get. A banker who issues his own notes, may, for different reasons, be unwilling, or unable, to lend them at less than a given rate of interest; but did he deal in metallic money the case would be different. If he paid nothing for his deposits, he would consider that no reason why he should get nothing for them; and if he could not get a high rate of interest, however low it might be, he would take the highest he could get. If he paid interest for them, he could not afford to keep the money in his coffers; but the less he could get, of course, the less he would give. Thus metallic money is always kept in circulation.

Hoarding to a small extent perhaps is generally practised, but not to be worth notice; and there is perhaps upon the average an equal sum applied in that way: as one hoard accumulates, another is brought into circulation, from one cause or other.

### Principles which govern the Demand for Bank Paper.

There are two principles which govern the

demand for bank paper : the value of money compared with the interest which banks charge, and the internal balance of trade.

## *The Value of Money compared with the Interest which Banks charge.*

There can be no question that if the banks at this moment were to lower the interest of money to one per cent. there would be a very extensive demand for bank paper upon the most unexceptionable securities. On the other hand, if they were to raise the rate of interest they charge to 10 or 15 per cent. there is as little doubt that all their creditors would pay off their debts as soon as possible, and they would find but very few new customers upon such terms.

The legal rate of interest, however, in this country, is 5 per cent. above which banks are not allowed to take; while they perhaps cannot afford to charge less than four. Bank notes are subject to a stamp duty which diminishes the profit of issuing them ; and it is found indeed by experience, that private banks would rather contract their issues, than take even less than five.

Now when money is worth more than 5 per cent. there is a great demand upon the banks for their notes, and when it is worth less, the demand declines ; in the first case they are enabled to extend their issues ; in the last they contract of themselves.

We have seen in a former chapter, that the value of money is determined by the demand for it, and that with the demand the rate of interest rises or falls. Previous to any general extension of bank issues, therefore, it will always be found that a demand for money has arisen which has increased the value of it; on the contrary, when the value of money has fallen below 5 per cent. we shall find that a contraction of bank issues has been the consequence.

Between the rate of interest paid by government and the value of money to individuals, there is probably about one per cent. difference : at least when government securities are above 60, and the usury law does not increase the distance : when they are beneath 60, the difference may be 3 or 4 per cent. At present, individuals, however, give 5 per cent. and the funds pay four.

Since 1793, until within these five years, money has always been worth 5 per cent. and upwards to individuals ; and no involuntary contraction of bank-issues has taken place : the banks have had as great a demand for their notes as they thought proper to supply, under the checks from other causes to which they were subject.

The circulation of the Bank of England is

not so liable to contraction from an alteration in the value of money. It is principally issued, not in loans to individuals, but to government upon exchequer bills. The interest of these bills, by a bargain with the bank, government may reduce, but they are not paid off in consequence of a fall in the value of money, as is the case with debts due by individuals.

## Internal Balance of Trade.

Each district has its balance of trade, as well as each nation : it is as necessary between two counties as two kingdoms : it is of no importance in what its circulating medium consists, whether in metallic money, Bank of England paper, or local notes, the principle is the same. A person whose property is in Northumberland, may live and spend his income in London. But in this case, a quantity of raw or manufactured produce must, directly or indirectly, be remitted from Northumberland to him : the balance of payments must upon the average be equal. This, however, can only be preserved by an equality of prices. If the prices of a district are above the general level, the balance of payments must be against it ; if below, in its favor.

When banks first began to issue notes, the

money in circulation must have been entirely metallic, and sufficient to maintain the level of the national prices. The only check, which, at that time, existed to the issues of banks, consisted in their obligation to pay their notes with gold on demand. As, however, gold must then have been very plentiful, if the credit of a bank was good, this could be hardly considered a check of a very positive nature ; the principal would perhaps arise from the doubts which, at least private bankers might then feel in the prudence of rendering their issues too extensive. But each banker would be governed by his own ideas on that point.

The first effect produced by the increased circulation of any particular bank, would be, of course, an elevation of prices in its own district; and this would determine the balance of trade against it. The consequence would, therefore, be, that metallic money equal to such increase, would be remitted to other parts of the country. This would elevate the prices of those districts, render the elevation more general, and money would be ultimately sent out of the kingdom equal to the issue which had taken place.

The limits, to which each bank would in the end be obliged to confine itself, would be the circulation, at the national prices, of that part of the country in which its notes would pass, If it exceeded this, and still determined the balance of trade against its own district, being obliged to pay its notes in metallic money, it would be called upon for gold, in order to make the necessary remittances. But the gold having previously disappeared, it would be obliged to import it from other parts of the country to meet this demand. This importation of gold on the one hand, would neutralize the remittance of it on the other, and the balance of trade would continue just as unfavourable. The bank would consequently be put to an endless expence until it reduced its circulation, and restored prices to the national level.

The superior credit of the Scotch Banks enabled them to issue their notes with confidence, and very early to occupy the principal circulation of Scotland. The theory of money and banking being at that time very little understood, they were not, at first, sufficiently cautious in keeping their issues within the necessary limits. The result was, that they had to purchase gold in London, and bring it to Scotland at a great expence, from whence it disappeared as soon as it was issued. They at last, however, discovered their mistake, and corrected it. Very interesting particulars, on this subject, will be found in Dr Smith's Chapter on Money.

London is the bullion market of the kingdom, where the exports and imports of it are made; and the Bank of England the mart of these transactions. When a demand for bullion to be sent abroad exists, the Bank of England is obliged to supply it; and when gold comes into the country, the bank generally replenishes its coffers for that purpose. By keeping its circulation, however, within the amount required to sustain the national prices, it can always prevent a demand which it is inconvenient to supply.

When paper money came to completely occupy the circulation of the kingdom, the issues of the Bank of England would govern those of the country banks. All the country banks have agents in London, and if a remittance is made from one part of the kingdom to the other, it is made by their drafts upon their London agents. When gold had disappeared from circulation, as the notes of each bank will only pass in its own district, there would be no other mode of remittance. The party wishing to remit, would take into a bank the notes current where he resided, and procure a bill upon London for them, which he would send to his correspondent. The bank would be obliged to furnish him this bill, or Bank of England notes. If it furnished him with the latter, it would have to procure them from London, so that there would be no advantage in refusing him a bill, were it so inclined.

The trade, however, between any particular district and London must balance. This balance, as we have before stated, can be preserved only by an equality of prices ; and this equality can only exist by the circulation of the district preserving a just proportion with that of the Bank of England. When the bills upon London received by a banker, and the demand for them are equal, he advances as many notes upon such bills on the one hand as he receives in demand for them on the other ; but if the demand exceeds the supply, he receives more notes than he advances ; while if the supply exceeds the demand, he advances more notes than he receives. When the balance of trade is therefore in favour of a district, the natural consequence is an extension of issues by the number of London bills presented for discount ; when against a district, a contraction of issues by the superior demand for London bills which the banks experience.

Bankers never have any hesitation in advancing their notes upon London bills. They are enabled, with the proceeds of them, to purchase into the funds, or increase their deposits at interest in their London agents' hands ; and though they may get less interest for their advances, and make less in this case by the circulation of their paper than if it were lent upon home securities at 5 per cent. yet the money is ready to meet the payment of their notes whenever they are returned, in demand either for those of the Bank of England, or London bills, without their suffering any material inconvenience.

If by a reduced home demand for money, in consequence of a reduction in its value, the circulation of country banks should continue to contract, keep down prices, and thus determine the balance of trade in favour of their respective districts, they would in time be enabled to re-advance their whole circulation upon deposits in London.

When, on the contrary, an excessive demand for London bills exists, a bank may have funds in London, from a previous favourable balance, or otherwise, with which to meet it, and if the demand for money at home is great, may re-advance its notes, and thus keep up the excessive circulation. In this case, the balance of trade would continue unfavourable, and fresh demands for bills on London would arise, and would continue until its funds in London were exhausted. It would then be obliged to allow its circulation to contract, or even to contract it forcibly, in order to reduce the demand for London bills upon it. This contraction would lower prices, restore the trade of the district to a balance, or probably determine the balance in its favour.

A banker's deposits in London, more particularly in his agent's hands, are usually termed cash. They do not, however, consist of cash, but of capital or credits. The money is lent out by his agents, and exists only in the shape of debts, the value of which has been consumed either actually or commercially. Or otherwise it rests on government securities, either in his own name or that of his agents, and government or the parties from whom the securities were purchased have done the same. The deposits which country banks have in London are considered money, because they can at any time be turned into it, not that they in reality consist of money, more than mortgages or any other description of capital.

When the bankers increase or withdraw their deposits from London, no permanent increase or diminution of property takes place. Each bill they remit is drawn for money purchased with commodities deposited, or to be deposited in the London market. That reduction of prices in the country which has determined the balance of trade in favour of London, has produced an actual exportation of consumable commodities to the London market, for the proceeds of which the bill is drawn. Or should a person go from the country to London, and purchase a bill upon London with which to pay his expences, by so doing he contracts the circulation of the district, reduces the prices below those of London, and an exportation of commodities to London is the consequence. Thus commodities always follow, if they do not precede, every bill upon London which is drawn. Accommodation bills, or bills not founded upon real transactions, must be met by other bills to the same amount, so that they never affect the real balance of payments.

Now when the balance of trade is in favour of the country, and bankers increase their deposits in London, these effects are produced by it: the prices of commodities are reduced in London; and so are the value of money and profits of trade; while the consumption is increased. In the country, on the other hand, the prices of commodities may have fallen, but the profits of trade and interest of money are kept up.

The prices of commodities in London, are not determined by the circulation of London, but by the circulation of the district from whence they come, upon the same principle that foreign commodities are not determined by the state of prices in this country, but in the country where they are produced. If the foreign trade in corn was thrown open, the prices of corn in this would be reduced to nearly a level with that of other countries, not by a reduced demand on our part, but by the reduced prices of the supply; and the principle is the same with our internal trade.

The commodities sent to London, therefore, in consequence of a contraction of currency, which enabled the country banker to increase his deposits, would merely reduce the prices in London, and increase its consumption. It would be a gain to London in consumable commodities, and a loss to the country. The money which the banker drew in London, by holding the bill, would represent a certain quantity of consumable commodities in the London market. It would not, however, be spent by him or his agent, but would be thrown into the money market. This would reduce the interest of money and profits of trade in London, and keep down its general economy, in order to make room for the expenditure of the money thus saved. But no immediate loss would result to those whose incomes were thus forcibly diminished; from the reduced price of commodities they would command as great a quantity as before.

In the country, the value of money and profits of trade would be kept up. If money was previously scarce, and the fall of prices proceeded from a forced contraction, on the part of the banks, the value of money would, of course, become greater. If it proceeded from the interest charged by the banks, being too high, the economy of the country, instead of reducing the interest of money and profits of trade, in order to reduce itself, would find vent in discharging the debts due to the banks, at the high rate of interest they imposed; and the value of money and profits of trade would thus be kept up to that level which rendered the general economy greater than the general expenditure.

Another effect, however, would also be produced. The principle laid down by bankers in the conduct of their business, and it is a very safe principle for themselves, is not to advance money on any other than mercantile bills, at least to any extent. If a person wished for money on an estate, though the security would be better, they would not, for they could not, prudently lend it him. The effect, however, of their lodging their money in London, by means of the balance of trade, would be to raise the price of the funds; whereas the effect of the contraction of their currency, would be to keep up the interest of money in the country. This would operate in two ways: while it raised the price of the funds on the one hand, it would on the other tempt the London capitalist, by keeping up the interest of money in the country, to lend his money in the country upon mortgage at this higher rate. The landed proprietor instead of borrowing of the banks, would therefore borrow of the London capitalist. So far as this effect was produced, the payments would balance. The notes of the banks would be virtually advanced to the landed proprietor, but it would be through the medium of the funds. A change of securities would take place between the banker and some fundholder. The banker would buy his stock, and he would advance the money to the country proprietor, who, could the bank have advanced it, would not have gone further.

Any contraction of currency, however local, would have the general effect of determining the balance of foreign trade in favour of the country. A contraction in one district would determine the balance of payments from other parts as well as London, in its favour. This would create in those places a demand for London bills to remit, which would curtail their respective circulations. Thus a general reduction of prices below the national standard would take place, and a balance of foreign trade and an influx of the precious metals would consequently follow.

This influx of precious metals would, however, very materially contribute to restore the circulation of the country banks to its proper level again.

All gold is either imported directly to London, or sent thither as soon as it is imported. A country bank can only receive gold in one of three ways : in payment of a debt; in exchange for its notes ; or by way of deposit. If in payment of a debt, the debt has been created by an advance of notes, and being repaid in gold, the notes extant represent the gold with which the debt is discharged. If in exchange for notes, the notes advanced represent the gold received ; or if by way of deposit, the deposit will be discharged with notes when it is withdrawn. Consequently gold cannot be received by a bank without giving currency to its value in paper. When received, it is not re-issued at home : the business of a bank is to issue its own notes. It is therefore sent to London, and purchases made with it into the funds. Or through the medium of the bank's agents it is advanced upon other securities, and the interest received in London ; and as with deposits by remittances of London bills, the gain of the bank by the notes put in circulation is the interest thus made. The gold thus sent to London is put in currency by means of these purchases or advances, or if it is sent to the Bank of England, it is in exchange for its notes to be so applied. In either case, circulation is extended, and prices increased in the London district. If it is imported by a country merchant, and sent to his own agents in London, in order to be coined or sold to the bank, he draws a bill upon his agent for the amount, and receives notes for the bill at a bank where he resides; which is the same to such bank as if the gold had passed through its hands. If, however, the gold is imported directly to London, it gives no immediate increase of country circulation, but in the first place swells that of the metropolis. This has the immediate effect of still further increasing the balance of trade in favour of the country; and of more speedily, in consequence, producing the re-issue of local paper to the extent necessary for restoring prices to their former level again.

A contraction of local currency must consequently be followed by these effects: the balance of foreign trade will be in our favour; the interest of money in London will be lower than in the country, and there will be more difficulty in finding employment for it; the consumption of London will be increased; and the quantity of money in circulation will be greater than usual; it will no doubt be found that the country banks have increased their deposits: at the same time, the circulation in the manufacturing districts will be less diminished, if it is not considerably extended; the quantity of goods manufactured for exportation will be greater than usual; while the consumption of those districts will be increased. If the present agricultural distress is the result of a contraction of country bank circulation, these effects

will be, and I have no doubt are, experienced
at the present moment. That some of them
are, is a matter of perfect notoriety.

### The Effects, in good and bad Harvests, of our present System of Currency.

As we have before shewn, in a good harvest
money is plentiful, in a bad one it is scarce ;
and that this is a wise disposition of Providence, by which additional employment to labour is given in the one case, and less in the
other. Now the effect of the present mode of
issuing the currency, obviously is to entirely
counteract this order of nature.

The additional demand for money in a scarcity, only creates an extension of bank issues.
Instead of merchants and manufacturers being
prevented from giving employment to labour,
by a contraction of bank accommodation, they
are induced by the cheapness of labour, and
the facility of raising money from the banks,
to give increased employment to it.

This additional employment of labour does
not increase the supply of provisions, it only
renders a greater quantity necessary ; while the
demand must still be kept down to the reduced
proportion there is for each individual, by an
excess of price. The dearness of provisions,

by inducing men to work double work in order to acquire even the limited proportion there is for them, cheapens labour. Thus misery meets the labouring classes in a two-fold shape,—they are worked to death on the one hand, and starved to death on the other.

In a plentiful season, on the contrary, unless the demand for money at the time exceed the supply, the effect is a contraction of currency, instead of a reduction of interest. The banks have already as much money lent as at the rate of interest they charge will be borrowed of them. The additional supply therefore will only contract their issues ; and instead of the farmer gaining by a good harvest, he stands a fair chance of losing by it. He places his corn in the market, and destroys its means of consumption by placing the money in a bank where it will be cancelled. By this means the party to whom it is sold loses by it, while from the reduced quantity of money in circulation, corn will not rise again, and the next he brings to market he must sell at a less price.

# CHAPTER XX.

*The Price of Corn not subject to material Fluctuations
from the Supply.*

I THINK this proposition will, without hesitation, be granted,—that if the price of corn depended upon the supply, it would be governed by it ; with an average crop it would be at an average price ; and as the crop was above or below the average, the price would fall or rise.

By the evidence of Mr Hodgson, of the house of Cropper, Benson, and Co. of Liverpool, before the agricultural committee of 1821, (an extract of which will be found in the Appendix) it appears that crops are subject in quantity to considerable variations. That house is in the habit of taking an annual survey of the principal corn districts of the kingdom, at an expence, and with a pains and accuracy which leave the truth of their results perfectly unquestionable ; and these, for six years, have been as follows :—

1815, 37 Winchester bushels per acre, quality good.

1816, 25 ditto, very bad in quality, nearly rotten.

1817, 33 ditto, the quality not very good.

1818, 32 ditto, quality very good.

1819, 27 ditto, quality very good, but not so good as the year before.

1820, 37 ditto, sound and dry, but not so good as the two preceding years.

6)191

32 Average say of the 6 years.

It is also understood that 1821 was an average crop, and this year rather less.

It must, however, be observed, that their object being merely to obtain a comparative estimate for commercial purposes, they appear only to take the most productive districts—those which are most likely to affect the market; while they make no allowance for furrows, hedges, loss by vermin, waste in harvesting, &c. They compute that in order to get the real produce, one-sixth at least ought to be deducted from their calculations. This however, would be no average for the kingdom, as they do not take the hilly and poorer districts. The average actual produce of the whole kingdom is supposed to be about 20 bushels per acre; and their surveys seem to support this supposition. Intelligent agriculturalists, I find, generally concur in thinking that the crops must at least be as variable in quantity as these surveys make them. I am further informed, that the variations must have been greater previous to the improvements which have taken place in agriculture: that great crops are now yielded upon soils which did not produce wheat before; and that a year which produces a good crop on these soils, is not favourable to those upon which, alone, above thirty or forty years ago, corn was grown, and *vice versa :* so that a failure on one description of soil is in some measure balanced by the productiveness of the other; and that there cannot be now such deficiencies as the crops must have been subject to in former times.

Now the average price of wheat during the last century, appears to have been about 40s. per quarter. Had the variations of price in that time therefore corresponded to the variations in supply, and had the difference in the crops only been equal to that exhibited by Messrs Cropper, Benson, and Co.'s surveys, taking 32 to be the average, the prices of that period must have presented fluctuations similar to the following :—

| | | Price per qr. | | Ann. variations. | | | |
|---|---|---|---|---|---|---|---|
| | | s. | d | s. | d. | s. | d. |
| 1815, 37 Winchester bushels | | 34 | 7 | | | *34 | 7 |
| 1816, 25 | ditto | 51 | 2 a rise of 16. | | 7 | | |
| 1817, 33 | ditto | 38 | 9 a fall of 12 | | 5 | | |
| 1818, 32 | ditto | 40 | 0 a rise of 1 | | 3 | | |
| 1819, 27 | ditto | 47 | 4 a rise of 7 | | 4 | | |
| 1820, 37 | ditto | 34 | 7 a fall of 12 | | 9 | *34 | 7 |
| 1821, 32 said to be an average crop. | | 40 | 0 a rise of 5 | | 4 | | |

This presumes that the crop each season
yielded alike. The quantity of flour however,
would be greater per quarter in good seasons
than in bad.

Now if we refer to the prices of the last century (see Appendix) we shall find that there are
no fluctuations at all corresponding to this.

In 1709, wheat was 69s. 9d. from whence it
gradually declined with trifling exceptions until 1724, when it was 32s. 10d. then rose at
once to 43s. 1d. and then gradually declined
again to 23s. 8d. and 25s. 2d. in 1732 and 3.
It then suddenly rose again to 34s. 6d.; but
ultimately fell, with the exception of a temporary rise produced by the scarcity of 1740, to
about the same prices in 1743, 4, and 5, as in
1732 and 3; after which, in 1746, it experienced another sudden elevation. The prices
of this period are as follow :—

* The 1st and 6th year, had the price been determined by
the supply, must have agreed in price as well as in quantity.

|  | *Price per qr.* | | *Ann. variations.* | | | | |
|---|---|---|---|---|---|---|---|
|  | *s.* | *d.* | | *s.* | *d.* | *s.* | *d.* |
| 1709, | 69 | 9 | | | | | |
| 1710, | 69 | 4 | a fall of | 0 | 5 | | |
| 1711, | 48 | 4 | a fall of | 11 | 0 | | |
| 1712, | 41 | 2 | a fall of | 7 | 2 | | |
| 1713, | 45 | 4 | a rise of | 4 | 2 | | |
| 1714, | 44 | 9 | a fall of | 0 | 7 | a fall of | 25 0 |
| 1715, | 38 | 2 | a fall of | 6 | 7 | | |
| 1716, | 42 | 8 | a rise of | 4 | 6 | | |
| 1717, | 40 | 7 | a fall of | 2 | 1 | | |
| 1718, | 34 | 6 | a fall of | 6 | 1 | | |
| 1719, | 31 | 1 | a fall of | 3 | 5 | a fall of | 13 8 |
| 1720, | 32 | 10 | a rise of | 1 | 9 | | |
| 1721, | 33 | 4 | a rise of | 0 | 6 | | |
| 1722, | 32 | 0 | a fall of | 1 | 4 | | |
| 1723, | 30 | 10 | a fall of | 1 | 2 | | |
| 1724, | 32 | 10 | a rise of | 2 | 0 | a rise of | 1 9 |
| 1725, | 43 | 1 | a rise of | 10 | 3 | | |

After this rise in 1725, prices continued high for a few
years and then declined again:

|  |  | | | | |  | |
|---|---|---|---|---|---|---|---|
| 1726, | 40 | 10 | a fall of | 2 | 3 | | |
| 1727, | 37 | 4 | a fall of | 3 | 6 | | |
| 1728, | 48 | 5 | a rise of | 11 | 1 | | |
| 1729, | 41 | 7 | a fall of | 6 | 10 | a rise of | 8 9 |
| 1730, | 32 | 5 | a fall of | 9 | 2 | | |
| 1731, | 29 | 2 | a fall of | 3 | 3 | | |
| 1732, | 23 | 8 | a fall of | 5 | 4 | | |
| 1733, | 25 | 2 | a rise of | 1 | 6 | | |

They now experienced another considerable rise:

Variations every 5 years,
being 6, inclusive of the 2
years enumerated.

| Prices per qr. | | | | Ann. variations. | | | | |
|---|---|---|---|---|---|---|---|---|
| | s. | d. | | | s. | d. | | |
| 1734, | 34 | 6 | a rise of | 9 | 4 | a fall of | 7 | 1 |
| 1735, | 38 | 2 | a rise of | 3 | 8 | | | |
| 1736, | 35 | 10 | a fall of | 2 | 4 | | | |
| 1737, | 33 | 9 | a fall of | 2 | 1 | | | |
| 1738, | 31 | 6 | a fall of | 2 | 3 | | | |
| 1739, | 34 | 2 | a rise of | 2 | 8 | a fall of | 0 | 4 |

1740 is the year of scarcity spoken of by Dr Smith, prices
therefore now rose, but fell immediately after.

| 1740, | 45 | 1 | a rise of | 10 | 11 | | | |
|---|---|---|---|---|---|---|---|---|
| 1741, | 41 | 5 | a fall of | 3 | 8 | | | |
| 1742, | 30 | 2 | a fall of | 11 | 3 | | | |
| 1743, | 22 | 1 | a fall of | 8 | 1 | | | |
| 1744, | 22 | 1 | the same, | | | a fall of | 12 | 1 |
| 1745, | 24 | 5 | a rise of | 2 | 4 | | | |

They now suddenly rose again:

| 1746, | 38 | 4 | a rise of | 10 | 3 | | | |
|---|---|---|---|---|---|---|---|---|
| 1747, | 30 | 11 | a fall of | 3 | 9 | | | |
| 1748, | 32 | 10 | a rise of | 1 | 11 | | | |
| 1749, | 32 | 10 | the same, | | | a rise of | 10 | 9 |
| 1750, | 28 | 10 | a fall of | 2 | 0 | | | |

I need not go through the whole table,
which the reader can refer to in the Appendix.
I take the early part of the century, more particularly, as there was then probably very little
paper in circulation. Here may be said to be
four periods, each of which commenced with a

sudden rise, followed with trifling exceptions, by
a gradual decline ; and it thus clearly appears,
that though there were great changes in price,
there were no such variations as would have
been produced by prices depending upon the
state of the crops, admitting them to be then
as variable as now.  Neither is it possible to
account for these changes, on the theory of
cycles of seasons referred to in the report of the
agricultural committee of 1821.  The changes
are not sufficiently regular and periodical for
the work of nature : Besides the principle of
population would equally tend to destroy their
effect upon prices; and as the crops of 1815
and 1820, were just of the same amount in
quantity, those six years of accurate admeasurement upset the hypothesis.

During the last century, there appears to
have been two years which were years of scarcity, 1740 and 1767.  The first is spoken of by
Dr Smith, and is proved by the table of exports and imports.  The last is proved by the
table of exports and imports, and by the fact
that the expedient of suspending distillation
from corn was resorted to that year for the first
time.  The stoppage of distillation has been
repeatedly resorted to since when prices were
high ; but under the presumption that high
prices were always a proof of scarcity.  That
these were scarce years is also proved by the

fact, that in both instances the rise was temporary. The prices from 1766 to 1769, were
as follow :—

|  | Price per Qr. |  | Ann. Variation. |  |
|---|---|---|---|---|
|  | s. | d | s. | d. |
| 1766, | 43 | 1 |  |  |
| 1767, | 57 | 4 | a rise of 14 | 3 |
| 1768, | 53 | 9 | a fall of 3 | 7 |
| 1769, | 40 | 7 | a fall of 13 | 2 |

I do not doubt, however, that this rise was
aggravated by the present system of currency
having become more general.

In 1740, the rise was 11s. per quarter; and
in 1767 it appears to have been 14s. 9d. Now,
if every rise in price during the last century
had proceeded from want of supply, every rise
to an equal extent must have been the result
of scarcity. That this was not the case, however, is proved by the table of exports and imports. A rise, no doubt, in the countries to
which our corn was exported, would have the
effect of increasing both our prices and exports
at the same time. But when it appears that a
rise took place, and our exports continued to a
limited extent, or suffered no material increase,
it is a proof that such rise was neither the result
of scarcity in other countries, nor in our own ;
for in the first case, our exports would have
been increased, in the last entirely suspended.

In 1702, 3, and 4, and also 1745, and subsequent years, rises as great as in these years of scarcity took place, without our exports being materially affected. Sudden elevations of price, produced by an alteration in the value of money, may take place, however, with a metallic currency, from increased demands for money by government, quickening its motions; but all declensions of price must be gradual, produced through the medium of the balance of trade, unless government were to take money out of circulation, and remit it abroad. The latter rises in price to which we have referred, were sudden, and just after the commencement, or during war; whereas the reductions which followed were gradual. We may consequently infer, that these alterations in price were changes in the value of the currency, produced by the sudden demands of government for money; that they were not fluctuations from variations in supply must be evident.

I shall not attempt, however, to account for changes in price at so remote a distance, and with a metallic currency. The precious metals are regardless of lines of demarcation; and a change in the value of money in one country will equally affect its value in all those which trade with it. In order to account for such changes, it would be necessary to know the economical history of other countries as well as our own ; while a correct knowledge, at this distance, is hardly possible of either. But within the last 30 years our currency has been principally paper, consequently the causes of the leading changes which have taken place in that time, may perhaps, in some measure at least, be accounted for.

# CHAPTER XXI.

*Probable Causes which have produced the leading **Changes** in the Prices of Corn, during the last 30 Years.*

AT the commencement of the late war, in 1793, there was a considerable quantity of metallic money in the country. The banks, however, had absorbed a considerable share of the circulation, and were very ready to occupy the remainder as soon as a sufficiently extensive demand for their notes should arise.

At this period, the economy and expenditure of the country would of course be equal, and the loans which were contracted would create a demand in the money market, that would fall upon trade, and compel merchants, traders, and others to reduce their stocks. Thus, though by the increased value of money, an accelerated motion would be given to the currency, yet a greater supply of commodities would be brought into the market, and until they were consumed, the more rapid movement of the money in circulation would not affect prices.

In 1795, however, the price of corn began to rise, and became very high. This might have happened from the increased motion of the currency alone, but to what extent, it would be difficult to say. The interest of money, however, had risen, and an increased demand upon bankers would be the natural result. In the early part of the year, the Bank of England had in consequence extended its issues very considerably, and the country banks had no doubt done the same.

As prices rose, the balance of trade would be determined against the country, and this would create a demand upon the Bank of England for gold, by which its notes would be run in upon it. Towards the end of the year, therefore, its issues appear to have been considerably contracted. This would not, perhaps, produce an equal contraction on the part of the country banks, as the balance of payments in favour of London would be met by remittances of gold then in circulation. The Bank of England, however, still continued to contract its issues, and this, together with the quantity of gold taken out of the circulation of London, in order to send abroad, or to supply the demands of the bank for the same purpose, would perhaps in the end check those of the country banks also. Towards the end of the following year, consequently, prices fell again to nearly their previous level, and the exchanges recovered.

It was thought at the time, that this rise was produced by a failing crop, as people were not then in the habit of thinking that money had any thing to do with price ; and perhaps the crop was worse than usual ; but as the exchanges fell immediately as the rise took place, this, to any extent at least, could not be the case. In a scarcity, the value of commodities, the produce of labour, is rather reduced than increased, and the foreign demand for them more likely to improve than decline. In 1667, as will be observed in the table of exchanges from the Encyclopedia Britannica, in the Appendix, which it is probable was a year of scarcity, the exchanges continued 8 per cent. in favour of London through the whole of it.

In 1799, the price of corn again began to rise. It is probable the crop of this year was a very bad one. The Bank of England, however, in 1797, had suspended cash payments, and was not now compelled to curtail its issues by any fear of demands upon it for gold ; and it had begun to increase them very considerably, in which it had no doubt been followed by the country banks. The price of wheat, which was 49s. in the beginning of 1799, rose in 1800 to 121s. and as the bank still continued to increase its issues, in April 1801 it had reached 156s.

The scarcity of 1799 might probably have raised the price of wheat in 1800 ten or fifteen shillings per quarter upon the average, as in former years of scarcity. But that these very high prices were the mere result of the extended circulation of the banks, is proved by the fact that prices were higher in 1801, after a good harvest, than they were in 1800, after a bad one.

Towards the end of 1801, however, prices began to fall, and in the following year nearly reached their former level. This does not seem to have been produced by any contraction of the bank issues. But peace with France took place the latter end of 1801 ; money became less valuable, and the funds rose. This would re- tard the motions of the currency, which would produce a reduction of prices. Perhaps the country banks might also have contracted their issues, from the sudden reduction in the value of money ; for it is the issues of country banks that regulate the price of corn. A principal cause, however, was no doubt an extension of trade, and an increase of commodities in circu- lation, which would just have the same effect in reducing prices as a diminished quantity of cur- rency would have. A great extension of til- lage, in consequence of the late rise, had also probably taken place. It must likewise be ob- served, that a considerable quantity of gold had no doubt been exported, for there was still a large amount in circulation.

War commenced again in the latter end of 1803, and about a year afterwards corn again began to rise. This rise would not take place until the stocks of commodities which had accumulated in consequence of the diminished value of money during the peace, had been considerably reduced. When this happened, the increased motion of the currency, from the high rate of interest and profits, together with the reduced demand for currency by the curtailment of our foreign trade, would be felt. At the same time, the issues of the bank had been rather increased. In August, 1805, wheat had therefore reached 100s. which was nearly double what it had been the August before. It after that declined to below 80s., and continued at and about that price the whole of the next year.

In 1807, a contraction of country circulation seems to have taken place (see table in the Appendix, of stamps issued to country banks, commencing the year 1805) and wheat declined to 73s. upon the average.

At the peace of Tilsit, in the latter end of 1807, Bonaparte succeeded in shutting us out of all direct trade with the continent of Europe, which would curtail our demand for currency ; but the issues of the banks were not reduced, and prices towards the end of the year 1808 began to rise considerably.

They continued high from 1808 to 1812, varying with the circumstances of our trade, and the extent of the circulation.

In 1813, a free trade took place with the north of Europe, and as no corresponding extension of Bank issues were made, corn began to decline : wheat fell from 122s. in March to 73s. in December, and continued at that average throughout the following year.

In 1815, a contraction of the circulation of the country banks took place, and wheat fell to an average of 64s. It continued low till the latter end of 1816, when probably the very bad harvest of that year had increased the demand for money in the country, as an extension of issues took place, and prices began to rise again. No extension of issues in the latter end of 1816 appears by the account of stamps ; but it must be presumed, from the previous contraction, that there was a balance of notes on hand, which would be first issued before that increased demand for stamps, which appears in 1817, would occur.

In 1817, the issues of the Bank of England were considerably extended, and the average price of wheat was 94s.

In 1818, the Bank of England circulation appears to have been curtailed. Money had become plentiful in London, and the 3 per cents. had rapidly risen to 80. This, however, had not been the case in the country, for the banks increased their issues ; and if we allow that prices were affected 20s. per quarter by the very bad harvest of 1816, which on 94s. is perhaps a fair estimate,—as the prices this year were 84s. it will make a national rise from the bank issues of 10s. per quarter.

The rise in the funds, however, induced many to sell out, and transfer their money to the country, which would create a demand for London bills, and curtail the issues of the country banks. Prices would consequently fall. In 1819, therefore, wheat fell to the average of 73s. Since then, the diminished value of money has continued, no doubt, to contract the country bank circulation, upon which the price of agricultural produce depends, and it has continued falling until it has reached its present depression.

For four or five years, commencing with 1809, the bullion and paper prices of corn were not the same. When gold had entirely disappeared from circulation, the issues of paper not being regulated by the state of the exchanges as before, prices rose above that level at which our foreign trade balanced ; and the price of bills upon England, or the exchanges, consequently fell to the extent of this difference. Corn may be said then to have had two prices governed by different principles : its price in paper governed by the quantity of it compared with the quantity of commodities in circulation ; and its price in gold, governed entirely by the circumstances of our trade at the moment.

During the operation of Bonaparte's continental system, it was much more easy to smuggle our lighter and more valuable goods to the continent, than to receive those bulky commodities of which our imports generally consist in return. A cargo of our exports to the north of Europe is worth twenty or thirty of the imports with which we are paid. This trade, therefore, could only be brought to a balance by the excessive price of our commodities. At the same time, as a very small quantity of gold would reduce its price where there was no demand for it, its price would be merely nominal, and would be determined by the demand for bills upon England, or the state of the Exchanges ; as this demand and the exchanges rose, the price of gold in bank paper would fall, and *vice versa*. At this time, therefore, the bullion price, as well as the paper price of corn was high. The following is a statement of the prices in both bullion and in paper, from 1809 to 1815 inclusive :—

| Paper Price per Quarter. | | | Bullion Price per Quarter. | | |
|---|---|---|---|---|---|
| 1809, | - | 95s. | 1809, | - | 82s. |
| 1810, | - | 106s. | 1810, | - | 95s. |
| 1811, | - | 94s. | 1811, | - | 83s. |
| 1812, | - | 125s. | 1812, | - | 97s. |
| 1813, | - | 108s. | 1813, | - | 80s. |
| 1814, | - | 74s. | 1814, | - | 59s. |
| 1815, | - | 64s. | 1815, | - | 53s. |

That these prices were entirely governed by different principles, is proved by the fluctuations not being parallel. For instance in 1814, the price of wheat in paper fell from 78s. to 70s. ; whereas the price in bullion rose from 56s. 6d. to 65s., and in 1815, the price of wheat in

| January was 60s. in paper, and 54s. in bullion. |
| May, | 70s. | ditto | 52s. | ditto. |
| December, | 55s. | ditto | 52s. | ditto. |

So that while the price in bullion remained nearly stationary, the price in paper within the year fluctuated considerably.

At that period of the war, when our foreign trade was so variable and uncertain, the bank restriction act would have been a great advantage, had the paper circulation been governed by any kind of principle.

# CHAPTER XXII.

*With a Paper Currency, Importations of Foreign Corn
cannot materially reduce Prices.*

DURING the high prices which have occurred
in the last 30 years, great importations of corn
have always taken place when the ports of Europe were open to us, and as they always diminished when corn fell, it has been supposed
that these importations reduced its price.
Great, however, as they may appear at different times to have been, they never could at
any time have had any very material effect upon
the market; and that in fact they had no such
effect, was proved in 1801, when, after a good
harvest, and in the teeth of the greatest importations at that time ever known, wheat rose to
a higher price than it ever was before, or has
been since. The principle however, will appear more evident upon further examination.

Dr Colquhoun, in 1812, estimates the quantity of grain produced in this kingdom as follows :—

*Quarters.*

| | | | |
|---|---|---|---|
| Wheat, | 9,170,000, | at 70s. 6d. | £32,324,250 |
| Barley, | 6,335,000, | at 37s. 6d. | 11,719,750 |
| Oats, | 16,950,000, | at 29s. 0d. | 24,577,500 |
| Rye, | 685,000, | at 43s. 10d. | 1,501,291 |
| Beans and Peas, | 1,860,000, | at 38s. 10d. | 3,611,500 |

£73,734,291

Now the total imports from foreign ports from 1813 to 1818 inclusive, after which the ports were finally shut, are as follows:—

1813. At prices corresponding to 108s. per quarter for wheat, £2,192,592
In order to put it upon a par with Dr Colquhoun's calculation at 70s. 6d. deduct say one-third - - - 730,864

£1,461,728

1814. At prices corresponding to 73s. 11d. for wheat, from which we shall make no deduction - - 2,815,319

1815. At prices corresponding to 64s. 4d. for wheat - 793,245
To which add one-tenth - 79,324

872,569

1816. At prices corresponding to 75s. 10d. for wheat, from which we shall make no deduction - - - 942,497

Carried over £6,092,113

|  | Brought forward | £6,092,113 |
|---|---|---|

1817. At prices corresponding
   to 94s. 9d. for wheat      6,403,893
From which deduct say two-
   ninths - - - - 1,423,086
                                          4,980,807

1818. At prices corresponding
   to 84s. 1d. for wheat - 10,908,140
From which deduct say one-
   eighth - - - 1,363,517
                                          9,544,623

                                          £20,617,543

Now the proportions which the imports each year bore to our average produce, are about as follows :—

1813 equal say to $\frac{1}{50}$
1814     ditto      $\frac{1}{26}$
1815     ditto      $\frac{1}{85}$
1816     ditto      $\frac{1}{77}$
1817     ditto      $\frac{1}{15}$ or say $\frac{2}{32}$
1818     ditto      $\frac{1}{8}$ or say $\frac{4}{32}$.
And the whole together equal to about $\frac{9}{32}$.

By comparing these importations with the difference in quantity there is between the crops of ordinary seasons, it will be seen how perfectly inadequate they are to produce any material effect upon prices. Altogether they do not amount to the difference between the harvests of 1819 and 1820, and these harvests were not, we should imagine, either so remarkably defective or abundant as naturally to produce any great effect upon prices. Presuming last year an average crop, the following gives the scale of produce and of prices since 1815. The crop of each year is of course sold the year after.

| | | | | | |
|---|---|---|---|---|---|
| 1815, | ........................... Average price of wheat | | | | 64s. |
| 1815, 37 quality good | | 1816 | ditto | | 75s. |
| 1816, 25 very bad in quality, nearly rotten | | 1817 | ditto | | 94s. |
| 1817, 33 quality not very good | | 1818 | ditto | | 83s. |
| 1818, 32 quality very good | | 1819 | ditto | | 72s. |
| 1819, 27 quality very good, but not so good as the year before | | 1820 | ditto | | 65s. |
| 1820, 37 sound and dry, but not so good as the two preceding years | | 1821 | ditto | | 54s. |
| 1821, 32 ................................. | | 1822 | ditto | | 43s. |

It will be observed that from 1817 to 1822, there has been an averge reduction of about ten shillings per quarter. Now adding the reduction from 1819 to 1820, and from 1820 to 1821 together, it amounts to 18s. per quarter which is 9s. per year. The crop of 1819, however, was $\frac{5}{32}$ below an average, and the fall only 7s. It appears therefore, to have been checked about two shillings per quarter; while the crop of 1820 being $\frac{5}{32}$ above an average crop, and the fall 11s. per quarter, it appears to have been increased in the same proportion. An increase of $\frac{5}{32}$ therefore seems to have reduced prices 2s. a decrease of $\frac{5}{32}$ to have increased them to the same extent, making a difference between the two harvests of 4s. per quarter. Assuming, therefore, the fall to be a question of currency, and this variation to be produced by the difference of the crops, we are led to conclude, that if all the importations for the six years enumerated, had taken place in one, they would have reduced wheat about 4s. per quarter. But if we say that they could not have produced an effect exceeding twice that, the correctness of the position will hardly be doubted.

We are willing, however, to allow it to be extremely possible that sudden importations to a great extent might with a metallic currency, have a considerable effect upon prices. It might determine the balance of trade against the country; and as the corn came into the market, the money which represented it might go out : as the supply increased, the consumption might be diminished; by which not only an immediate, but a permanent fall of prices would be the result. But in this case it would not be the importations of corn, but the exportation of money, that would produce the material effect. The depression of the markets would still be more a question of currency than supply. It is impossible, indeed, unless we suppose that a supply of foreign corn will frighten a market out of its wits, that with a paper currency it can either affect the market after it is consumed and out of it, or can have a greater effect in reducing prices when in it, than a corresponding increase of supply by a good harvest.

It is even very possible that importations of foreign corn may have the effect of raising its price, by giving rise to a demand for bank accommodation. If a merchant imports a thousand pounds worth of corn, and borrows a thousand pounds worth of notes in consequence, he puts as much money into circulation as perhaps would promote the consumption of ten times the quantity; and I have no doubt that the late rise was at the moment rather increased than diminished by the importations which took place. This to a certain extent, at least, has evidently been the case with foreign corn in bond. The banks in Newcastle are at this time under considerable advances upon security of this description of corn; and to the extent of that advance the currency must have been extended, or prevented from contracting. If this corn was brought into the market, or all the bonded corn in the kingdom, it is hardly probable that, so far as the additional supply operated, it would affect prices one shilling per quarter. But if the money which it produced, was taken out of consumptive circulation, and paid to the banks, or placed in their hands, which would probably be done, and the consumption in consequence diminished as the supply was increased, a great reduction of price would no doubt be the result.

The ports were closed against further importations in February, 1819. Since then, of course, no more supplies of foreign corn have been brought into the market. Now admitting that one half of the foreign corn imported in 1818 was unconsumed when the harvest of that year was gathered, it would make the total supply for 1819, 34 by Messrs Cropper, Benson, and Co.'s scale. If we further assume 72s. the price of that year, to be proportioned to the supply and state of the currency at the time, had the prices since then been governed by the state of the crops alone, they must have been as follows :—

|  |  |  | *Average of Wheat.* |  |  |
|---|---|---|---|---|---|
| 1818. | 34 bushels per acre. | | 1819, | ... | 72s. |
| 1819. | 27 | ditto | 1820, | ... | 90s. |
| 1820. | 37 | ditto | 1821, | ... | 66s. |
| 1821. | 32 | ditto | 1822, | ... | 76s. |

Whereas the actual prices were :—

| | |
|---|---|
| 1819, | 73s. |
| 1820, | 65s. 7d. |
| 1821, | 54s. |
| 1822, | 44s. |

Nothing can be more clear from the above statement, than that the present low prices are produced by alterations in the currency. The reduction never could proceed from the supply, when the supply within this year or two has fallen off; nor yet from importations of foreign corn, for there has been none.

A good deal has been said about the effect produced by the large supplies of corn from Ireland; but I do not see how an increase of growth in Ireland is to have a different effect from an increase of growth in Yorkshire or Northumberland. The reasoning which applies to the one applies to the other. If it is wished to lay an exclusive tax upon Ireland, tax her produce imported into this country, and keep down her national prices below the level of ours; but if not, and she is to enjoy all the advantages of our manufacturing superiority, having a sea to cross does nct affect the principles we have endeavoured to establish. It is a shorter carriage, and less expensive, to send corn from Ireland to Liverpool, than from Berwick to London.

# CHAPTER XXIII.

*The present Price of Stocks a Proof of a Contraction*
*of Currency.*

THAT the present agricultural distress must be
caused by a contraction of the circulation of
the country banks, is a proposition which, I
trust, is now almost self-evident; but a further
proof of it is afforded by the present low price
of the funds.

If we examine the stock table, in the Appendix, and compare it with the table of the rise of
the national debt, since the revolution, from Dr
Hamilton's Inquiry, we shall have sufficient
reason to conclude that, without some particular cause, the 3 per cents. ought, by this time,
to have been far above 80.

At the commencement of the war, in 1740,
they were about 100. The stock table commences 1731, and gives, up to that period, the
following yearly averages:—

```
1731,  95
1732,  98
1733,  98
1734,  92
1735,  94
1736, 105
1737, 106
1738, 105
1739, 100
1740,  99
```

At the commencement of the war, in the year 1740, the national debt appears to have been £47,954,623, and at the peace of Aix-la-Chapelle, eight years afterwards, it had increased to £79,193,313, that is about twenty-one millions; in which time, the prices of stock were as follow :—

```
1741,  97
1742, 100
1743, 101
1744,  94
1745,  89
1746,  83
1747,  84
1748,  86
```

It is not improbable that government had not begun to borrow until 1744, as the funds did not fall until then. They were at the lowest, at the commencement of 1746, and, in that year, as we have before stated, wheat, without

any scarcity, rose very considerably. In the
eight years of peace which followed, the debt
was reduced between five and six millions, and
the prices of stock were—

1749,   98
1750,   99
1751,  100
1752,  104
1753,  104
1754,  103
1755,   95
1756,   88

In the latter year, war commenced again,
and, probably, preparations for it had begun
the year before. It continued seven years, during which the debt was increased sixty millions. In this period, the prices of stock were—

1757,   89
1758,   93
1759,   82
1760,   81
1761,   77
1762,   75
1763,   89

From this time to the American war in 1775,
a space of ten years, ten millions of debt were
discharged, in which interval stocks were,—

| | |
|---|---|
| 1764, | 82 |
| 1765, | 88 |
| 1766, | 88 |
| 1767, | 89 |
| 1768, | 90 |
| 1769, | 87 |
| 1770, | 84 |
| 1771, | 85 |
| 1772, | 89 |
| 1773, | 86 |
| 1774, | 87 |
| 1775, | 88 |

The American war lasted eight years, and an addition of £115,000,000. was made to the debt. In this war stocks were,—

| | |
|---|---|
| 1776, | 85 |
| 1777, | 78 |
| 1778, | 64 |
| 1779, | 60 |
| 1780, | 61 |
| 1781, | 57 |
| 1782, | 57 |
| 1783, | 53 |

Peace now continued to 1793, in which ten years the debt was reduced ten millions, and stocks were,—

| | |
|---|---|
| 1784, | 55 |
| 1785, | 62 |
| 1786, | 72 |
| 1787, | 72 |

1788,   75
1789,   76
1790,   77
1791,   84
1792,   90
1793,   75

In 1792, they had attained 96, but fell in contemplation of the war which broke out the year following.

Since the termination of the late war, the three per cents. have never risen except in a trifling degree above 80 ; yet from this brief review, it must be evident that with the immense reduction of expenditure by government which has taken place, stocks by this time ought to have been at much higher prices. It is not at all probable, that as government reduced its expenditure, individuals would increase theirs in exactly the same proportion, even keeping the sinking fund out of view. The consequence in that case would have been, that the economy of government would have reduced the interest of money and profits of trade, and have raised the price of the funds, had it not contracted the currency.

While the interest of money to individuals is kept up to five per cent. it is certain that the value of government securities will bear a determinate proportion to it : in the money market, the respective securities must, like other commodities, the quality of which are known, have their relative prices; and government securities, according to the present state of opinion, appear to be worth one per cent. per annum more than those of individuals. It is probable, therefore, that until the currency is principally re-issued upon deposits in London, the three per cents. will not rise much above 80.

Up to this price, however, they have risen without difficulty, Even in 1809 and 1810, during the war, they were at 70. In 1817, eighteen months after the termination of hostilities, they were 80, and occasionally 1 or 2 per cent. above it; from whence they declined in the latter part of 1818, probably in consequence of the foreign loans, until 1820, when they began to rise again; and in Oct. 1821 they were at 78; between which and 80, or a trifle above it, they have continued ever since.

By the contraction of the currency the value of money is kept up, while the prices of commodities are reduced, and the balance of trade determined in favour of the country; by which an importation of the precious metals to supply the deficiency is caused. But though by this importation the currency will be re-extended, and the prices of commodities ultimately raised to what they were before, the value of money will not, of course, be reduced by the same means. The money which comes into the country is received in payment for commodities, and will be spent in consumption by those who receive it, the same as if it had been in previous circulation. It will only be that proportion which is saved out of the incomes of those who receive it, that will tend to reduce the interest of money, and that must be but a trifling part of the whole. If, therefore, the currency were to annually contract four or five millions, and four or five millions were received by the balance of trade, whatever the immediate effect upon prices might be, which we shall again speak of hereafter, the interest of money would still be kept up, and the contraction would still go on.

Opinion, we have no doubt, has some effect in keeping the stocks at their present prices. I remember hearing that the Scotch banks sold out of the funds very largely when the 3 per cents. were at 80, in 1817 and 1818, and it was thought a wonderful instance of financial sagacity; and it seems now a pretty general opinion that 80 is about their maximum. If they were expected to be higher, capitalists would not be desirous to place their money on mortgage, until they had attained the expected price, and this would cause them to rise to it.

What prices stocks might by this time have

attained, with a metallic or an incontractable paper currency, it is impossible to say with certainty. The value of money is different in different countries; but it appears to be always the lowest in the most commercial nations, and in the most advanced state of society. In Dr Smith's time, the government of Holland borrowed at 2 per cent.* I should imagine, however, that three per cent. was about the natural rate for this country, the rate which may be termed its par. Money never seems to have been worth much more than three per cent., whereas during peace, the funds have been oftener at or above 100, than below it. In the ten years of peace which preceded the American war, they did not indeed rise much above 90, and were oftener below than above that price; but the high prices of corn in 1767, and those which followed in 1771, 2, 3, 4, and 5, appear to have given a great stimulus to agriculture, which would absorb capital, and keep the funds from attaining that price to which they would otherwise have probably arrived. In 1792, just before the war broke out, they had very nearly reached 100 : they were at 96, when they began to decline, in prospect of the war, which was declared the year following.

* Wealth of Nations, Book I. Chap. 9.

If the capitalists of society are a country's greatest economists, it must necessarily follow that the more society advances, and the greater is the proportion of its income which capitalists enjoy, the greater will be the number of its economists, and the lower the interest of money. In Russia, where society is considerably behind, at least the commercial part of Europe, interest of money is high. The Commercial Bank of St. Petersburgh, I understand, gives 5 per cent. for deposits made with it, and discounts at from 6 to 10, according to the supply and demand for money at the time. This bank only deals in money; it does not make it. It therefore necessarily regulates its charge for discounts according to the state of its funds, and the demand for money at the moment; which from some peculiarity in the trade of St Petersburgh (if there is so great a difference in the interest charged at different times) is perhaps very variable.

There is, however, no reason why money should be worth less in this country now than it was 100 years ago. The capitalists, in proportion, are more numerous than they were then, and our agricultural improvements are at a stand; and when we take into account the forced economy produced by the sudden and enormous reduction of government expenditure, there seems little reason to doubt, that with a different system of currency, the 3 per cents. must have been at 100 by this time; even though they should have subsided after the effects of the economy of government had ceased to be felt in the market. Their present price is, however, a sufficient proof of a contraction of currency, as without that they must at least before this have risen above 80.

# CHAPTER XXIV.

*Sinking Fund.*

It is not, I believe, until within these twelve months, or two years at most, that the actual receipts of government, since the return of peace, have exceeded its expenditure, that is, since the sinking fund began to operate. We now, however, have a *sinking* fund, and I have no doubt it has proved one to the agriculturists. They were sunk low enough before, but since it was added to the general excess of economy, many of them I dare say, have found themselves entirely ruined.

The fall was greater last year than in any year since the last declension of prices began. It was 11s. upon 54. A contraction numerically as great with wheat at 54 as at 84, must throw upwards of half as much more in quantity into the market without its means of consumption, and in a similar proportion with any other price: so that there must have been a greater quantity of corn thrown into the market last year, without its means of consumption, than any year before.

There can be little doubt indeed, that the

economy of the last session of parliament was most unfortunate for those it was intended to serve. It is not an impossible supposition that they might lose ten millions for every one added to the sinking fund.

But independent of the effects upon the currency, under the present system, produced by government contracting large loans, and afterwards attempting to discharge them, the principles of which have been sufficiently illustrated, the policy of this plan of finance is in other respects extremely questionable. It is, in fact, absurd on the one hand, and unjust on the other.

More than the income of society cannot be spent, and a loan is nothing but a tax through the interest of money and profits of trade. It is even more—it is a double tax. For every million saved by the economist out of their increased profit, it is probable that another, at least, is spent. When people make money with more ease, they naturally spend it with more freedom; and the additional interests and profits created must not only be equal to furnish the loan, but to cover this additional expenditure also. Consequently the borrowers furnish out of their own pockets, probably, twice the amount of the sum they borrow, and saddle themselves with an annual charge besides. It may be almost laid down as a principle, that a nation which can regularly supply its government with loans, to any particular extent, could with half the ease pay, within the year, direct taxes to the same amount.

On the other hand, with a proper currency, a sinking fund would be no loss but a gain to the ultimate payers of the taxes. If the whole income of society must be spent, the sinking fund cannot be saved, but must necessarily curtail the incomes of the economists. If not more than a certain amount of money is wanted, both the economists and government cannot save it. Indeed the idea of saving corn, cabbages, and other consumable commodities which the income of the sinking fund represents, appears quite ridiculous, and would be nonsense were it possible. It may be good housewifery to economise by hoarding commodities for any thing I know, more especially if there be plenty of pigs and ducks to gobble up the victuals that spoil, and other equally thrifty means of disposing of the other descriptions of commodities that may be wasted; but a nation cannot economise in this manner: the savings of one class or body must curtail those of another.

Nothing indeed could be a finer speculation to the ultimate payers of taxes with a proper currency, than a sinking fund. It would not merely curtail the interest of money and profits of trade to the amount of itself, but probably to many times that amount. It would reduce, in fact, in an equal degree, all income throughout the kingdom, the value of which depended upon that of capital : buildings, ships, mines, and every description of created property would be affected by it. So that every million thrown into the market would be felt from one end of the nation to the other.

All those whose incomes depend upon the value of money, ought to resist by every means in their power the continuance of this fund, properly called sinking, so far as they are affected. To continue it would be nothing but a a very ingenious method of taking so much money out of their pockets, by robbing them of that due share of the national income to which they are naturally entitled.

Perhaps it may be said that they have had great gains during the war, and a sinking fund would now be but a fair retaliation. Would it, however, be fair to feed a servant on very rich food until he could not live without it, and then say, Now, Sir, you have for a long time been fed too well, and in order to balance accounts, you must be fed on turnips and carrots? No—the reply would naturally be,—You have given me habits which I cannot easily change, and if that is not an argument why the style of living is to be continued, it is none why

I should be starved to death. The great profits enjoyed by the mercantile classes for so long a period during the war, is the very reason why they should not be artificially reduced now. The mercantile classes have acquired habits of expenditure which they cannot easily alter, and they will no doubt find them sufficiently low without the expedient of a sinking fund. And as to the debt, unless the mortgagees can be put in possession of that part of the property of the nation to which they are entitled, nothing can with justice to all parties be done, but allow it to remain as it is.

# CHAPTER XXV.

*Plan for the Government of the Currency.*

I⊤ is at present a general opinion with all our
political economists and statesmen, that there
is a demand for money by the country, which
as regularly presents itself to the banks in discount of good commercial bills, as the demand
for any other commodity presents itself in
the market, and is determined by the consumption of it; and that the issues of bank
paper are the consequence of high prices and
not the cause. The fallacy of this opinion,
it is, we trust, unnecessary further to illustrate.
Money comes into the market by the balance
of foreign trade, not in consequence of the
high, but in consequence of the low price of
commodities; and from the banks, either from
the same cause producing a balance of payment in London bills to their respective districts, or in consequence not of a demand for
currency, but of a demand for capital, determined by the interest which the banks charge
proportioned to the market rate. And in all
cases the influx of money into the market,
whether it proceed from the balance of fo-

reign trade, or the issues of banks, is not the effect, but the cause of high prices.

It is also the general opinion, that the circulation of the bank of England controuls that of the country banks; and it no doubt did so during the war, when the issues of the country banks were made upon home bills, and they had no means of providing against an unfavourable balance of payments. But when their issues come to be founded upon deposits in London, at a low rate of interest, they will be glad to avail themselves of any demand for money, either from a bad harvest or otherwise, to withdraw their deposits from London and lend them out on better interest at home. It may consequently be two or three years or more before the balance of payments in favour of London, after a demand for money has arisen, exhausts their deposits. In the mean time an artificial scarcity might be caused, or a real one aggravated; while probably before their deposits were exhausted, the sudden demand for money might cease; a contraction of currency follow; and prices fall as much below the national level until the deposits in London were restored, as they had been above it. Thus prices might be kept in a state of great vacillation without the issues of the country banks ever coming within the controul of the Bank of England's circulation.

Independent of this, every contraction of bank issues necessarily determines the balance of foreign payments in favour of the nation, and a spring tide of metallic currency, if we may so term it, flows to the metropolis. This the more effectually of course determines the balance of payments in favour of the country, and enables the country banks the more speedily to re-issue their notes upon deposits in London. But the balance of payments will continue in favour of the country until its circulation is upon a level with that of London, however much it may have been increased above the amount necessary, with its ordinary consumption, to maintain the national prices. Thus every low state of prices will be as necessarily followed by a state of prices proportionately high. Prices will rise as much above the national level as they were previously below it, until the metallic money which has come into the country has again disappeared, and the circulation of London is brought to its proper level. The gold which is now flowing into the country in such abundance, is only a temporary visitor : it will be ultimately re-expelled, if the present system of currency continues, by prices as high as they are now low ; and without some change, the lovers of gold and cheap corn will find themselves most sadly deceived.

With a metallic or a paper currency, which could not be issued by country banks at pleasure, these effects would not be produced. When the circulation of London exceeded that of the country, and determined the balance of payments in its favour, if the country banks could not increase their issues, money, with which to pay the balance, would have to be sent from the metropolis, and its circulation would be diminished as that of the country increased. No mountain of currency would therefore rise in London to be re-expelled by excessive prices; but by the internal balance of payments, the circulation would equalize itself, and when prices came to the national level, they would not rise above it.

Now to put the currency on this footing, seems absolutely necessary, unless we wish corn to continue subject to those fluctuations in price which we have experienced during the last 30 years.

It is perhaps unnecessary to contend that paper is a better circulating medium than gold. It is determined by practice, which at least in practical matters, is the only correct mode of coming at the truth. People in this country who have no theories upon the subject, universally prefer paper. It is more portable, forgeries are more easily detected, at least with the notes of country banks, and it is in all respects more convenient; while every plain man sees that bank notes answer the purpose of money just as well as a metallic currency. In Russia also, I understand, paper is preferred. Before it was issued in excess, and the precious metals were still in circulation, it bore a premium or agio of one per cent. and in this country I am persuaded that merchants would on the average rather give 5 or 10 shillings per cent. for paper, than submit to the inconvenience of receiving their payments in metallic money.

Presuming, therefore, that the present notes of the country banks are found to be as good a description of money as need, for any useful purpose, to be invented, I venture to submit the following Plan for the government of the currency :—

1st. Let an enquiry be made by a committee of parliament into the circulation of all the banks in the kingdom, at different periods, in order to ascertain, as far as possible, the amount of currency necessary in different districts, to maintain any given level of prices.

2nd. Let public banks be established in different parts of the country, with proper capitals, and to each bank a certain amount of circulation be assigned; for which, let both the bank and the state be security to the public.

3rd. Let each bank pay government for this

currency, a per centage, say 3 per cent., lend it out in the manner most agreeable to its interests, and keep it in circulation or not at its own pleasure.

4th. Let a board of commissioners be established in London, under whose management the currency may be placed; and to this board let every bank send weekly or monthly returns of the state of the circulation, the supply and demand for London bills, and such other information as the commissioners deem necessary for their government.

5th. Let these commissioners have an office for the deposit of bullion, and purchase all that comes into the country, at the mint price, or a little above the mint price. Let them pay for it by receipts or notes of not less, say, than a £100 each; and let any bank, either in London or any other part of the country, to which these notes or bullion receipts may be presented, be obliged to discount them, not with old notes, but by an issue of new notes over and above their stated circulation, and then return them to the board of commissioners.

6th. When a demand for bills upon London, exceeding the supply, occurs in any district, let the demand be met by the drafts of its bank upon the commissioners for bullion, and let the notes received in demand for these bills be cancelled. If these drafts are presented for payment in bullion to be exported, or for any other purpose, let them be paid ; but if they are remitted to any other part of the kingdom, let the banks, to whom they are presented for discount, issue fresh notes to their amount. In the same manner, let the Bank of England, or such banks of circulation as may be established in London, pay their notes by drafts upon the commissioners for bullion when required, and also issue fresh notes in discount of such drafts when presented, the same as the country establishments.

Now by this plan, while banks could not manufacture money at pleasure, the currency would dilate and contract in the same manner as with a metallic circulation. But, however, we shall take the liberty of considering it more in detail.

1. *Let an Enquiry be made by a Committee of Parliament, into the Circulation, at different Periods, of all the Banks in the Kingdom, in order to ascertain, as far as possible, the Amount of Currency necessary in different Districts to maintain any given Level of Prices.*

The obvious necessity of some such preliminary investigation by a committee of parliament, or by the commissioners intended to carry the measure into effect, renders any argument on the subject superfluous. The public welfare requires that private banks should be called upon for the information necessary; though justice will of course require that the information thus obtained, be kept secret, and only the general results be published.

*2nd. Let Public Banks be established in different Parts of the Country, with proper Capitals, and to each Bank a certain Amount of Circulation be assigned, for which let both the State and the Bank be Security to the Public.*

Public banks, with proper encouragement, might be established in six months, in every part of the kingdom; and that is as soon as any great national change could be expected to be made. National affairs, like great bodies, must necessarily move slowly. In the great commercial towns, such as Liverpool, it might be necessary to grant charters; as in the minds of some there are prejudices against entering into banks, which charters would obviate. But government cannot possibly have any objection to meet a little prejudice with a little parchment: in fact it is understood that ministers have no such objection. The charters might be granted for 21 years, and a fine levied upon their renewal. Let those banks that wish for the bauble pay for it. There never was a speculation proposed more to the public taste than these joint stock companies; and I am enabled to say, that there will be no want of subscriptions to them when they are allowed to be set up, even though charters should not be granted.

The currency should also be put upon the most stable footing, so that no demand for gold should ever arise from want of confidence.

This would be most effectually done by both the bank and government being pledged to the public; and as government would have an inspection of the bank affairs, no possible loss could ever arise to the state from it; while the bank being also pledged, no want of confidence in the faith of government could ever materially influence the credit of the currency.

*3rd. Let the Bank pay Government for this Currency a per Centage, say 3 per Cent. and lend it out in the Manner most agreeable to its Interests, and keep it in Circulation or not, at its own Pleasure.*

The currency belongs to no individual, and is therefore the property of the state. Government ought to receive the profits derived from that which is so properly its own. It is the object to make the taxes as little objectionable to individuals as possible, and no tax could fall more imperceptibly upon the public than this would do. The proper business of banks is not to manufacture, but to trade in money. To take from banks, therefore, either private or public, the precarious source of profit which they derive from the circulation of notes, and oblige them to charge a commission upon their discounts instead, would be doing them good and not harm. Experience has proved that those private banks have made the most money upon the average, that have had nothing to do with the circulation at all. I should imagine, that if the banks in Newcastle did not issue notes, but conducted their present business upon the same principles as the banks in Manchester, Liverpool, or London, they would make twice the money.

The per centage which government will be enabled to charge, will depend, in the first place, upon whether they allow more than one public bank in each place or not. If banks are allowed to be set up unlimitedly, of course the bank which conducts the circulation cannot afford to do it for nothing; and the interest must be sufficiently below the common rate to pay with a profit, for the expence and trouble incurred. In the next place, the per centage they can afford will in some measure depend upon the size of the banks. If banks are of sufficiently moderate size to be enabled to make their profits by the business of banking alone, they can pay more for the currency. But if any magnificent scheme is entered into of making wonderful grand banks, on the principle of the Bank of England, which shall perhaps embrace the circulation of a large county, government will have to support them, more or less, by charging them a lower rate of interest. The success and usefulness of a bank to commerce and agriculture, is determined by the knowledge which its directors may possess of the individuals who trade with it; and the more limited the business the more intimate that knowledge. As a bank increases in magnificence, therefore, it diminishes in utility. Two small banks in a county will be both more useful to the public, and profitable to their stock-holders, than one large one; and the more profitable they are, the more interest they will be enabled to pay government.

I do not mean to say, however, that there ought to be more than one bank in each town, even though it should be a large one. The greatest possible frauds are often committed upon the public, to which banks are sometimes the unconscious, and generally the unwilling instruments, which I see no mode of preventing, except by the existence of one bank only. Merchants are very often tempted to speculate beyond their depth by the facilities of raising money which too great banking competition generates ; while with more banks than one they are enabled to cloak their transactions. When they get wrong, therefore, instead of stopping at once, which they seldom have courage to do, they by means of accommodation bills, which carry fraud upon the face of them, are enabled through the banks, to support their credit and involve themselves deeper and deeper, until their debts become very large, while their means of paying them become very small ; and the public are dreadful sufferers. If there was, however, but one public bank, towards which all bills would naturally gravitate, and where every merchant might be sure his transactions would be seen through, a salutary check would be thus imposed, which would improve the general character of mercantile transactions, and prevent many a fraud of this description from even taking root.

The banks ought also to be allowed to lend the money as they thought proper, the same as if it were the deposits of individuals. If they paid interest to government for the circulation, they would not let it lie idle, for their own sakes. If they could not lend it at one rate of interest, they would take another, and would lend it upon any description of sufficient securities that offered, rather than suffer the loss of keeping it unemployed. Money would sometimes be plentiful, at other times scarce. At one period, they would be able to accommodate all their friends, at another, would be obliged to curtail their accommodations. If they chose to purchase into the funds, they would do so. Their transactions in that respect would only produce the same effect as those of other individuals. But to compel them to invest their stock or money in the funds, on the same principles as the Bank of England, which I think has been suggested, it is evident would be of no advantage to government, would only disturb unnecessarily the internal balance of trade, and would be meddling to no good purpose.

4. *Let a Board of Commissioners be established in London, under whose Management let the Currency be placed, and to this Board let every Bank send Weekly or Monthly Returns of the state of the Circulation, the Supply and Demand for London Bills, and such other Information as the Commissioners deem necessary for their Government.*

Little need be said in advocation of this measure ; it is involved in the principle that an in-

terference on the part of government is necessary. Circulation is a science yet to be understood; and no proper management could be
exercised, except by proper persons devoted to
the subject, who shall have proper accounts regularly sent them. They ought also to have
the power of determining the amount of capital
required for each bank ; to regulate their respective boundaries ; and be in fact a kind of
board of controul, without whose approbation
no vital changes at least, in any of the banks
ought to be made. The proper duties of this
board, however, it would be extremely difficult
at once fully to determine ; but a principal
duty, though it will be merely a mechanical
one, is involved in the next proposition.

5. *Let the Commissioners have an Office for the
Deposit of Bullion, and purchase all that comes
into the Country at the Mint Price, or a little
above the Mint Price. Let them pay for it by
Receipts or Notes of not less, say, than £100
each ; and let any Bank either in London or any
other Part of the Country, to which these Notes
or Bullion Receipts may be presented, be obliged to discount them, by an Issue of Notes
over and above their stated Circulation, and return them to the Board of Commissioners.*

Gold ought not to be allowed to circulate;

though the best way to prevent it would be by giving for it the Mint price, or perhaps a trifle more than that price. It would always be put into circulation first in London, where it is coined, and under any system of currency would produce a considerable derangement of the balance of trade. These bullion receipts, however, making a convenient remittance, would at once be sent to those parts of the country where the circulation was most deficient, and discharge as it were an additional quantity of notes from the banks of those districts. If a merchant, for instance, with a metallic currency, sent bullion up to London to be coined, he would draw a bill against it, and the gold would be put into circulation in payment of this bill. A temporary rise of prices would in consequence be produced, until the exchange with the county fell sufficiently to pay for the exporting this gold back to the country. But, by the present plan, a bullion receipt would be sent him at once, and the circulation would be increased only where it was wanted. Besides which, with a mixed currency of gold and paper, the commissioners would not have that perfect knowledge of the circulation which would be desirable.

*6. When a Demand for Bills upon London by any of the Banks arises, exceeding the Supply, let the Demand be met by Drafts upon the Commissioners for Bullion, and the Notes received in Demand for these Bills be cancelled. If these Drafts are presented for Payment in Bullion, for Exportation or any other Purpose, let them be paid ; but if they are remitted to any other Part of the Kingdom, let the Banks to whom they are presented for Discount, issue fresh Notes to their Amount. In the same Manner let the Bank of England, or such Banks of Circulation as may be established in London, pay their Notes by Drafts upon the Commissioners for Bullion when required, and also issue fresh Notes in Discount of such Drafts when presented, the same as the Country Establishments.*

As long as the banks had bills on London, or funds in their agents' hands to meet the drafts for which there was a demand, they would, for the sake of their own interests, supply such demand by drafts upon their own agents. But when the demand for London bills in any district exceeded the supply, it would be a proof that its circulation to the extent of this demand was excessive.

By the bank, therefore, drawing a bullion draft (at the same date, we shall say, as their drafts upon their agents, by which they would make nothing, and would not in consequence be tempted to draw unnecessarily,) the circulation would be contracted to the extent required. If these drafts, instead of being sent to London, were sent to any other part of the country, it would be in consequence of a deficient circulation in the part to which they were sent, and an extension would immediately take place. If, however, they were presented for payment in bullion, and that bullion was exported, it would be in consequence of prices being above the national level, and they would be reduced accordingly.

In the chances of trade it would probably happen that a bank might have an excess of bills on London without any bullion drafts amongst them. Nevertheless, however, a quantity of bullion drafts equal to this excess must have been drawn in that district from whence this balance of payment would have come.

We shall suppose, therefore, that these drafts were sent to another part of the country where the balance of trade was equal, and where they were of course not wanted, but that they were presented for payment, and fresh issues took place upon them. There would, in consequence, immediately be a deficiency of London bills to their extent, and notes would necessarily be taken in again to purchase fresh drafts of equal value. These would be sent to London as an ordinary remittance, and be discounted there, and fresh issues would be made upon them. But in the mean time, the country bank which had an excess of London bills, without any bullion drafts among them, must have sent these bills to its London agents for payment, but not wanting the money in London, would necessarily order its agents to return the balance in bullion drafts, the same as it would have ordered them to remit gold, had the circulation been metallic. Its agents would, therefore, take an equal amount of notes into the Bank of England to procure such drafts, and remit them accordingly. Thus with the Bank of England, the discount of bullion drafts on the one hand, and demand for them on the other, would balance; while the country district in whose favour the balance of payment had been determined, would experience an increase of circulation by the fresh issues which would be made upon the bullion drafts received from London in return for the other bills sent thither for payment.

To the extent that the balance of payments was in favour of London, the circulation of London would be increased in the same manner as other districts; and when the circulation of London was excessive, the balance of payments against it would create a demand for bullion drafts, which would be sent into the country, or be presented for payment in bullion to be sent out of it, according as the balance of payments was against the country generally, or against London, in favour of some particular district.

The various bullion drafts thus drawn would never be presented in demand for bullion until it was wanted to be remitted abroad, and it would be hardly necessary for the commissioners to be put to the trouble of accepting them. They need know nothing of them except by the accounts remitted from the different banks, unless presented for actual payment.

Now this plan is the essence of simplicity ; and if it has any merit it is that of being strictly a copy of nature. A paper circulation, by this system, would dilate and contract precisely in the same manner as a metallic currency. The demand for currency in different places is continually varying. We shall suppose for instance, that a gentleman who has been living in Northumberland, goes to reside in London. His income would in consequence have to be remitted him by his agent in London bills. This would determine the balance of payments in favour of London, and with a metallic circulation the balance would be settled by a remittance of money. The circulation of Northumberland would be thereby contracted, while that of London would be increased to the same extent. The effect upon the price of commodities would be that they would be lowered in Northumberland and increased in London sufficiently to induce an exportation to London from Northumberland, equal to the consumption of the individual who had changed his residence. A certain amount of currency would be transported to London first, and the produce of his estate, or an equal value in other commodities the produce of Northumberland, would follow it. Now just the same effects would be produced by this plan. The balance of payments in favour of London, which with a metallic currency, would be followed by a remittance of money, would be met by a contraction of currency in Northumberland, and a remittance of bullion bills, upon which a corresponding issue would be made in London. As the currency contracted in the one place, it would be dilated in the other. At present whether these effects were produced or not would be a mere chance. The currency might contract in Northumberland without being at all extended in London. The tendency, in this case, would be to produce a balance of foreign payments, in favour of the country by lowering prices generally, and thus increase the circulation of London, by an importation of the precious metals. But this would be effecting, in an indirect and disadvantageous manner, what nature intended should be done in the simplest manner that can be conceived : viz.—By merely sending the money from where it was not wanted, to where it was.

# CHAPTER XXVI.

## *Bank of England.*

THE charter of the Bank of England has to be altered before any steps can be taken either to improve our banks, as commercial business establishments, or to adopt a new system, for the management of the currency, the necessity for which, at least, has been, we trust, sufficiently established.

During the last session of parliament, the directors gave considerable opposition to the views of government. They conceived that the alteration of the charter was a measure vitally injurious to the interests of the bank; and that being the case, it was proper for them so to do.

Any scheme, however, which diminishes the importance of the bank, in the monied system of the country, is injurious to its interests; and whatever may be the individual wishes of the bank directors, must officially be opposed by them, in discharge of their duty to their constituents, unless an opposite conduct would be more advantageous.

But a person, with firm standing, may be confident and at ease in his position, while if, when he conceives himself upon solid ground, you are enabled to shew him that he is upon very thin ice, you may be certain that at least he will cease to cut capers.

I cannot help thinking that the Bank of England stands upon very thin ice, and that it would, therefore, be exceeding dangerous for the directors to caper. Perhaps, the following reasons, for this opinion, may not appear altogether absurd :—

In the first place, the bank is too large for a commercial institution, and too expensive for a government establishment; and, in the next, its charter is not, for the purpose of securing its monopoly, worth the parchment it is written upon.

The proper use of a bank to trade, we have sufficiently pointed out in the Essay on the Principles of Banking, to which we have before referred, and which forms part of this volume. Human institutions must have their limits. One bank could not undertake the business of the world; nor yet of a nation; nor yet it appears of London. Experience proves that the Bank of England is too large for commercial purposes. The only service which it is of to commerce, is in discounting commercial bills. But a very small part of its issues are so applied, except when money is very much in demand. Nor is it, probably, at any time, of much use in checking accommodation paper. Its observation must necessarily be confined to a few leading houses. The trade of London is too extensive for that kind of knowledge of the transactions of individuals, which country banks possess. Besides in London, merchants receive less accommodation from banks. Their credit, in a great measure, depends upon their having capital to spare, in their banker's hands. Their bankers are more obliged to them, than they are to their bankers. Therefore the Bank of England can, in no respect, be of the same use to commerce, as a similar establishment would be in a smaller place.

The bank, properly, is a government establishment, for the management of the national debt, keeping its cash accounts, and conducting the circulation of London. It is the bank of the state. Much has been said about the trafficking of government with the bank, as if it were criminal. It would, however, just be as proper to blame the trafficking of government with the exchequer, or the traffic of a person's hand with his pocket, or to blame a merchant for trafficking with his banker. If a merchant had business to require nearly a bank to himself, he must have transactions with it daily. But it would never occur to him as a necessary consequence, that if he only wanted one bank, there should be no more than one. No merchant would surely be so unwise, though he did transact with one bank alone, as to prevent, if he had the power, any other competitor, and render himself dependent upon it, both as to the amount of its charges, and the accommodation it gave him. Butler, in his Hudibras, somewhere speaks of a man, who " catched the itch, on purpose to be scratched," and this conduct would certainly be something like it, only we may add—and skinned into the bargain. This, however, is just what is done with respect to the Bank of England. A commercial monopoly is given to it, of which it can make no adequate use ; which is the cause of immense loss and inconvenience to the country ; and by which government is rendered dependent upon it, without either government or the country gaining any one advantage therefrom, that, at least with my limited perceptions, I can make out.

The usual result of want of competition is dearness, and this the government feels in its transactions with the bank in no small degree. When interest of money in government securities was at 5 per cent. by lending its capital of £14,686,800 to the state at three, the bank may be said to have paid annually about £300,000 per annum for its monopoly and the business of the state. Now that interest is at 4 per cent. it does not pay more than half that sum. For this it enjoyed the circulation of London, which would amount since the present charter to, say £25,000,000 upon the average, and this at 5 per cent. would leave £1,250,000 per annum. I have no means at this moment of estimating what it may have realized from the balances of government in its hands, or have cleared by the management of the national debt ; but if we state this at £300,000 a year, it would leave a gain of £1,250,000 from the circulation.

Now, if instead of one public bank in London, there had been half a dozen, of size sufficiently extensive for security, but sufficiently limited for commercial business, and the government account had been subject to a fair competition, while the circulation had been divided amongst them, or given to those only who would give the most for it, there is no man of business can entertain a doubt, that when money was so scarce, $3\frac{1}{2}$ or 4 per cent. would have been given for both the circulation and the balances of government. I have no doubt also, that the national debt would have been managed for less money ; but as it is a mere matter of accounting, it would perhaps have been both better and cheaper to have put it at once into the hands of commissioners. If we, therefore, say that government must have lost one million per annum for want of competition, we shall not, perhaps, be far from the truth.

Now, in addition to this, when we consider all the inconveniences to commerce and agriculture that have resulted from the rickety system of banking to which the monopoly has given rise, and the number of failures that have been the consequence, we shall be surprised that in the present century any thing so absurd could have existed.

The ingenuity of man may be defied to point out any peculiar advantage which is derived from the bank. Indeed the ingenuity of man has been most sadly puzzled upon the subject.

Mr Mc'Cay, who has lately published a general view of the history and object of the bank of England, which is a very sensible publication, and who, as is perfectly natural, is very much disposed to say all that can be said for it ; after stating that it is a most valuable institution to commerce, thinks it necessary, for want of better arguments, to support his opinion by a reference to authorities. " Many great authorities upon " the subject might," he says, " be adduced in " support of this opinion ; among many, I shall " produce two writers of considerable cele- " brity, Mr Rolt, in his Dictionary of Trade " and Commerce, under the head of Bank of " England, finishes that article in these words :

" ' Thus firmly established is this glori-
" ' ous superstructure of the national cre-
" ' dit of Great Britain, having the legislative
" ' power of the kingdom for its foundation ;
" ' a security sufficient for so noble, so exten-
" ' sive a fund ; a security coeval with the li-
" ' berties of the people, that cannot perish
" ' without the extinction of freedom, and
" ' which has so closely riveted the constitu-
" ' tion of the bank with the common interests
" ' of the country, that they should now co-ope-
" ' rate against the extended arm of ambition,
" ' —the designing eye of avarice,—the envy
" ' of surrounding enemies,—and the force of
" ' future invasions.' "

This, I dare say, may be depended upon as
a very clear account of the matter, the whole
of which is, no doubt, implicitly believed by
the directors ; for I myself heard one of them,
in his place in parliament, either quote some
other great authority, or from himself gravely
compare it to the sun in the hemisphere.

But " Dr Adam Smith, in his Wealth of
" Nations," alluding to the bank, " says, with
" greater sobriety, that

" The stability of the bank of England is
" equal to that of the British government. All
" that it has advanced to the public must be
" lost before its creditors can sustain any loss."

This is certainly sober enough for a choice
eulogium, out of so many great authorities ; but

it is unfortunately not true. It is quite possible
that the directors might ruin the bank, and
the British government remain just as stable as
ever. The eulogy, at the same time, is rather
a doubtful one; it amounts to this :—that the
capital of the bank is lent to one creditor, with
whom it consequently must either stand or fall;
and the sponge that wipes off the national debt,
makes a clean sweep in Threadneedle-street.
The quotation, however, shows that Dr Smith
would have said something in favour of the
bank, had it been possible.

But the charter of the bank does not secure
it the circulation of London : there is no law to
prevent other banks competing with it; and
when I found the directors opposing the views
of government, (see letters from the Times, in
the Appendix to the Pamphlet on Banking,) it
occurred to me that they might be brought to
their senses in another way. I immediately
drew out a plan for the establishment of a private bank, for the circulation of notes, in competition with the Bank of England ; and through
a channel which gave it weight, submitted it to
some of the leading monied men in London.
They were unanimous in thinking that it would
be a most advantageous speculation, as well as
a measure of public utility. The plan, or at
least that which was thought practicable, was
simply this : that five or six individuals should

subscribe a million of capital, establish a bank, and issue notes, in discount of commercial bills, &c. ; and that the affairs of the concern should be examined every six or twelve months, by gentlemen of known character and respectability, and published to the world. By these means, the credit of the bank would never be questioned, and considerable profit would be realised, without any considerable risk. Its merits in the public estimation would be, that it possessed an actual subscribed capital, and publicity was given to its affairs. The above plan was thought the most simple and practicable. Mine, however, was originally much more involved. It was to form the outlines of a public bank, which was to be carried on as a private concern, until the bank charter was altered, and then resolve itself into a public establishment. I had proposed only half a million, but it was thought that if the plan was approved, there would be no difficulty whatever with respect to the amount of capital.

As this would at once have brought the bank directors to reason, and have induced them to apply for an alteration of their charter, with a view to secure their monopoly, which would, I have no doubt, have been granted, the defect of the plan was, that after the expence of fitting up an office, preparing the establishment, &c. had been incurred, it might be rendered useless.

This, however, I proposed to obviate, by suggesting that when this happened, which would of course be immediately followed by the establishment of joint stock companies in different parts of the country, the concern should immediately offer itself to undertake exclusively, without doing any other business, the agencies of these banks, and propose to submit annually to their directors, a statement of its affairs, inspected and verified by deputies from a few of them, annually sent to London for the purpose, in the event of their not having a public bank to draw upon. This I was aware would fall in with the ideas of the stock holders and directors of the proposed companies, and I even thought that as I should probably have some interest in the concern, the new banks might have pleasure on that account in giving it a preference, as they would perhaps readily acknowledge that they were under more obligations to me than to any person connected with any other establishment. Consequently there seemed little reason to doubt that these agencies, if gone properly about, might be secured; and as I understand that the agencies of considerable banks are worth from one to three or four thousand pounds each, supposing them not to be worth more than a thousand upon the average, forty or fifty of such, or even half the number, would form a valuable business to any concern, and would be unattended with the usual risk and trouble of banking. I further would have proposed, that the capital of the bank should, as far as possible, be vested in country bank stock, by which 50 or even a 100 per cent. would, in all probability, be made.

These plans and views, however, did not occur until other duties rendered my longer stay in London impossible, and as the gentleman to whom I originally communicated them was about to leave it for six months, the matter was left to a future opportunity. I, however, was satisfied that proper people might be very easily found in London to enter into such an establishment, and this was what I was in the first instance desirous to ascertain.

I had not long left London, however, until a still better idea presented itself. I saw that it would be perfect nonsense for such a bank to trouble itself with discounting commercial bills, with stocks at their present price. Its best plan would evidently be to purchase into the funds at once, by which as much interest might be made as by discounting bills, without any risk or trouble.

Notes issued in purchase of stock could never be returned upon the bank, if it maintained its credit, until the balance of foreign trade was turned against the country. No payments, either in its own notes or any other, would be made to it. It would hold stock equal to the amount of its notes in circulation; and they would never be presented in a demand for gold until it was wanted to send out of the country ; by which time it was evident, at least to me, that the 3 per cents. would probably be a 100, or 90 at all events; while as the stocks could not be lower than they are at present, the speculation would be perfectly safe.

My views upon the subject generally, however, had now so much improved, at least I could not help supposing so, that after some little hesitation, I determined to give them to the public. But as it will help to strengthen my argument, that the present charter is but a very slippery dependance for the bank, and the plan may not be in itself, perhaps, an entirely uninteresting speculation to men of business, I shall take the liberty of detailing the steps which it appears to me it would have been proper to have taken, and the measures which it would have been the best, with such a speculation, to have pursued.

In order to prove, to a few individuals, the advantage of a private speculation, it would not have been necessary to have gone through the whole range of subject contained in this Essay. After the fourth chapter it might have been proved by a much shorter process of reasoning, that the contraction of the currency kept down the funds, and that the exchanges must continue favourable until corn attained the average of 80s. per quarter; and that an issue of currency would produce this effect. Only a very small pamphlet would have been necessary for the purpose.

Having first proved the plan to be both advantageous to the individuals who might engage in it, and the public, the following might have been submitted as the most judicious mode of carrying it into effect :—

1st. That the bank should commence with declaring, that it was the opinion of those who established it, that the present distress arose from the contraction of the issues of the bank of England and country banks, which they expected in some measure to relieve. That it was not the intention to interfere with the business of the existing private banks ; and that in consequence no bills would be discounted except through them ; and that whenever it appeared that the public good required it, this bank would at any time make arrangements for withdrawing its circulation and close its doors. That a million of capital had been subscribed, and that its affairs should be annually submitted to the inspection of proper persons chosen for that purpose.

By these means, the other bankers would be conciliated, and this pledge to the public would inspire confidence, while it would be no loss to the concern. For the public good could not require the bank to withdraw its notes, until it would be the interest of the establishment to realize its profits, and withdraw from the speculation.

2nd. That it should confine itself principally to the issue of £100 notes, and to none less than £20.

This would have several important advantages. First, it would keep the circulation in the hands of respectable people, put the bank out of all danger of a run, and enable it to issue ten millions with much more confidence than it could issue one in small notes. The large notes of the bank of England would in consequence be changed for small ones, the consumptive circulation would thus be occupied by the Bank of England, and the abstract circulation by the notes of this bank. In the second place, they would make a good remittance to the country, whither, in consequence, they would with greater readiness be sent; and in the third place, they would be both much cheaper and issued with less trouble. It would take 200,000 five pound notes to make a million of money, and the stamps would cost £12,500, whereas it would take only 10,000 one hundred pound notes, and the stamps would cost only £4,250; with twenty, thirty, and fifty pound notes, the stamps would cost £5,000.; so that if upon the average, including other expences, which would be comparatively trifling, we say £5000 per million, we should perhaps exceed the actual cost. A hundred pound note is as easily made as one of one pound ; consequently the trouble of keeping ten millions in circulation could not exceed that of a country bank with an issue of a hundred, or a hundred and twenty, thousand pounds in one pound notes, and might be done with the most perfect ease with two or three clerks. Six weeks interest in the funds, at 4 per cent. would pay the whole expence, while the trouble would not be worth the naming.

3rd. That accounts should be opened with ten or a dozen principal banks, more or less, as it might be deemed expedient, in whose hands the notes should be placed, with which the stock was to be purchased, and checks given upon these banks for the purchases when they were made ; different brokers on the stock exchange should also be employed. By these means the extent of the purchases would not be discovered, and any expedient by which this could be prevented, as a matter of prudence ought to be adopted, to prevent any speculative rise founded upon a knowledge of the intentions of the concern.

4th. Having made these preparations, it would then be proper to purchase as largely as could be done, without affecting the funds more than three or four per cent. But whether this would take one million, five millions, or ten, my practical knowledge does not enable me to surmise.

We shall suppose, however, that the partners are fully possessed with both the safety and goodness of the speculation, are men of firmness of purpose, and clearness of head, and have made up their minds to purchase ten millions of stock, if they find the scheme work well.

We must also presume they have made up their minds that an addition of ten millions to the circulation of London, would have a very rapid effect in extending the circulation of the country banks, by determining the balance of payments against London, producing remittances of these notes into the country, upon which issues would be immediately made, and that they would then be returned to the London money market again, would further increase the price of the funds, would again travel down into the country, perform the same operation, and again return to London as before, that therefore, if ten millions of stock could be purchased under we shall say 85, it would be desirable to purchase at once to that extent, and put that quantity of notes in circulation.

We shall therefore suppose that purchases of stock to the extent of ten millions, without raising the funds above 85, could be and was made. All that the partners would then have to do, would be to remain quiet until agricultural produce had nearly attained the national level, when the bank ought to sell out and realize at such price as the funds had attained, whatever that might be, before the demand for gold for exportation arose. If, however, the funds by this time had risen 20 per cent. the concern would have made 2 millions ; if 10 per cent. one.

But we shall suppose that not more than a million could be thrown into the market without raising the funds to 85. In that case, they might conclude that if the funds, from such a supply of money, would quickly rise, they would quickly fall. It cannot be supposed that one million could raise the value of capital 5 per cent. throughout the whole country. After, therefore, purchasing a million, the bank would wait until the funds fell again, then purchase another million, &c. until they had permanently risen as high as the partners chose to speculate further at. All these purchases, however, would be made at the lowest rates ; the funds would rise in consequence of them ; not before, but after. When they had thus extended their purchases as far as they thought proper, they might then wait until the time for selling out arrived.

It must be observed, that the effect upon the funds by the issues of the Bank of England form no criterion by which to judge of the effect which would be produced by the issues of this bank. When the bank of England extends its circulation, it is in consequence of an increasing demand for money, and though it equally raises prices of agricultural produce, its effect upon the funds is to keep them from falling. But these issues would not be the result of an increased demand for money, and would therefore have the effect of raising the funds. The effect would also be infinitely greater than during the war, when the demand and supply of money was so much more extensive. In a market with an actual demand for ten thousand bushels of wheat, an additional supply of one thousand must have less effect upon prices than if the demand and supply in that market were not more than three thousand; and upon the same principles, a greater effect would be produced in the stock market now, than would be produced by the same supply of money during the war, when the demands of government were great, and the annual economy, and supply of money in the market, so much greater than at present.

Should the partners, however, think that waiting until the country circulation was extended, too slow an operation, they might quicken it in this manner: Having made all the purchases of stock they were disposed to do, they might then throw as much money into the market as they could, by increasing their deposits with their bankers, and by discounting at a low rate of interest. They need have no hesitation as to the quantity of money they thus lent out upon good bills. The amount of interest they got would be of no importance. Their profit would arise from the speculation in the funds, and the lower the interest the better : it would have a greater effect in raising them. The securities, however, would have to be at short dates, and of course perfectly good. In this case they would perhaps have to employ bill brokers to purchase bills, as the bankers, from the previous issues in purchase of stock, would be overflowing with money, and would not discount with them. If they were to lower the rate of discount, say, to $2\frac{1}{2}$ per cent. and glut the market with money, on these terms the 3 per cents must necessarily rise to a hundred. They might then sell out, taking care to push the money they received from the sale of the stock into the market again, by which to keep it up until they had sold out the whole.

If they did not wish to speculate on so great a scale, and instead of making millions, they were willing to be content with hundreds of thousands, they might, we shall say, purchase, one, two, or three millions of stock, as they thought proper, then throw an equal quantity of money, as already described, by way of discount, into the market, &c. They would have always to keep in mind, of course, that when they sold out, they would have still to keep the money in the market, if they even lent it without interest; or by withdrawing it, they would both lower the price of the funds, and agricultural produce also. If they did good to themselves, they should take care to do as little harm to others as possible.

If, however, they were not influenced by quite such liberal principles, they might play upon the market by taking all the money at once out of circulation after they had got rid of their stock. This would produce a corresponding reduction in the funds; when they might buy in again, and do the same as before. In order to this it would not be necessary for them to withdraw their own notes; the bills discounted, would be paid them perhaps principally in those of the bank of England, as it would have the greatest circulation. But if they locked up Bank of England notes, it would be just the same; and by their own notes continuing in circulation, these operations upon the market would not be so fully seen through; which, with such Machiavelian policy, would at least be prudent. Without, however, losing sight of the interest of the country, (for to raise the funds quickly to what they will ultimately attain, could be no evil,) a considerable sum, there is no doubt, might have been made, even if the plan did not work so smoothly as we have laid down, and the bank was sometimes obliged to sell out against its inclination. It must be kept in view, that its selling out would always produce the fall, its buying in the rise in the funds *that would fol-low* : as it would therefore come into the market before both the fall and the rise, it would always have the advantage ; while at the same time, the extended circulation would produce a gradual permanent rise, and they would always sell out more or less to a profit. In any case, therefore, the speculation must have been attended with gain, and that not inconsiderable.

The whole of their circulation would be either in stock or short dated bills, and they consequently never could have been placed in any very aukward situation. No run upon them could have taken place without actual fears of security, which at any moment might have been dissipated ; while they would know and feel their credit as they went along, and govern themselves accordingly.

It is probable, however, that two consequences would have resulted from such a speculation. First, that other banks would follow its example, and begin to issue large notes also ; and next, that government would interfere. If other banks began to make issues, it would be done blindly, and without measure, by which the price of stock would be more rapidly increased; and as upon the stability of their operations no reliance could be placed, it would be prudent to sell out, and realize as their issues increased, and terminate the speculation. Or, if government interfered, it would not be for the purpose of contracting the circulation. In this case, they ought to be ready and willing, conformably to their first declaration, to turn their issues over to the Bank of England, if required. The bank taking their stock at its existing value, or holding it as security, and bringing it into the market at such periods, and in such a manner as, for making the most of the speculation, might be agreed upon.

Both the principle and the plan of this speculation are sufficiently simple. There can be no doubt that the power of making money at pleasure, would give any house of sufficient credit the power of lowering its value by increasing the supply; and as the supply in the country is now less than is wanted, they could with confidence for a limited time make issues to almost any extent.

The trouble would be quite trivial, so far as making and issuing the notes, &c. went. The principal management would lie in the operations of the stock market. That it is a speculation which would very much suit the tastes of many of the monied men in London, there cannot perhaps be a doubt; and that consequently if it had been properly gone about, such a plan might have been carried into effect, I think extremely possible, and by those also who would have carried it through to any extent practicable, great as the scheme is, without the vibration of a nerve.

That the plan is possible, however, is a sufficient argument both with the bank and government, for an immediate alteration of the present charter. If the law is left as it now stands, government cannot expect that individuals will lose any fair opportunity of making money by establishing paper mints of this description in London, as well as in other places.

THE END.

# Appendix.

# APPENDIX, No. I.

An ACCOUNT of the Quantity of British Wheat and Wheat Flour, exported from England, and of Foreign Wheat and Wheat Flour imported into England, in the following Years.

*(From Mr Rose's Pamphlet.)*

| YEARS. | British Wheat and Flour exported. | | Foreign Wheat and Flour imported. | |
|---|---|---|---|---|
| | Quarters. | Bushels. | Quarters. | Bushels. |
| 1697 . . | 14,698 | 6 | 400 | 0 |
| 1698 . . | 6,857 | 1 | 845 | 0 |
| 1699 . . | 557 | 2 | 486 | 3 |
| 1700 . . | 49,056 | 5 | 4 | 6 |
| 1701 . . | 98,323 | 7 | 1 | 1 |
| 1702 . . | 90,230 | 4 | 0 | 0 |
| 1703 . . | 106,615 | 4 | 50 | 0 |
| 1704 . . | 90,313 | 5 | 1 | 6 |
| 1705 . . | 96,185 | 1 | 0 | 0 |
| 1706 . . | 188,332 | 3 | 77 | 1 |
| 1707 . . | 74,155 | 1 | 0 | 0 |
| 1708 . . | 83,406 | 3 | 86 | 4 |
| 1709 . . | 169,679 | 7 | 1,552 | 3 |
| 1710 . . | 13,924 | 1 | 400 | 0 |
| 1711 . . | 76,949 | 0 | 0 | 0 |
| 1712 . . | 145,191 | 0 | 0 | 0 |
| 1713 . . | 176,227 | 0 | 0 | 0 |
| 1714 . . | 174,821 | 1 | 15 | 7 |
| 1715 . . | 166,490 | 2 | 0 | 4 |
| 1716 . . | 74,926 | 1 | 0 | 0 |
| 1717 . . | 22,953 | 7 | 0 | 0 |
| 1718 . . | 71,800 | 0 | 0 | 0 |
| 1719 . . | 127,762 | 4 | 20 | 1 |
| 1720 . . | 83,084 | 2 | 0 | 0 |
| 1721 . . | 81,632 | 6 | 0 | 0 |

| YEARS. | British Wheat and Flour exported. | | Foreign Wheat and Flour imported. | |
|---|---|---|---|---|
| | Quarters. | Bushels. | Quarters. | Bushels. |
| 1722 . . | 178,880 | 1 | 0 | 0 |
| 1723 . . | 157,719 | 6 | 0 | 0 |
| 1724 . . | 245,864 | 6 | 148 | 2 |
| 1725 . . | 204,413 | 3 | 12 | 2 |
| 1726 . . | 142,183 | 3 | 0 | 0 |
| 1727 . . | 30,315 | 3 | 0 | 0 |
| 1728 . . | 3,817 | 0 | 74,574 | 2 |
| 1729 . . | 18,993 | 3 | 40,315 | 2 |
| 1730 . . | 93,970 | 7 | 75 | 7 |
| 1731 . . | 130,025 | 2 | 4 | 0 |
| 1732 . . | 202,058 | 4 | 0 | 0 |
| 1733 . . | 427,199 | 0 | 7 | 4 |
| 1734 . . | 498,196 | 4 | 6 | 5 |
| 1735 . . | 153,343 | 5 | 9 | 1 |
| 1736 . . | 118,170 | 0 | 16 | 5 |
| 1737 . . | 461,602 | 0 | 32 | 4 |
| 1738 . . | 580,596 | 4 | 2 | 5 |
| 1739 . . | 279,542 | 4 | 22 | 7 |
| 1740 . . | 54,390 | 4 | 5,468 | 5 |
| 1741 . . | 45,416 | 7 | 7,540 | 2 |
| 1742 . . | 293,259 | 6 | 0 | 7 |
| 1743 . . | 371,431 | 3 | 2 | 5 |
| 1744 . . | 231,984 | 5 | 2 | 0 |
| 1745 . . | 324,839 | 5 | 5 | 6 |
| 1746 . . | 130,646 | 2 | 0 | 0 |
| 1747 . . | 266,906 | 7 | 0 | 0 |
| 1748 . . | 543,387 | 5 | 385 | 0 |
| 1749 . . | 629,049 | 0 | 382 | 0 |
| 1750 . . | 947,602 | 1 | 279 | 5 |
| 1751 . . | 661,416 | 4 | 3 | 0 |
| 1752 . . | 429,279 | 4 | 0 | 0 |
| 1753 . . | 299,608 | 7 | 0 | 0 |
| 1754 . . | 356,270 | 1 | 201 | 0 |
| 1755 . . | 237,459 | 2 | 0 | 0 |
| 1756 . . | 101,936 | 4 | 5 | 0 |
| 1757 . . | 11,226 | 0 | 130,343 | 2 |
| 1758 . . | 9,233 | 6 | 19,039 | 7 |
| 1759 . . | 226,426 | 0 | 82 | 1 |
| 1760 . . | 390,710 | 4 | 0 | 0 |
| 1761 . . | 440,746 | 2 | 0 | 0 |
| 1762 . . | 294,500 | 0 | 56 | 2 |

| YEARS. | British Wheat and Flour exported. | | Foreign Wheat and Flour imported. | |
|---|---|---|---|---|
| | Quarters. | Bushels. | Quarters. | Bushels. |
| 1763 . . | 427,074 | 3 | 8 | 1 |
| 1764 . . | 396,537 | 5 | 1 | 1 |
| 1765 . . | 167,030 | 0 | 89,642 | 5 |
| 1766 . . | 165,953 | 1 | 9,387 | 0 |
| 1767 . . | 5,071 | 0 | 444,029 | 0 |
| 1768 . . | 7,433 | 1 | 272,307 | 6 |
| 1769 . . | 49,892 | 1 | 2,903 | 1 |
| 1770 . . | 75,400 | 5 | 15 | 2 |
| 1771 . . | 10,477 | 0 | 2,509 | 0 |
| 1772 . . | 6,974 | 0 | 27,114 | 0 |
| 1773 . . | 7,802 | 0 | 57,786 | 0 |
| 1774 . . | 16,731 | 0 | 278,039 | 0 |
| 1775 . . | 90,413 | 0 | 575,250 | 0 |
| 1776 . . | 220,210 | 0 | 21,568 | 0 |
| 1777 . . | 90,932 | 0 | 233,905 | 0 |
| 1778 . . | 146,637 | 0 | 106,616 | 0 |
| 1779 . . | 232,925 | 0 | 5,254 | 0 |
| 1780 . . | 250,434 | 0 | 4,242 | 0 |
| 1781 . . | 117,247 | 0 | 162,278 | 0 |
| 1782 . . | 163,579 | 0 | 81,259 | 0 |
| 1783 . . | 56,502 | 0 | 584,041 | 0 |
| 1784 . . | 99,039 | 0 | 215,817 | 0 |
| 1785 . . | 141,394 | 0 | 107,968 | 0 |
| 1786 . . | 215,102 | 0 | 50,999 | 0 |
| 1787 . . | 126,960 | 0 | 60,245 | 0 |
| 1788 . . | 89,731 | 0 | 149,667 | 0 |
| 1789 . . | 146,951 | 0 | 109,762 | 0 |
| 1790 . . | 33,822 | 0 | 219,351 | 0 |
| 1791 . . | 74,968 | 0 | 463,591 | 0 |
| 1792 . . | 300,278 | 0 | 22,417 | 0 |
| 1793 . . | 76,869 | 0 | 490,398 | 0 |
| 1794 . . | 155,048 | 0 | 327,902 | 0 |
| 1795 . . | 18,839 | 0 | 313,793 | 0 |
| 1796 . . | 24,679 | 0 | 879,200 | 0 |
| 1797 . . | 54,522 | 0 | 461,767 | 0 |
| 1798 . . | 59,782 | 0 | 396,721 | 0 |
| 1799 . . | 39,362 | 0 | 463,185 | 0 |
| 1800 . . | 22,013 | 0 | 1,264,520 | 0 |
| 1801 . . | 28,406 | 0 | 1,424,766 | 0 |
| 1802 . . | 149,304 | 0 | 647,664 | 0 |

| YEARS. | British Wheat and Flour exported. | | Foreign Wheat and Flour imported. | |
|---|---|---|---|---|
| | Quarters. | Bushels. | Quarters. | Bushels. |
| 1803 . . | 76,580 | 0 | 373,725 | 0 |
| 1804 . . | 63,073 | 0 | 461,140 | 0 |
| 1805 . . | 77,959 | 0 | 920,834 | 0 |
| 1806 . . | 29,566 | 0 | 310,342 | 0 |
| 1807 . . | 24,365 | 0 | 400,759 | 0 |
| 1808 . . | 77,567 | 0 | 81,466 | 0 |
| 1809 . . | 31,278 | 0 | 448,487 | 0 |
| 1810 . . | 75,785 | 0 | 1,530,691 | 0 |
| 1811 . . | 97,765 | 0 | 292,038 | 0 |
| 1812 . . | 46,325 | 0 | 129,866 | 0 |

## No. II. PRICES of WHEAT, per Quarter, at Windsor Market.*

*( From Mr Rose's Pamphlet. )*

| YEARS. | Prices of Wheat at Windsor, 9 Gallons to the Bushel. | | | Prices of Wheat reduced to the Winchester Bushel of 8 Gallons. | | | Average of 10 Years, according to the Winchester Bushel of 8 Gallons. | | |
|---|---|---|---|---|---|---|---|---|---|
| | £. | s. | d. | £. | s. | d. | £. | s. | d. |
| 1646 . . | 2 | 8 | 0 | 2 | 2 | 8 | | | |
| 1647 . . | 3 | 13 | 8 | 3 | 5 | $5\frac{1}{4}$ | | | |
| 1648 . . | 4 | 5 | 0 | 3 | 15 | $6\frac{3}{4}$ | | | |
| 1649 . . | 4 | 0 | 0 | 3 | 11 | $1\frac{1}{4}$ | | | |
| 1650 . . | 3 | 16 | 8 | 3 | 8 | $1\frac{3}{4}$ | | | |
| 1651 . . | 3 | 13 | 4 | 3 | 5 | $2\frac{1}{4}$ | | | |
| 1652 . . | 2 | 9 | 6 | 2 | 4 | 0 | | | |
| 1653 . . | 1 | 15 | 6 | 1 | 11 | $6\frac{3}{4}$ | | | |
| 1654 . . | 1 | 6 | 0 | 1 | 3 | $1\frac{1}{4}$ | | | |
| 1655 . . | 1 | 13 | 4 | 1 | 9 | $7\frac{1}{2}$ | 2 | 11 | $7\frac{3}{4}$ |
| 1656 . . | 2 | 3 | 0 | 1 | 18 | $2\frac{3}{4}$ | | | |
| 1657 . . | 2 | 6 | 8 | 2 | 1 | $5\frac{3}{4}$ | | | |
| 1658 . . | 3 | 5 | 0 | 2 | 17 | $9\frac{1}{4}$ | | | |
| 1659 . . | 3 | 6 | 0 | 2 | 18 | 8 | | | |
| 1660 . . | 2 | 16 | 6 | 2 | 10 | $2\frac{1}{4}$ | | | |
| 1661 . . | 3 | 10 | 0 | 3 | 2 | $2\frac{3}{4}$ | | | |
| 1662 . . | 3 | 14 | 0 | 3 | 5 | $9\frac{1}{4}$ | | | |
| 1663 . . | 2 | 17 | 0 | 2 | 10 | 8 | | | |
| 1664 . . | 2 | 0 | 6 | 1 | 16 | 0 | | | |
| 1665 . . | 2 | 9 | 4 | 2 | 3 | $10\frac{1}{4}$ | 2 | 10 | $5\frac{3}{4}$ |
| 1666 . . | 1 | 16 | 0 | 1 | 12 | 0 | | | |
| 1667 . . | 1 | 16 | 0 | 1 | 12 | 0 | | | |
| 1668 . . | 2 | 0 | 0 | 1 | 15 | $6\frac{3}{4}$ | | | |
| 1669 . . | 2 | 4 | 4 | 1 | 19 | 5 | | | |

\* These are the prices of Mealing Wheat; which is understood, at Eton College, to be of a middling quality.

| YEARS. | Prices of Wheat at Windsor, 9 Gallons to the Bushel. | | | Prices of Wheat reduced to the Winchester Bushel of 8 Gallons. | | | Average of 10 Years, according to the Winchester Bushel of 8 Gallons. | | |
|---|---|---|---|---|---|---|---|---|---|
| | £. | s | d. | £. | s. | d. | £. | s. | d. |
| 1670 . . | 2 | 1 | 8 | 1 | 17 | 0½ | | | |
| 1671 . . | 2 | 2 | 0 | 1 | 17 | 4 | | | |
| 1672 . . | 2 | 1 | 0 | 1 | 16 | 5¼ | | | |
| 1673 . . | 2 | 6 | 8 | 2 | 1 | 5¾ | | | |
| 1674 . . | 3 | 8 | 8 | 3 | 1 | 0½ | | | |
| 1675 . . | 3 | 4 | 8 | 2 | 17 | 5¾ | 2 | 0 | 11¾ |
| 1676 . . | 1 | 18 | 0 | 1 | 13 | 9¼ | | | |
| 1677 . . | 2 | 2 | 0 | 1 | 17 | 4 | | | |
| 1678 . . | 2 | 19 | 0 | 2 | 12 | 5¼ | | | |
| 1679 . . | 3 | 0 | 0 | 2 | 13 | 4 | | | |
| 1680 . . | 2 | 5 | 0 | 2 | 0 | 0 | | | |
| 1681 . . | 2 | 6 | 8 | 2 | 1 | 5¾ | | | |
| 1682 . . | 2 | 4 | 0 | 1 | 19 | 1¼ | | | |
| 1683 . . | 2 | 0 | 0 | 1 | 15 | 6¾ | | | |
| 1684 . . | 2 | 4 | 0 | 1 | 19 | 1¼ | | | |
| 1685 . . | 2 | 6 | 8 | 2 | 1 | 5¾ | 2 | 1 | 4¼ |
| 1686 . . | 1 | 14 | 0 | 1 | 10 | 2¾ | | | |
| 1687 . . | 1 | 5 | 2 | 1 | 2 | 4½ | | | |
| 1688 . . | 2 | 6 | 0 | 2 | 0 | 10¾ | | | |
| 1689 . . | 1 | 10 | 0 | 1 | 6 | 8 | | | |
| 1690 . . | 1 | 14 | 8 | 1 | 10 | 9¾ | | | |
| 1691 . . | 1 | 14 | 0 | 1 | 10 | 2¾ | | | |
| 1692 . . | 2 | 6 | 8 | 2 | 1 | 5¾ | | | |
| 1693 . . | 3 | 7 | 8 | 3 | 0 | 1¾ | | | |
| 1694 . . | 3 | 4 | 0 | 2 | 16 | 10¾ | | | |
| 1695 . . | 2 | 13 | 0 | 2 | 7 | 1¼ | 1 | 19 | 6¾ |
| 1696 . . | 3 | 11 | 0 | 3 | 3 | 1¼ | | | |
| 1697 . . | 3 | 0 | 0 | 2 | 13 | 4 | | | |
| 1698 . . | 3 | 8 | 4 | 3 | 0 | 9 | | | |
| 1699 . . | 3 | 4 | 0 | 2 | 16 | 10¾ | | | |
| 1700 . . | 2 | 0 | 0 | 1 | 15 | 6¾ | | | |
| 1701 . . | 1 | 17 | 8 | 1 | 13 | 5¾ | | | |
| 1702 . . | 1 | 9 | 6 | 1 | 6 | 2¾ | | | |
| 1703 . . | 1 | 16 | 0 | 1 | 12 | 0 | | | |
| 1704 . . | 2 | 6 | 6 | 2 | 1 | 4 | | | |
| 1705 . . | 1 | 10 | 0 | 1 | 6 | 8 | 2 | 2 | 11 |
| 1706 . . | 1 | 6 | 0 | 1 | 3 | 1¼ | | | |
| 1707 . . | 1 | 8 | 6 | 1 | 5 | 4 | | | |
| 1708 . . | 2 | 1 | 6 | 1 | 16 | 10¾ | | | |

| YEARS. | Prices of Wheat at Windsor, 9 Gallons to the Bushel. | | | Prices of Wheat reduced to the Winchester Bushel of 8 Gallons. | | | Average of 10 Years, according to the Winchester Bushel of 8 Gallons. | | |
|---|---|---|---|---|---|---|---|---|---|
| | £. | s. | d. | £. | s. | d. | £. | s. | d. |
| 1709 . . | 3 | 18 | 6 | 3 | 9 | $9\frac{1}{4}$ | | | |
| 1710 . . | 3 | 18 | 0 | 3 | 9 | 4 | | | |
| 1711 . . | 2 | 14 | 0 | 2 | 8 | 0 | | | |
| 1712 . . | 2 | 6 | 4 | 2 | 1 | $2\frac{1}{4}$ | | | |
| 1713 . . | 2 | 11 | 0 | 2 | 5 | 4 | | | |
| 1714 . . | 2 | 10 | 4 | 2 | 4 | 9 | | | |
| 1715 . . | 2 | 3 | 0 | 1 | 18 | $2\frac{1}{4}$ | 2 | 4 | $2\frac{1}{4}$ |
| 1716 . . | 2 | 8 | 0 | 2 | 2 | 8 | | | |
| 1717 . . | 2 | 5 | 8 | 2 | 0 | $7\frac{1}{4}$ | | | |
| 1718 . . | 1 | 18 | 10 | 1 | 14 | $6\frac{3}{4}$ | | | |
| 1719 . . | 1 | 15 | 0 | 1 | 11 | $1\frac{1}{4}$ | | | |
| 1720 . . | 1 | 17 | 0 | 1 | 12 | $10\frac{1}{4}$ | | | |
| 1721 . . | 1 | 17 | 6 | 1 | 13 | 4 | | | |
| 1722 . . | 1 | 16 | 0 | 1 | 12 | 0 | | | |
| 1723 . . | 1 | 14 | 8 | 1 | 10 | $10\frac{1}{4}$ | | | |
| 1724 . . | 1 | 17 | 0 | 1 | 12 | $10\frac{1}{4}$ | | | |
| 1725 . . | 2 | 8 | 6 | 2 | 3 | $1\frac{1}{4}$ | 1 | 15 | $4\frac{3}{4}$ |
| 1726 . . | 2 | 6 | 0 | 2 | 0 | $10\frac{1}{4}$ | | | |
| 1727 . . | 2 | 2 | 0 | 1 | 17 | 4 | | | |
| 1728 . . | 2 | 14 | 6 | 2 | 8 | $5\frac{1}{4}$ | | | |
| 1729 . . | 2 | 6 | 10 | 2 | 1 | $7\frac{1}{4}$ | | | |
| 1730 . . | 1 | 16 | 6 | 1 | 12 | $5\frac{1}{4}$ | | | |
| 1731 . . | 1 | 12 | 10 | 1 | 9 | $2\frac{1}{4}$ | | | |
| 1732 . . | 1 | 6 | 8 | 1 | 3 | $8\frac{1}{2}$ | | | |
| 1733 . . | 1 | 8 | 4 | 1 | 5 | $2\frac{1}{4}$ | | | |
| 1734 . . | 1 | 18 | 10 | 1 | 14 | $6\frac{1}{4}$ | | | |
| 1735 . . | 2 | 3 | 0 | 1 | 18 | $2\frac{1}{4}$ | 1 | 15 | 2 |
| 1736 . . | 2 | 0 | 4 | 1 | 15 | $10\frac{1}{4}$ | | | |
| 1737 . . | 1 | 18 | 0 | 1 | 13 | $9\frac{1}{4}$ | | | |
| 1738 . . | 1 | 15 | 6 | 1 | 11 | $6\frac{1}{4}$ | | | |
| 1739 . . | 1 | 18 | 6 | 1 | 14 | $2\frac{1}{4}$ | | | |
| 1740 . . | 2 | 10 | 8 | 2 | 5 | $1\frac{1}{4}$ | | | |
| 1741 . . | 2 | 6 | 8 | 2 | 1 | $5\frac{1}{4}$ | | | |
| 1742 . . | 1 | 14 | 0 | 1 | 10 | $2\frac{1}{4}$ | | | |
| 1743 . . | 1 | 4 | 10 | 1 | 2 | 1 | | | |
| 1744 . . | 1 | 4 | 10 | 1 | 2 | 1 | | | |
| 1745 . . | 1 | 7 | 6 | 1 | 4 | $5\frac{1}{4}$ | 1 | 12 | 1 |
| 1746 . . | 1 | 19 | 0 | 1 | 14 | 8 | | | |
| 1747 . . | 1 | 14 | 10 | 1 | 10 | $11\frac{1}{4}$ | | | |

| YEARS. | Prices of Wheat at Windsor, 9 Gallons to the Bushel. | | | Prices of Wheat reduced to the Winchester Bushel of 8 Gallons. | | | Average of 10 Years, according to the Winchester Bushel of 8 Gallons. | | |
|---|---|---|---|---|---|---|---|---|---|
| | £. | s. | d. | £. | s. | d. | £. | s. | d. |
| 1748 . . | 1 | 17 | 0 | 1 | 12 | 10¾ | | | |
| 1749 . . | 1 | 17 | 0 | 1 | 12 | 10¾ | | | |
| 1750 . . | 1 | 12 | 6 | 1 | 8 | 10¾ | | | |
| 1751 . . | 1 | 18 | 6 | 1 | 14 | 2¾ | | | |
| 1752 . . | 2 | 1 | 10 | 1 | 17 | 2¼ | | | |
| 1753 . . | 2 | 4 | 8 | 1 | 19 | 8½ | | | |
| 1754 . . | 1 | 14 | 8 | 1 | 10 | 9¾ | | | |
| 1755 . . | 1 | 13 | 10 | 1 | 10 | 1 | 1 | 13 | 2¾ |
| 1756 . . | 2 | 5 | 2 | 2 | 0 | 1¾ | | | |
| 1757 . . | 3 | 0 | 0 | 2 | 13 | 4 | | | |
| 1758 . . | 2 | 10 | 0 | 2 | 4 | 5¼ | | | |
| 1759 . . | 1 | 19 | 8 | 1 | 15 | 3 | | | |
| 1760 . . | 1 | 16 | 6 | 1 | 12 | 5¼ | | | |
| 1761 . . | 1 | 10 | 2 | 1 | 6 | 9¾ | | | |
| 1762 . . | 1 | 19 | 0 | 1 | 14 | 8 | | | |
| 1763 . . | 2 | 0 | 8 | 1 | 16 | 1¾ | | | |
| 1764 . . | 2 | 6 | 8 | 2 | 1 | 5¾ | | | |
| 1765 . . | 2 | 14 | 0 | 2 | 8 | 0 | 1 | 19 | 3¼ |
| 1766 . . | 2 | 8 | 6 | 2 | 3 | 1¼ | | | |
| 1767 . . | 3 | 4 | 6 | 2 | 17 | 4 | | | |
| 1768 . . | 3 | 0 | 6 | 2 | 13 | 9¼ | | | |
| 1769 . . | 2 | 5 | 8 | 2 | 0 | 7 | | | |
| 1770 . . | 2 | 9 | 0 | 2 | 3 | 6¾ | | | |
| 1771 . . | 2 | 17 | 0 | 2 | 10 | 8 | | | |
| 1772 . . | 3 | 6 | 0 | 2 | 18 | 8 | | | |
| 1773 . . | 3 | 6 | 6 | 2 | 19 | 1¼ | | | |
| 1774 . . | 3 | 2 | 0 | 2 | 15 | 1¼ | | | |
| 1775 . . | 2 | 17 | 8 | 2 | 11 | 3¼ | 2 | 11 | 3¾ |
| 1776 . . | 2 | 8 | 0 | 2 | 2 | 8 | | | |
| 1777 . . | 2 | 15 | 0 | 2 | 8 | 10¼ | | | |
| 1778 . . | 2 | 9 | 6 | 2 | 4 | 0 | | | |
| 1779 . . | 2 | 0 | 8 | 1 | 16 | 1¾ | | | |
| 1780 . . | 2 | 8 | 6 | 2 | 3 | 1¼ | | | |
| 1781 . . | 2 | 19 | 0 | 2 | 12 | 5¼ | | | |
| 1782 . . | 3 | 0 | 6 | 2 | 13 | 9¼ | | | |
| 1783 . . | 3 | 1 | 0 | 2 | 14 | 2¾ | | | |
| 1784 . . | 3 | 0 | 6 | 2 | 13 | 9¼ | | | |
| 1785 . . | 2 | 14 | 0 | 2 | 8 | 0 | 2 | 7 | 8½ |
| 1786 . . | 2 | 7 | 6 | 2 | 2 | 2¾ | | | |

| YEARS. | Prices of Wheat at Windsor, 9 Gallons to the Bushel. | | | Prices of Wheat reduced to the Winchester Bushel of 8 Gallons. | | | Average of 10 Years, according to the Winchester Bushel of 8 Gallons. | | |
|---|---|---|---|---|---|---|---|---|---|
| | £. | s. | d. | £. | s. | d. | £. | s. | d. |
| 1787 . . | 2 | 11 | 6 | 2 | 5 | $9\frac{1}{4}$ | | | |
| 1788 . . | 2 | 15 | 6 | 2 | 9 | 4 | | | |
| 1789 . . | 3 | 3 | 2 | 2 | 16 | $1\frac{3}{4}$ | | | |
| 1790 . . | 3 | 3 | 2 | 2 | 16 | $1\frac{3}{4}$ | | | |
| 1791 . . | 2 | 15 | 6 | 2 | 9 | 4 | | | |
| 1792* . . | | | | 2 | 13 | 0 | | | |
| 1793 . . | | | | 2 | 15 | 8 | | | |
| 1794 . . | | | | 2 | 14 | 0 | | | |
| 1795 . . | | | | 4 | 1 | 6 | 2 | 14 | $3\frac{1}{4}$ |
| 1796 . . | | | | 4 | 0 | 2 | | | |
| 1797 . . | | | | 3 | 2 | 0 | | | |
| 1798 . . | | | | 2 | 14 | 0 | | | |
| 1799 . . | | | | 3 | 15 | 8 | | | |
| 1800 . . | | | | 6 | 7 | 0 | | | |
| 1801 . . | | | | 6 | 8 | 6 | | | |
| 1802 . . | | | | 3 | 7 | 2 | | | |
| 1803 . . | | | | 3 | 0 | 0 | | | |
| 1804 . . | | | | 3 | 9 | 6 | | | |
| 1805 . . | | | | 4 | 8 | 0 | 4 | 1 | $2\frac{1}{4}$ |
| 1806 . . | | | | 4 | 3 | 0 | | | |
| 1807 . . | | | | 3 | 18 | 0 | | | |
| 1808 . . | | | | 3 | 19 | 2 | | | |
| 1809 . . | | | | 5 | 6 | 0 | | | |
| 1810 . . | | | | 5 | 12 | 0 | | | |
| 1811 . . | | | | 5 | 8 | 0 | | | |
| 1812 . . | | | | 6 | 8 | 0 | | | |
| | | | | | | | Aver. of 8 years | | |
| 1813 . . | | | | 6 | 0 | 0 | 5 | 1 | $9\frac{1}{4}$ |

* From this year, inclusive, the account at Eton College has been kept according to the bushel of eight gallons, under the provision of the act of 31 G. 3. c. 30. sect. 82.

12

No. III. TABLE of the YEARLY and MONTHLY
AVERAGE PRICES of Corn in England and Wales,
from 1792 to 1822 inclusive.

YEARLY AVERAGES.

| 1792 | - | 43s. | 1808 | - | 79s. |
|------|---|------|------|---|------|
| 1793 | - | 49s. | 1809 | - | 94s. |
| 1794 | - | 51s. | 1810 | - | 105s. |
| 1795 | - | 71s. | 1811 | - | 93s. |
| 1796 | - | 76s. | 1812 | - | 125s. |
| 1797 | - | 52s. | 1813 | - | 107s. |
| 1798 |   | 50s. | 1814 | - | 74s. |
| 1799 | - | 69s. | 1815 | - | 64s. |
| 1800 | - | 105s. | 1816 | - | 75s. |
| 1801 | - | 120s. | 1817 | - | 94s. |
| 1802 | - | 67s. | 1818 | - | 83s. |
| 1803 | - | 56s. | 1819 | - | 72s. |
| 1804 | - | 59s. | 1820 | - | 65s. |
| 1805 | - | 87s | 1821 | - | 54s. |
| 1806 | .. | 77s. | 1822 | - | 43s. |
| 1807 | - | 73s. |      |   |      |

## MONTHLY AVERAGES.

| | 1792. | 1793. | 1794. | 1795. |
|---|---|---|---|---|
| January - | 42s. | 46s. | 50s. | 57s. |
| February - | 41s. | 46s. | 50s. | 58s. |
| March - | 41s. | ... | 50s. | 59s. |
| April - | 39s. | 50s. | 51s. | 62s. |
| May - | 38s. | ... | 51s. | 64s. |
| June - - | 39s. | 51s. | 51s. | 67s. |
| July - - | 39s. | 51s. | 51s. | 81s. |
| August - | 42s. | 50s. | 52s. | 103s. |
| September - | 44s. | 49s. | 51s. | 75s. |
| October - | 49s. | ... | 51s. | 76s. |
| November - | 49s. | ... | 52s. | 73s. |
| December - | 49s. | ... | 55s. | 86s. |

| | 1796. | 1797. | 1798. | 1799. |
|---|---|---|---|---|
| January - | 92s. | 54s. | 51s. | 49s. |
| February - | 93s. | 52s. | 49s. | 50s. |
| March - | 101s. | 49s. | 50s. | 50s. |
| April - - | ... | 49s. | 51s. | ... |
| May - | 75s. | 49s. | 51s. | 61s. |
| June - - | 80s. | 50s. | 50s. | 64s. |
| July - - | 81s. | 51s. | 51s. | 67s. |
| August - | 75s. | 52s. | 51s. | 73s. |
| September - | 64s. | 58s. | 50s. | 74s. |
| October - | 61s. | 59s. | 48s. | 86s. |
| November - | 59s. | 56s. | 47s. | 89s. |
| December - | 57s. | 52s. | ... | 93s. |

|  |  | 1800. | 1801. | 1802. | 1803. |
|---|---|---|---|---|---|
| January | - | 94s. | 133s. | 76s. | 56s. |
| February | - | 95s. | 136s. | 75s. | 56s. |
| March | - | 103s. | 145s. | 72s. | 56s. |
| April | - - | 108s. | 156s. | 68s. | 56s. |
| May | - | 118s. | 150s. | 64s. | 57s. |
| June | - - | 121s. | 91s. | 67s. | 64s. |
| July | - - | 121s. | 129s. | 67s. | 59s. |
| August | - - | 76s. | 136s. | 69s. | 55s. |
| September | - | 96s. | 124s. | 67s. | 55s. |
| October | - | 107s. | 88s. | 61s. | 54s. |
| November | - | 108s. | 77s. | 59s. | 54s. |
| December | - | 119s. | 74s. | 58s. | 53s. |

|  |  | 1804. | 1805. | 1806. | 1807. |
|---|---|---|---|---|---|
| January | - | 51s. | 86s. | 75s. | 77s. |
| February | - | 50s. | 89s. | 74s. | 75s. |
| March | - | 50s. | 93s. | 74s. | 76s. |
| April | - - | 51s. | 91s. | 77s. | 76s. |
| May | - - | 51s. | 87s. | 84s. | 75s. |
| June | - - | 51s. | 89s. | 84s. | 74s. |
| July | - - | 53s. | 90s. | 82s. | 73s. |
| August | - | 60s. | 100s. | 81s. | 74s. |
| September | - | 64s. | 89s. | 80s. | ... |
| October | - | 67s. | 81s. | 78s. | 68s. |
| November | - | 81s. | 78s. | 77s. | 65s. |
| December | - | 84s. | 76s. | 77s. | 68s. |

|  |  | 1808. | 1809. | 1810. | 1811. |
|---|---|---|---|---|---|
| January | - | 68s. | 91s. | 101s. | 96s. |
| February | - | 69s. | 92s. | 99s. | 95s. |
| March | - | 69s. | 94s. | 102s. | 92s. |
| April | - - | 71s. | 92s. | 104s. | 88s. |
| May | - - | 78s. | 90s. | 110s. | 88s. |
| June | - - | 80s. | 88s. | ... | 86s. |

| | 1808. | 1809. | 1810. | 1811. |
|---|---|---|---|---|
| July - - | 81s. | 88s. | 114s. | 87s. |
| August - | 81s. | 94s. | 116s. | 91s. |
| September - | 84s. | 101s. | 116s. | 97s. |
| October - | 87s. | 103s. | 101s. | 100s. |
| November - | 92s. | 101s. | 101s. | 105s. |
| December - | 90s. | 102s. | 95s. | ... |

| | 1812. | 1813. | 1814. | 1815. |
|---|---|---|---|---|
| January - | 105s. | 118s. | 78s. | 60s. |
| February - | 105s. | 120s. | 78s. | 64s. |
| March - | 113s. | 122s. | 78s. | 66s. |
| April - | 126s. | 119s. | 76s. | 71s. |
| May - - | 133s. | 117s. | 68s. | 70s. |
| June - - | 133s. | 117s. | 69s. | 69s. |
| July - - | 146s. | 116s. | 67s. | 67s. |
| August - | 155s. | 112s. | 74s. | 68s. |
| September - | 132s. | 98s. | 77s. | 64s. |
| October - | 110s. | 93s. | 75s. | 57s. |
| November - | 122s. | 85s. | 73s. | 56s. |
| December - | 121s. | 73s. | 70s. | 55s. |

| | 1816. | 1817. | 1818. | 1819. |
|---|---|---|---|---|
| January - | 52s. | 103s. | 85s. | 79s. |
| February - | 56s. | 102s. | 85s. | 80s. |
| March - | 54s. | 102s. | 84s. | 79s. |
| April - - | 60s. | 102s. | 90s. | 74s. |
| May - - | 76s. | 105s. | 86s. | 72s. |
| June - - | 74s. | 111s. | 84s. | 68s. |
| July - - | 73s. | 100s. | 87s. | 75s. |
| August - | 82s. | 86s. | 79s. | 74s. |
| September - | 85s. | 76s. | 81s. | 72s. |
| October - | 93s. | 78s. | 81s. | 66s. |
| November - | 98s. | 80s. | 82s. | 67s. |
| December - | 103s. | 84s. | 80s. | 65s. |

|  | 1820. | 1821. | 1822. |
|---|---|---|---|
| January - - | 63s. | 54s. | 49s. |
| February - | 65s. | 53s. | 49s. |
| March - - | 71s. | 54s. | 46s. |
| April - - | 69s. | 54s. | 44s. |
| May - - - | 70s. | 51s. | 47s. |
| June - - | 70s. | 52s. | 44s. |
| July - - - | 67s. | 52s. | 43s. |
| August - - | 72s. | 56s. | 43s. |
| September - - | 68s. | 61s. | 39s. |
| October - - | 58s. | 58s. | 38s. |
| November - - | 57s. | 55s. | 39s. |
| December - | 54s. | 49s. | 38s. |

No. IV. TABLE of the PRICES of 3 PER CENT.
STOCKS, from 1731 to 1822 inclusive.

MONTHLY PRICES.

| | 1731. | 1732. | 1733. | 1734. |
|---|---|---|---|---|
| January . - - | 95 | 96 | 100 | 92 |
| February - - - | 94 | 97 | ... | ... |
| March - - | 90 | ... | ... | 90 |
| April . - - | ... | ... | 102 | ... |
| May - - - | ... | ... | ... | ... |
| June - - - | 99 | ... | 103 | 94 |
| July - - - | 95 | 98 | 100 | 92 |
| August - - - | 96 | 99 | 97 | 93 |
| September - - | ... | ... | 97 | 94 |
| October - - - | 94 | ... | 92 | 92 |
| November - - | 95 | 101 | ... | ... |
| December - - | 97 | ... | ... | 94 |

| | 1735. | 1736. | 1737. | 1738. |
|---|---|---|---|---|
| January - - | 94 | 100 | ... | 106 |
| February - - | 92 | 102 | ... | ... |
| March - - - | 94 | 104 | ... | 105 |
| April - - - | ... | ... | 105 | ... |
| May - - - | ... | ... | ... | ... |
| June - - - | ... | 105 | 107 | ... |
| July - - - | 97 | 113 | 105 | 102 |
| August - - - | 94 | 105 | 106 | 105 |
| September - - | ... | ... | ... | ... |
| October - - - | ... | ... | ... | ... |
| November - - | 98 | ... | ... | ... |
| December - - | 93 | ... | ... | 106 |

|            |   |   | 1739. | 1740. | 1741. | 1742. |
|------------|---|---|-------|-------|-------|-------|
| January    | - | - | 104   | 98    | 98    | 98    |
| February   | - | - | ...   | 99    | 99    | 99    |
| March      | - | - | 105   | 100   | ...   | 100   |
| April      | - | - | ...   | 101   | 101   | 101   |
| May        | - | - | ...   | ...   | ...   | ...   |
| June       | - | - | 100   | 100   | ...   | 102   |
| July       | - | - | 98    | ...   | 99    | 100   |
| August     | - | - | 99    | 101   | 98    | 101   |
| September  | - | - | 98    | 100   | 99    | 100   |
| October    | - | - | 97    | 99    | 89    | ...   |
| November   | - | - | 98    | ...   | 101   | 101   |
| December   | - |   | 100   | ...   | 100   | 102   |

|            |   |   | 1743. | 1744. | 1745. | 1746. |
|------------|---|---|-------|-------|-------|-------|
| January    | - | - | 101   | 99    | 89    | 76    |
| February   | - | - | 100   | 96    | ...   | 75    |
| March      | - | - | ...   | 90    | ...   | ...   |
| April      | - | - | 101   | 93    | 92    | 82    |
| May        | - | - | 103   | ...   | 93    | ...   |
| June       | - | - | 102   | ...   | 92    | 83    |
| July       | - | - | 103   | ...   | 90    | 85    |
| August     | - | - | 102   | ...   | 87    | 89    |
| September  | - | - | 101   | ...   | 85    | 88    |
| October    | - | - | 102   | ...   | 86    | 85    |
| November   | - | - | ...   | ...   | ...   | 83    |
| December   | - | - | ...   | ...   | ...   | 84    |

|            |   |   | 1747. | 1748. | 1749. | 1750. |
|------------|---|---|-------|-------|-------|-------|
| January    | - | - | 83    | 79    | 91    | 98    |
| February   | - | - | 84    | 82    | 94    | 99    |
| March      | - | - | 86    | 76    | 95    | ...   |
| April      | - | - | 85    | 80    | ...   | 100   |
| May        | - | - | 86    | 88    | 100   | ...   |
| June       | - | - | ...   | 90    | 99    | 101   |

| | 1747. | 1748. | 1749. | 1750. |
|---|---|---|---|---|
| July - - - | ... | 89 | 100 | ... |
| August - - - | 82 | 90 | 100 | 100 |
| September - - | ... | 88 | 101 | ... |
| October - - - | ... | 91 | 102 | 101 |
| November - - | ... | 90 | 99 | ... |
| December - - | 81 | 89 | 100 | 99 |

| | 1751. | 1752. | 1753. | 1754. |
|---|---|---|---|---|
| January - - | 97 | 101 | 106 | 104 |
| February - - | 98 | 102 | 104 | 102 |
| March - - | 99 | ... | ... | ... |
| April - - | 100 | 103 | 105 | 103 |
| May - - - | 99 | 104 | ... | ... |
| June - - - | 101 | 105 | ... | 104 |
| July - - - | 103 | 106 | ... | ... |
| August - - - | 100 | 105 | 103 | ... |
| September - - | 99 | ... | 104 | ... |
| October - - - | 100 | 104 | ... | 103 |
| November - | 101 | ... | ... | 102 |
| December - - | 102 | 106 | 105 | ... |

| | 1755. | 1756. | 1757. | 1758. |
|---|---|---|---|---|
| January - - | 100 | 89 | 86 | 91 |
| February - - | 101 | ... | 87 | 94 |
| March - - - | 99 | ... | 89 | ... |
| April - - - | 98 | 90 | 88 | 93 |
| May - - - | 97 | 89 | 89 | 94 |
| June - - - | 99 | ... | 90 | 95 |
| July - - - | ... | 87 | 88 | 97 |
| August - - | 92 | 89 | 89 | 90 |
| September - - | 90 | 88 | 91 | 89 |
| October - - | 93 | ... | ... | 90 |
| November - - | 91 | 89 | 89 | 91 |
| December - - | 92 | 88 | 90 | 98 |

|  | 1759. | 1760. | 1761. | 1762. |
|---|---|---|---|---|
| January - - | 88 | 82 | 74 | 63 |
| February - - | 86 | 81 | 73 | 68 |
| March - - - | 82 | 82 | 76 | 67 |
| April - - - | 80 | ... | 88 | 70 |
| May - - - | ... | ... | 87 | 73 |
| June - - - | 79 | ... | 86 | 72 |
| July - - - | ... | 83 | 81 | 75 |
| August - - - | 82 | ... | 76 | 79 |
| September - - | 81 | 82 | 74 | 81 |
| October - - - | ... | 83 | 72 | 80 |
| November - - | 84 | 80 | 71 | 86 |
| December - - | ... | 76 | 66 | 87 |

|  | 1763. | 1764. | 1765. | 1766. |
|---|---|---|---|---|
| January - - | 90 | 82 | 85 | 89 |
| February - - - | 93 | 84 | 87 | 87 |
| March - - - | 96 | 86 | ... | 88 |
| April - - - | 92 | 83 | ... | 89 |
| May - - - | 91 | ... | ... | 90 |
| June - - - | ... | ... | 86 | ... |
| July - - - | 89 | 81 | ... | 88 |
| August - - - | 87 | 82 | 87 | 90 |
| September - - | 84 | 83 | 89 | 87 |
| October - - - | ... | 80 | 91 | 89 |
| November - - | 83 | 82 | 92 | ... |
| December - - | ... | 83 | 92 | ... |

|  | 1767. | 1768. | 1769. | 1770. |
|---|---|---|---|---|
| January - - | 88 | 91 | 88 | 85 |
| February - - | 89 | 92 | ... | 87 |
| March - - | 88 | 93 | ... | ... |
| April - - - | ... | ... | ... | ... |
| May - - - | ... | ... | 89 | 86 |
| June - - - | 87 | 92 | 89 | 84 |

| | 1767. | 1768. | 1769. | 1770. |
|---|---|---|---|---|
| July - - - | ... | 90 | ... | 83 |
| August - - - | ... | 89 | ... | 78 |
| September - - | 88 | ... | 88 | ... |
| October - - - | 90 | ... | ... | ... |
| November - - | 91 | 88 | 84 | ... |
| December - - | 90 | 89 | ... | 84 |

| | 1771. | 1772. | 1773. | 1774. |
|---|---|---|---|---|
| January - - | 86 | 87 | 87 | 87 |
| February - - - | 85 | .... | .... | 86 |
| March - - - | 87 | .... | .... | .... |
| April - - - | 88 | 88 | 86 | .... |
| May - - - | 81 | .... | .... | 87 |
| June - - - | 86 | .... | 87 | .... |
| July - - - | .... | 95 | .... | 88 |
| August - - - | .... | 89 | .... | .... |
| September - - | 87 | .... | .... | .... |
| October - - - | .... | 88 | 86 | .... |
| November - - | .... | .... | .... | 89 |
| December - - | 86 | .... | .... | .... |

| | 1775. | 1776. | 1777. | 1778. |
|---|---|---|---|---|
| January - - | 90 | 90 | 80 | 72 |
| February - - - | .... | 89 | 78 | 70 |
| March - - - | 87 | 87 | 79 | 64 |
| April - - - | 88 | 86 | .... | 61 |
| May - - - | .... | 85 | .... | .... |
| June - - - | .... | 84 | 76 | 62 |
| July - - - | .... | 82 | .... | 61 |
| August - - - | 89 | .... | .... | 63 |
| September - - | .... | 83 | 78 | 64 |
| October - - - | .... | 81 | .... | 66 |
| November - - | 88 | .... | .... | 63 |
| December - - | .... | 82 | 76 | 62 |

| | 1779. | 1780. | 1781. | 1782. |
|---|---|---|---|---|
| January - - | 60 | 61 | 57 | .... |
| February - - - | 59 | .... | 58 | 53 |
| March - - - | 61 | .... | 59 | 54 |
| April - - - | 64 | 60 | .... | 57 |
| May - - - | 63 | .... | .... | 59 |
| June - - - | 60 | .... | 57 | 60 |
| July - - - | 59 | 63 | .... | 55 |
| August - - - | 61 | .... | .... | 56 |
| September - - | .... | .... | 56 | 57 |
| October - - - | .... | 61 | .... | 58 |
| November - - | .... | .... | .... | 59 |
| December - - | 60 | .... | .... | 61 |

| | 1783. | 1784. | 1785. | 1786. |
|---|---|---|---|---|
| January - - | 64 | 57 | 56 | 70 |
| February - - - | 66 | 56 | 55 | 69 |
| March - - - | 68 | 55 | 57 | .... |
| April - - - | .... | 56 | 58 | .... |
| May - - - | .... | 57 | .... | 70 |
| June - - - | 66 | .... | .... | 71 |
| July - - - | 67 | 55 | .... | 70 |
| August - - - | .... | 54 | 59 | 73 |
| September - - | 66 | .... | 65 | 74 |
| October - - - | 63 | .... | 66 | 76 |
| November - - | 62 | 55 | 70 | 78 |
| December - - | 58 | .... | 71 | 74 |

| | 1787. | 1788. | 1789. | 1790. |
|---|---|---|---|---|
| January - - | 73 | 76 | 72 | 78 |
| February - - - | 70 | 75 | 73 | .... |
| March - - - | 74 | .... | 74 | .... |
| April - - - | 76 | .... | .... | 80 |
| May - - - | 77 | .... | 75 | 73 |
| June - - - | 73 | 76 | 77 | .... |

|  | 1787. | 1788. | 1789. | 1790. |
|---|---|---|---|---|
| July - - - | 70 | .... | .... | .... |
| August - - - | 72 | 74 | 78 | 77 |
| September - - | 69 | .... | 80 | .... |
| October - - - | 70 | .... | .... | 74 |
| November - - | 72 | .... | 78 | 79 |
| December - - | 75 | 73 | .... | 80 |

|  | 1791. | 1792. | 1793. | 1794. |
|---|---|---|---|---|
| January - - | 80 | 90 | 77 | 70 |
| February - - - | .... | 94 | 72 | 67 |
| March - - - | 81 | 96 | 75 | .... |
| April - - - | 78 | 95 | 78 | 69 |
| May - - - | 81 | 92 | 76 | 70 |
| June - - - | 82 | 91 | 77 | .... |
| July - - - | 81 | 92 | .... | 67 |
| August - - - | 86 | 91 | .... | .... |
| September - - | 89 | 90 | 74 | 76 |
| October - - - | 88 | .... | 75 | 64 |
| November - - | 87 | 88 | 74 | 67 |
| December - - | 89 | 76 | .... | 65 |

|  | 1795. | 1796. | 1797. | 1798. |
|---|---|---|---|---|
| January - - | 63 | 69 | 54 | 48 |
| February - - - | 62 | 68 | 53 | 49 |
| March - - - | .... | .... | 50 | 50 |
| April - - - | 63 | 67 | .... | 49 |
| May - - - | 65 | 65 | 48 | 48 |
| June - - - | 67 | 63 | 50 | 49 |
| July - - - | 68 | 60 | 53 | 48 |
| August - - - | .... | 59 | 52 | 49 |
| September - - | 69 | 56 | 50 | 50 |
| October - - - | 68 | 58 | 49 | 51 |
| November - - | 68 | 56 | 48 | 55 |
| December - - | 70 | 57 | 49 | 52 |

|  | 1799. | 1800. | 1801. | 1802. |
|---|---|---|---|---|
| January - - | 53 | 61 | 60 | 68 |
| February - - - | .... | .... | 57 | 69 |
| March - - - | 54 | 62 | 56 | .... |
| April - - - | 54 | 63 | 59 | 76 |
| May - - - | 55 | .... | 60 | 75 |
| June - - - | 59 | 62 | 61 | .... |
| July - - - | 62 | 63 | 60 | 73 |
| August - - - | 65 | 64 | .... | 69 |
| September - - | 64 | 65 | .... | .... |
| October - - - | 60 | 64 | 67 | 68 |
| November - - | 61 | .... | 68 | .. . |
| December - - | 62 | 63 | 67 | * |

|  | 1803. | 1804. | 1805. | 1806. |
|---|---|---|---|---|
| January - - | 72 | 56 | 61 | 60 |
| February - - - | 71 | 55 | 58 | 60 |
| March - - - | 65 | 56 | 58 | 60 |
| April - - - | .... | 55 | 58 | 60 |
| May - - - | 59 | 57 | 58 | 60 |
| June - - - | 57 | 55 | 59 | 63 |
| July - - - | 55 | 57 | 60 | 64 |
| August - - - | 54 | 56 | 57 | 62 |
| September - - | 54 | 57 | 58 | 63 |
| October - - - | 52 | 57 | 58 | 61 |
| November - - | 53 | 58 | 60 | 61 |
| December - - | 54 | 59 | 62 | 60 |

|  | 1807. | 1808. | 1809. | 1810. |
|---|---|---|---|---|
| January - - | 60 | 63 | 65 | 68 |
| February - - - | 62 | 63 | 67 | 67 |
| March - - - | 62 | 64 | 67 | 68 |

\* Up to this date is taken from Sir John Sinclair's work upon the Revenue. The prices after this, are the prices, upon, or about the 20th of each month, exclusive of fractional parts.

| | 1807. | 1808. | 1809. | 1810. |
|---|---|---|---|---|
| April - - - | 62 | 66 | 67 | 69 |
| May - - - | 63 | 68 | 68 | 70 |
| June - - - | 61 | 70 | 69 | 71 |
| July - - - | 61 | 68 | 68 | 68 |
| August - - | 62 | 67 | 68 | 68 |
| September - - | 62 | 66 | 68 | 65 |
| October - - | 62 | 66 | 68 | 66 |
| November - - | 63 | 66 | 70 | 67 |
| December - - | 64 | 66 | 71 | 67 |

| | 1811. | 1812. | 1813. | 1814. |
|---|---|---|---|---|
| January - - | 66 | 62 | 60 | 67 |
| February - - - | 66 | 62 | 59 | 70 |
| March - - - | 65 | 60 | 59 | 71 |
| April - - - | 64 | 60 | 59 | 67 |
| May - - - | 65 | 61 | 59 | 67 |
| June - - - | 64 | .... | .... | .... |
| July - - - | 63 | 56 | 56 | 68 |
| August - - - | 62 | 58 | 58 | 66 |
| September - - | 63 | 59 | 58 | 64 |
| October - - - | 63 | 58 | 58 | 65 |
| November - - | 64 | 59 | 59 | 65 |
| December - - | .... | .... | .... | .... |

| | 1815. | 1816. | 1817. | 1818. |
|---|---|---|---|---|
| January - - | 66 | 60 | 62 | 80 |
| February - - - | 65 | 62 | 66 | 79 |
| March - - - | 61 | 61 | 70 | 78 |
| April - - - | 57 | 61 | 72 | 80 |
| May - - - | 58 | 62 | 73 | 79 |
| June - - - | .... | .... | .... | .... |
| July - - - | 57 | 64 | 82 | 77 |
| August - - - | 56 | 62 | 79 | 76 |
| September - - | 57 | 62 | 80 | 74 |

|  |  | 1815. | 1816. | 1817. | 1818. |
|---|---|---|---|---|---|
| October | - - | 61 | 62 | 82 | 77 |
| November | - - | 62 | 63 | 83 | 77 |
| December | - - | .... | .... | .... | .... |

|  |  | 1819. | 1820. | 1821. | 1822. |
|---|---|---|---|---|---|
| January | - - | 78 | 77 | 69 | 76 |
| February | - - - | 77 | 68 | 72 | 78 |
| March | - - - | 74 | 68 | 70 | 80 |
| April | - - - | 73 | 70 | 72 | 78 |
| May | - - - | 71 | 69 | 74 | 79 |
| June | - - - | .... | .... | .... | .... |
| July | - - - | 70 | 69 | 76 | 79 |
| August | - - - | 71 | 68 | 76 | 80 |
| September | - - | 70 | 66 | 76 | 81 |
| October | - - - | 77 | 67 | 78 | 81 |
| November | - - | 67 | 69 | 78 | 81 |
| December | - - | .... | .... | .... | 78 |

YEARLY AVERAGES.

| | | | |
|---|---|---|---|
| 1731, | 95 | 1760, | 81 |
| 1732, | 98 | 1761, | 77 |
| 1733, | 98 | 1762, | 75 |
| 1734, | 92 | 1763, | 89 |
| 1735, | 94 | 1764, | 82 |
| 1736, | 105 | 1765, | 88 |
| 1737, | 106 | 1766, | 88 |
| 1738, | 105 | 1767, | 89 |
| 1739, | 100 | 1768, | 90 |
| 1740, | 99 | 1769, | 87 |
| 1741, | 97 | 1770, | 84 |
| 1742, | 100 | 1771, | 85 |
| 1743, | 101 | 1772, | 89 |
| 1744, | 94 | 1773, | 86 |
| 1745, | 89 | 1774, | 87 |
| 1746, | 83 | 1775, | 88 |
| 1747, | 84 | 1776, | 85 |
| 1748, | 86 | 1777, | 78 |
| 1749, | 98 | 1778, | 64 |
| 1750, | 99 | 1779, | 60 |
| 1751, | 100 | 1780, | 61 |
| 1752, | 104 | 1781, | 57 |
| 1753, | 104 | 1782, | 57 |
| 1754, | 103 | 1783, | 53 |
| 1755, | 95 | 1784, | 55 |
| 1756, | 88 | 1785, | 62 |
| 1757, | 89 | 1786, | 72 |
| 1758, | 93 | 1787, | 72 |
| 1759, | 82 | 1788, | 75 |

| | | | |
|---|---|---|---|
| 1789, | 76 | 1806, | 61 |
| 1790, | 77 | 1807, | 62 |
| 1791, | 84 | 1808, | 66 |
| 1792, | 90 | 1809, | 68 |
| 1793, | 75 | 1810, | 68 |
| 1794, | 67 | 1811, | 64 |
| 1795, | 66 | 1812, | 59 |
| 1796, | 61 | 1813, | 58 |
| 1797, | 50 | 1814, | 67 |
| 1798, | 50 | 1815, | 60 |
| 1799, | 59 | 1816, | 62 |
| 1800, | 63 | 1817, | 75 |
| 1801, | 61 | 1818, | 77 |
| 1802, | 71 | 1819, | 72 |
| 1803, | 58 | 1820, | 68 |
| 1804, | 56 | 1821, | 74 |
| 1805, | 59 | 1822, | 79 |

No. V. AMOUNT of the NATIONAL FUNDED DEBT at the Revolution, and at the Commencement and Termination of each War, to 1812.

*(From Dr Hamilton's Inquiry concerning the National Debt).*

| | | |
|---|---|---|
| National debt at the Revolution - | 1689 | £1,054,925 |
| Funded debt at the peace of Ryswick, | 1697 | 21,515,772 |
| — at the commencement of the war, | 1701 | 16,394,701 |
| — at the peace of Utrecht, - | 1714 | 55,282,978 |
| including annuities afterwards subscribed to the South Sea stock. | | |
| — at the commencement of the war, | 1740 | 47,954,623 |
| — at the peace of Aix-la-Chapelle, | 1748 | 79,193,313 |
| — at the commencement of the war, | 1756 | 73,289,673 |
| — at the peace of Paris, - | 1763 | 133,959,270 |
| including £9,839,957, which was funded in the subsequent years. | | |
| Besides this, there was about £6,000,000 of debt paid off without being funded. | | |
| — at the commencement of the American war, - - - | 1775 | 123,644,500 |
| — at the peace of Versailles, - | 1783 | 211,363,524 |
| Besides this, there was a large unfunded debt, which being funded in the following years, raised the amount to - | | 238,231,248 |
| And this was reduced by purchases for the redemption of the national debt, at the commencement of the war, | 1793 | 227,989,148 |
| Funded debt at the peace of Amiens, 1802, including the loan of that year, £567,008,978 | | |
| Of which redeemed, - 67,255,915 | | |
| | | 499,753,063 |
| There was no reduction of the national debt in the short peace which followed the treaty of Amiens. | | |
| Funded debt 1st Feb. 1812, £769,764,356 | | |
| Of which redeemed, - 189,538,480 | | |
| | | 580,225,876 |

No. VI. An ACCOUNT of the AMOUNT of BANK
NOTES in CIRCULATION on the under-mentioned
Days.

*( From the Report of the Committee of the House of Commons, in
1819, on the Bank resuming Cash Payments.)*

|      |   |          |   |    |   | Total.        |
|------|---|----------|---|----|---|---------------|
| 1792 | - | February | - | 25 | - | £11,149,809   |
|      |   | August   | - - | 25 | - | 11,006,969  |
| 1793 | - | February | - | 26 | - | 11,428,381    |
|      |   | August   | - - | 26 | - | 10,838,214  |
| 1794 | - | February | - | 26 | - | 10,697,924    |
|      |   | August   | - - | 26 | - | 10,628,220  |
| 1795 | - | February | - | 26 | - | 13,539,163    |
|      |   | August   | - - | 26 | - | 11,458,382  |
| 1796 | - | February | - | 26 | - | 10,909,694    |
|      |   | August   | - - | 26 | - | 9,531,335   |
| 1797 | - | February | - | 25 | - | 8,601,964     |
|      |   | August   | - - | 26 | - | 10,568,216  |
| 1798 | - | February | - | 26 | - | 12,850,085    |
|      |   | August   | - - | 25 | - | 12,191,025  |
| 1799 | - | February | - | 26 | - | 12,636,145    |
|      |   | August   | - - | 26 | - | 13,259,873  |
| 1800 | - | February | - | 25 | - | 15,236,676    |
|      |   | August   | - - | 26 | - | 14,735,378  |
| 1801 | - | February | - | 26 | - | 16,577,514    |
|      |   | August   | - - | 26 | - | 14,970,321  |
| 1802 | - | February | - | 26 | - | 15,458,876    |
|      |   | August   | - - | 26 | - | 16,887,113  |
| 1803 | - | February | - | 26 | - | 15,576,932    |
|      |   | August   | - - | 26 | - | 17,035,959  |

| | | | | | _Total._ |
|---|---|---|---|---|---|
| 1804 | - | February | - | 25 | - | £17,577,352 |
| | | August | - - | 25 | - | 17,323,994 |
| 1805 | - | February | - | 26 | - | 17,234,466 |
| | | August | - - | 26 | - | 16,296,178 |
| 1806 | - | February | - | 25 | - | 17,148,446 |
| | | August | - - | 26 | - | 19,072,893 |
| 1807 | - | February | - | 26 | - | 17,205,344 |
| | | August | - - | 26 | - | 20,034,112 |
| 1808 | - | February | - | 26 | - | 18,593,054 |
| | | August | - - | 26 | - | 17,365,266 |
| 1809 | - | February | - | 25 | - | 18,014,677 |
| | | August | - - | 26 | - | 19,357,241 |
| 1810 | - | February | - | 26 | - | 20,429,281 |
| | | August | - - | 25 | - | 24,446,175 |
| 1811 | - | February | - | 26 | - | 23,384,833 |
| | | August | - - | 26 | - | 23,793,115 |
| 1812 | - | February | - | 26 | - | 22,998,197 |
| | | August | - - | 26 | - | 23,482,910 |
| 1813 | - | February | - | 26 | - | 23,307,471 |
| | | August | - - | 26 | - | 24,024,869 |
| 1814 | - | February | - | 26 | - | 25,095,415 |
| | | August | - - | 26 | - | 28,979,876 |
| 1815 | - | February | - | 25 | - | 26,673,370 |
| | | August | - - | 26 | - | 27,024,049 |
| 1816 | - | February | - | 26 | - | 25,680,069 |
| | | August | - - | 26 | - | 27,075,854 |
| 1817 | - | February | - | 26 | - | 27,058,578 |
| | | August | - - | 26 | - | 30,099,908 |
| 1818 | - | February | - | 26 | - | 28,279,043 |
| | | August | - - | 26 | - | 26,602,837 |
| 1819 | - | February | - | 11 | - | 25,947,637 |

No. VII. An ACCOUNT of the DUTIES on PROMISSORY NOTES re-issuable; distinguishing the Rate of Duty, and the Amount received for each Class of Promissory Notes, in each Quarter, from 5th January, 1798, to the latest Period to which the same can be made up.

*(From the Report of the Bullion Committee.)*

| Quarter ended | Not exceeding £1. 1s. 3d. | | | DUTIES imposed by Act 44 GEO. III. | | | | | | | | |
| --- | --- | --- | --- | --- | --- | --- | --- | --- | --- | --- | --- | --- |
| | | | | Exceeding £1. 1s. and not exceeding £2. 2s. 6d. | | | Exceeding £2. 2s. and not exceeding £5. 5s. 9d. | | | Exceeding £5. 5s. and not exceeding £20. 1s. | | |
| | £ | s. | d. | £ | s. | d. | £ | s. | d. | £ | s. | d. |
| Quarter ended 5th Jan. 1805 | 7,807 | 13 | 6 | 194 | 15 | 6 | 5,458 | 18 | 3 | 3,517 | 14 | 0 |
| —— 5th April —— | 7,781 | 4 | 6 | 285 | 12 | 0 | 5,032 | 11 | 6 | 2,042 | 16 | 0 |
| —— 5th July —— | 6,610 | 1 | 3 | 143 | 2 | 0 | 6,794 | 12 | 6 | 3,065 | 7 | 0 |
| —— 10th Oct. —— | 14,121 | 10 | 3 | 176 | 19 | 6 | 13,595 | 4 | 3 | 6,504 | 5 | 0 |
| Quarter ended 5th Jan. 1806 | 12,066 | 16 | 9 | 494 | 0 | 6 | 12,537 | 15 | 0 | 6,705 | 14 | 0 |
| —— 5th April —— | 9,397 | 9 | 9 | 387 | 5 | 6 | 8,689 | 10 | 9 | 4,068 | 14 | 0 |
| —— 5th July —— | 6,443 | 3 | 0 | 432 | 10 | 0 | 6,323 | 15 | 6 | 3,713 | 0 | 0 |
| —— 10th Oct. —— | 7,218 | 5 | 3 | 339 | 17 | 0 | 3,684 | 15 | 9 | 1,668 | 10 | 0 |
| Quarter ended 5th Jan. 1807 | 6,905 | 19 | 3 | 465 | 4 | 0 | 5,559 | 15 | 0 | 2,138 | 19 | 0 |
| —— 5th April —— | 7,274 | 18 | 3 | 521 | 10 | 6 | 5,062 | 16 | 9 | 1,809 | 1 | 0 |
| —— 5th July —— | 5,193 | 9 | 9 | 227 | 17 | 0 | 3,759 | 2 | 3 | 1,499 | 18 | 0 |
| —— 10th Oct. —— | 7,452 | 8 | 3 | 305 | 3 | 0 | 3,734 | 12 | 6 | 1,754 | 1 | 0 |
| Quarter ended 5th Jan. 1808 | 6,853 | 2 | 0 | 354 | 1 | 0 | 4,597 | 12 | 3 | 2,042 | 2 | 0 |
| —— 5th April —— | 7,609 | 11 | 9 | 938 | 13 | 6 | 5,419 | 9 | 3 | 2,411 | 1 | 0 |
| —— 5th July —— | 6,198 | 11 | 9 | 457 | 3 | 6 | 5,570 | 17 | 0 | 2,371 | 5 | 0 |
| —— 10th Oct. —— | 3,000 | 6 | 6 | 209 | 18 | 6 | 9,389 | 14 | 9 | 3,099 | 5 | 6 |

No. VIII. A TABLE of the ISSUES of the COUNTRY BANKS, calculated from an ACCOUNT (in the Appendix to the Report of the Commons in 1819, upon the Bank resuming Cash Payments) of STAMPS for their PROMISSORY NOTES, delivered from the Stamp-Office.

The stamps of one, two, and five pound notes, will admit notes of the one, two, and five guineas to be drawn upon them; but paper of this description is not often circulated. With this exception, the stamps are always issued at the full value which they will bear, and this table is calculated accordingly. During the period comprised in this table, the stamps were allowed to circulate three years. A change of this arrangement has recently taken place, but I understand it was since the date of the report from which this table is taken. Consequently, by adding three years together, a tolerably correct estimate of the circulation of each year is obtained.

| | Fresh Notes issued Quarterly. | Fresh Notes issued Yearly. | Total Amount in Circulation. |
|---|---|---|---|
| 1810. | | | |
| Quarter ending 5th April, 1810,............ | £3,321,770 | | |
| ......... 5th July, ............... | 3,540,620 | | |
| ......... 10th October, ............... | 2,078,053 | £10,997,066 | |
| ......... 5th Jan. 1811,............... | 2,056,623 | | |

| Quarter ending | Fresh Notes issued Quarterly. | Fresh Notes issued Yearly. | Total Amount in Circulation. |
|---|---|---|---|
| **1811.** | | | |
| 5th April, | £2,286,378 | | |
| 5th July, | 2,752,906 | | |
| 10th October, | 3,643,630 | | |
| 5th Jan. 1812, | 3,622,670 | £12,305,584 | |
| **1812.** | | | |
| 5th April, | 3,143,861 | | |
| 5th July, | 3,495,550 | | |
| 10th October, | 2,811,557 | | |
| 5th Jan. 1813, | 5,053,411 | 14,504,379 | 37,807,029 |
| **1813.** | | | |
| 5th April, | 4,249,579 | | |
| 5th July, | 3,446,804 | | |
| 10th October, | 2,465,435 | | |
| 5th Jan. 1814, | 4,308,756 | 14,470,574 | 41,280,537 |
| **1814.** | | | |
| 5th April, | 2,900,836 | | |
| 5th July, | 2,992,478 | | |
| 10th October, | 2,641,441 | | |
| 5th Jan. 1815, | 2,859,614 | 11,394,360 | 40,369,322 |

| Quarter | Fresh Notes issued Quarterly. | Fresh Notes issued Yearly. | Total Amount in Circulation. |
|---|---|---|---|
| 1815. | | | |
| Quarter ending 5th April, 1815, | £2,008,006 | | |
| 5th July, | 1,825,049 | | |
| 10th October, | 2,089,987 | | |
| 5th Jan. 1816, | 1,924,969 | £7,848,011 | £33,712,945 |
| 1816. | | | |
| 5th April, | 1,536,057 | | |
| 5th July, | 1,762,381 | | |
| 10th October, | 1,140,037 | | |
| 5th Jan. 1817, | 2,000,202 | 6,438,677 | 25,681,057 |
| 1817. | | | |
| 5th April, | 2,273,016 | | |
| 5th July, | 2,252,781 | | |
| 10th October, | 2,550,059 | | |
| 5th Jan. 1818, | 3,542,024 | 10,617,880 | 24,904,568 |
| 1818. | | | |
| 5th April, | 3,161,105 | | |
| 5th July, | 2,667,950 | | |
| 10th October, | 2,945,789 | | |
| 5th Jan. 1819, | 2,671,087 | 11,445,931 | 28,502,488 |

3

No. IX. The Amount of ADVANCES made by the Bank of England to Government, on Exchequer Bills and other Securities, including Exchequer Bills, Navy Bills, Victualling Bills, &c. purchased.

*( From the Report of the Committee of the House of Commons, in 1819, on the Bank resuming Cash Payments.)*

|      |          |    | Total. |
|------|----------|----|--------|
| 1792 | February | 25 | £10,968,306 |
|      | August   | 25 | 11,684,484 |
| 1793 | February | 26 | 10,529,828 |
|      | August   | 26 | 11,851,388 |
| 1794 | February | 26 | 10,816,867 |
|      | August   | 26 | 8,737,806 |
| 1795 | February | 26 | 13,118,013 |
|      | August   | 26 | 13,460,144 |
| 1796 | February | 26 | 12,717,239 |
|      | August   | 26 | 10,454,614 |
| 1797 | February | 25 | 10,181,862 |
|      | August   | 26 | 7,145,134 |
| 1798 | February | 26 | 9,807,814 |
|      | August   | 25 | 9,444,976 |
| 1799 | February | 26 | 10,082,739 |
|      | August   | 26 | 8,986,439 |
| 1800 | February | 25 | 13,201,639 |
|      | August   | 26 | 12,899,239 |
| 1801 | February | 26 | 15,289,439 |
|      | August   | 26 | 11,948,539 |

|      |   |          |   |    |   | *Total.*      |
|------|---|----------|---|----|---|---------------|
| 1802 | - | February | - | 26 | - | £14,284,239   |
|      |   | August   | - | 26 | - | 13,552,339    |
| 1803 | - | February | - | 26 | - | 9,595,939     |
|      |   | August   | - | 26 | - | 13,635,239    |
| 1804 | - | February | - | 25 | - | 14,715,239    |
|      |   | August   | - | 25 | - | 15,304,439    |
| 1805 | - | February | - | 26 | - | 17,202,739    |
|      |   | August   | - | 26 | - | 11,745,339    |
| 1806 | - | February | - | 25 | - | 14,663,339    |
|      |   | August   | - | 26 | - | 14,445,339    |
| 1807 | - | February | - | 26 | - | 13,763,539    |
|      |   | August   | - | 26 | - | 13,665,339    |
| 1808 | - | February | - | 26 | - | 14,364,939    |
|      |   | August   | - | 26 | - | 15,677,539    |
| 1809 | - | February | - | 25 | - | 15,400,139    |
|      |   | August   | - | 26 | - | 16,009,339    |
| 1810 | - | February | - | 26 | - | 15,017,839    |
|      |   | August   | - | 25 | - | 17,689,739    |
| 1811 | - | February | - | 26 | - | 18,068,439    |
|      |   | August   | - | 26 | - | 22,696,239    |
| 1812 | - | February | - | 26 | - | 22,551,739    |
|      |   | August   | - | 26 | - | 21,957,639    |
| 1813 | - | February | - | 26 | - | 25,893,939    |
|      |   | August   | - | 26 | - | 25,731,239    |
| 1814 | - | February | - | 26 | - | 24,484,039    |
|      |   | August   | - | 26 | - | 35,814,539    |
| 1815 | - | February | - | 25 | - | 28,032,739    |
|      |   | August   | - | 26 | - | 24,955,839    |
| 1816 | - | February | - | 26 | - | 19,865,039    |
|      |   | August   | - | 26 | - | 27,222,845    |

| 1817 | - | February | - | 26 | - | 26,373,570 |
|------|---|----------|---|----|---|------------|
|      |   | August   | - - | 26 | - | 28,300,200 |
| 1818 | - | February | - | 26 | - | 28,035,523 |
|      |   | August   | - - | 26 | - | 28,087,865 |
| 1819 | - | February | - | 11 | - | 23,028,820 |

No. X. An ACCOUNT of the AGGREGATE VALUE (as calculated at the Average Market Prices in England and Wales) of all CORN, GRAIN, MEAL, and FLOUR, imported from Foreign Parts into Great Britain during each of the last six Years.

*(From the Report of the Committee of the House of Commons, in 1819, on the Bank resuming Cash Payments.)*

|       |   |   |   | £. | s. | d. |
|-------|---|---|---|----|----|----|
| 1813  | - | - | - | 2,192,592 | 3 | 6 |
| 1814  | - |   | - | 2,815,319 | 4 | 0 |
| 1815  | - | - | - | 793,245 | 8 | 11 |
| 1816  | - |   | - | 942,497 | 19 | 7 |
| 1817  | - | - | - | 6,403,893 | 10 | 6 |
| 1818  | - |   | - | 10,908,140 | 0 | 2 |

## No. XI. Account of the Finances of the Bank of England, on the 26th of February, 1797.

| DR. | | CR. | |
|---|---|---|---|
| Bank Notes in circulation | £8,640,250 | Bills and Notes discounted, Cash and Bullion | £4,176,080 |
| Drawing Account | 2,389,600 | Exchequer Bills | 8,228,000 |
| Exchequer Bills deposited | 1,676,000 | Lands and Tenements | 65,000 |
| Audit Roll (or unpaid Dividends) | 983,730 | Money lent on Mortgage on Annuities of £1,200,000 to the East India Company | 700,000 |
| Bank Stock Dividends unclaimed | 45,150 | Stamps | 1,510 |
| Dividends unclaimed on East India Annuities | 10,210 | Navy and Victualling Bills | 15,890 |
| Sundry small articles unclaimed | 1,330 | American Debentures, 1790 | 54,150 |
| Due from Chief Cashier on the Loan of 1797 | 17,060 | Petty Cash in the House | 5,320 |
| Unpaid Irish Dividends | 1,460 | Sundry Articles | 24,150 |
| Ditto on the Imperial Loan | 5,600 | 5 per Cent. Navy Annuities | 795,800 |
| Balance in favour of the Bank | 3,826,890 | 5 per Cents. 1797 | 1,000,000 |
| | | Treasury Bills paid for Government | 1,512,270 |
| | | Loan to Government without Interest | 376,000 |
| | | Bills discounted unpaid | 88,120 |
| | | Treasury and Exchequer Fees | 740 |
| | | Interest due on different sums advanced to Government | 554,250 |
| | £17,597,280 | | £17,597,280 |
| | | Balance in favour of the Bank | £3,826,890 |

No. XII. An ACCOUNT of the Total Amount of OUT-STANDING DEMANDS on the Bank of England, and likewise the Funds for discharging the same, 30th January, 1819.

*(From the Report of the Committee of the House of Commons, in 1819, on the Bank resuming Cash Payments.)*

DR. - The Bank, - 30th January, 1819. - CR.

| | £. | | £. |
|---|---|---|---|
| TO Bank Notes out | 26,094,430 | BY Advances on Government Securities, viz. | |
| To other Debts, viz. Drawing Accounts } Audit Roll - Exchequer Bills deposited - And various other Debts - - } | 7,800,150 | On Exchequer Bills } on Malt, &c. 1818 Bank Loan, 1808 Supply, 1816, at £4 per cent. - Growing Produce of the Consolidated } Fund to 5th April, 1819, and Loans to Government on unclaimed Dividends - } | 8,438,660 |
| | 33,894,580 | | |
| Balance of Surplus in favour of the Bank of England, exclusive of the Debt from Government, at £3. per cent. £11,686,800 } And the Advance to Government, per 56 Geo. III. cap. } 96 at £3. per cent. £3,000,000 } | 5,202,320 | By all other Credits, viz. Cash and Bullion } Exchequer Bills purchased & Interest Bills and Notes discounted - Treasury Bills for } the Service of Ireland - - Money lent, and various other Articles } | 30,658,240 |
| | £39,096,900 | | £39,096,900 |
| | | By the permanent Debt due from Government, for the Capital of the Bank at £3. per cent. per Annum | 11,686,800 |
| | | By the Advance to Government, per Act 56 Geo. III. cap. 96, at £3 per cent. per Annum | 3,000,000 |

WILLIAM DAWES, Accountant General.

*Bank of England, 22nd February, 1819.*

No. XIII. ACCOUNT of the Market Prices of STAND-
ARD GOLD, the *real par* and course of exchange between London and Hamburgh, and the *per centage* in
favour of and against London.*

*( From the Article Exchange, in the Supplement to the Encyclopædia
Britannica.)*

| | | Price of Standard Gold per oz. | | | Par of Exchange with Hambro'. | | Course of exchange with Hambro'. | | Per cent. in favour of London. | Per cent. against London. |
|---|---|---|---|---|---|---|---|---|---|---|
| | | £. | s. | d. | sch. | gr. | | | | |
| 1760 | Jan. 1 | 3 | 18 | 6 | 32 | 9.9 | 36 | 4 | 10.6 | |
| | May 2 | 3 | 19 | 1 | 33 | 3.7 | 35 | 6 | 6.5 | |
| | Sept. 2 | 4 | 0 | 1 | 33 | 6.0 | 32 | 2 | | 4 |
| 1 | Jan. 2 | 3 | 18 | 10 | 32 | 0.1 | 32 | 0 | | 0.1 |
| | May 1 | 4 | 0 | 0 | 32 | 0.1 | 32 | 2 | 0.4 | |
| | Sept. 1 | 4 | 0 | 6 | 33 | 0.9 | 32 | 5 | | 2 |
| 2 | Jan. 1 | 3 | 19 | 0 | 33 | 1.8 | 32 | 11 | | 2.0 |
| | May 4 | 3 | 19 | 3 | 32 | 7.9 | 34 | 3 | 4.8 | |
| | Sept. 3 | 3 | 19 | 4 | 33 | 11.2 | 35 | 0 | 3.6 | |
| 3 | Jan. 4 | 4 | 0 | 0 | 33 | 10.1 | 34 | 2 | 0.9 | |
| | May 3 | 4 | 1 | 3 | 33 | 2.6 | 34 | 2 | 2.7 | |
| | Sept. 2 | 4 | 1 | 6 | 34 | 4.0 | 34 | 7 | 0.7 | |
| 4 | Jan. 3 | 3 | 18 | 3 | 33 | 8.7 | 34 | 5 | 1.9 | |

* " This table, with the exception of the column of the Bank of
" England notes, from 1760 to 1809, is extracted from the second
" edition of Mr Mushet's pamphlet. The last ten years have been
" filled up from the accounts given in the *Reports on the Expediency*
" *of the Bank resuming Cash Payments*, laid before parliament in 1819.
" The *fixed par* is taken at 34 schillings, 11 grotes, and ¼, which is
" esteemed the true *par* by the merchants, though it differs about ⅜
" *per cent.* from the par (35s. 1d. Hamburgh currency), as estimated
" by Dr Kelly from the Mint regulations. The bills on Hamburgh
" from the negociation of which this table has been formed, have
" been invariably drawn at 2½ usances."

| | | Price of Standard Gold per oz. | | | Par of Exchange with Hambro'. | | Course of Exchange with Hambro'. | | Per cent. in favour of London. | Per cent. against London. |
|---|---|---|---|---|---|---|---|---|---|---|
| | | £. | s. | d. | sch. | gr. | | | | |
| 1764 | May 1 | 3 | 18 | 3 | 34 | 3.1 | 34 | 11 | 1.1 | |
| | Sept. 4 | 3 | 18 | 0 | 34 | 2.0 | 35 | 0 | 2.4 | |
| 5 | Jan. 1 | 3 | 18 | 0 | 34 | 2.0 | 35 | 1 | 2.6 | |
| | May 3 | 3 | 18 | 0 | 33 | 9.0 | 34 | 11 | 3.4 | |
| | Sept. 3 | 3 | 18 | 8 | 33 | 7.9 | 34 | 4 | 2.0 | |
| 6 | Jan. 3 | 3 | 18 | 7 | 33 | 2.9 | 34 | 6 | 3.7 | |
| | May 2 | 3 | 19 | 2 | 33 | 1.2 | 34 | 11 | 5.4 | |
| | Sept. 2 | 3 | 19 | 0 | 32 | 9.6 | 35 | 3 | 8.2 | |
| 7 | Jan. 2 | 3 | 19 | 3 | 32 | 9.3 | 35 | 6 | 8.3 | |
| | May 1 | 3 | 19 | 10 | 32 | 10.7 | 35 | 10 | 8.9 | |
| | Sept. 1 | 3 | 19 | 5 | 33 | 2.6 | 35 | 11 | 8.1 | |
| 8 | Jan. 1 | 3 | 18 | 8 | 33 | 4.8 | 34 | 11 | 4.4 | |
| | May 3 | 3 | 19 | 1 | 33 | 0.9 | 34 | 8 | 4.8 | |
| | Sept. 2 | 3 | 19 | 6 | 33 | 4.6 | 34 | 5 | 3.0 | |
| 9 | Jan. 3 | 3 | 19 | 7 | 33 | 3.7 | 33 | 2 | | 0.5 |
| | May 2 | 4 | 0 | 3 | 33 | 2.3 | 33 | 8 | 1.4 | |
| | Sept. 1 | 4 | 0 | 4 | 33 | 1.2 | 33 | 6 | 1.2 | |
| 1770 | Jan. 2 | 4 | 0 | 6 | 33 | 0.4 | 33 | 2 | 0.4 | |
| | May 1 | 4 | 0 | 4 | 32 | 10.1 | 33 | 3 | 1.3 | |
| | Sept. 4 | 4 | 0 | 0 | 33 | 5.4 | 33 | 2 | | 0.1 |
| 1 | Jan. 1 | 3 | 18 | 9 | 32 | 8.2 | 33 | 8 | .5 | |
| | May 3 | 3 | 19 | 2 | 32 | 6.0 | 33 | 6 | .5 | |
| | Sept. 3 | 4 | 0 | 8 | 33 | 4.3 | 33 | 11 | | 1.4 |
| 2 | Jan. 3 | 4 | 1 | 0 | 33 | 2.9 | 32 | 7 | | 2.0 |
| | May 1 | 4 | 0 | 9 | 32 | 10.7 | 32 | 10 | | 2 |
| | Sept. 1 | 3 | 19 | 0 | 33 | 9.6 | 33 | 5 | | 1.2 |
| 3 | Jan. 5 | 3 | 18 | 0 | 33 | 7.5 | 34 | | 1.1 | |
| | May 4 | 3 | 17 | 11 | 33 | 10.1 | 34 | 9 | 2.6 | |
| | Sept. 3 | 3 | 17 | 9 | 34 | 0.1 | 34 | 8 | 1.9 | |
| 4 | Jan. 4 | 3 | 17 | 9 | 34 | 7. | 34 | 9 | 0.4 | |
| | May 3 | 3 | 17 | 9 | 33 | 11. | 34 | 7 | 1.9 | |
| | Sept. 2 | 3 | 17 | 7 | 34 | 2.8 | 34 | 5 | 0.5 | |
| 5 | Jan. 3 | 3 | 17 | 7 | 33 | 8.5 | 34 | 3 | 1.6 | |
| | May 2 | 3 | 17 | 7 | 33 | 2.3 | 34 | 4 | 3.4 | |
| | Sept. 1 | 3 | 17 | 7 | 34 | 0.6 | 34 | 4 | 0.8 | |
| 6 | Jan. 5 | 3 | 17 | 7 | 33 | 3.7 | 34 | 1 | 4.8 | |
| | May 3 | 3 | 17 | 7 | 32 | 8.2 | 33 | 8 | 3. | |
| | Sept. 3 | 3 | 17 | 7 | 32 | 11.3 | 33 | 5 | 1.4 | |
| 7 | Jan. 3 | 3 | 17 | 7 | 31 | 11.6 | 33 | 2 | 3.7 | |
| | May 2 | 3 | 17 | 7 | 32 | 2.9 | 32 | 10 | 1.8 | |

| | | Price of Standard Gold per oz. | | | Par of Exchange with Hambro'. | | Course of Exchange with Hambro'. | | Per cent. in favour of London. | Per cent. against London. |
|---|---|---|---|---|---|---|---|---|---|---|
| | | £. | s. | d. | sch. | gr. | | | | |
| 1777 | Sept. 2 | 3 | 17 | 7 | 32 | 7.5 | 32 | 2 | 1.4 | |
| 8 | Jan. 2 | 3 | 17 | 7 | 31 | 3.2 | 32 | 4 | 3.4 | |
| | May 1 | 3 | 17 | 7 | 32 | 11.3 | 34 | 2 | 3.7 | |
| | Sept. 1 | 3 | 17 | 7 | 33 | 5.4 | 34 | 5 | 2.8 | |
| 9 | Jan. 1 | 3 | 17 | 7 | 34 | 9.5 | 35 | 6 | 2.9 | |
| | May 4 | 3 | 17 | 6 | 34 | 5.9 | 36 | 2 | 4.8 | |
| | Sept. 3 | 3 | 17 | 6 | 33 | 4.8 | 33 | 9 | 1. | |
| 1780 | Jan. 4 | 3 | 17 | 6 | 34 | 2.5 | 34 | 6 | 0.8 | |
| | May 2 | 3 | 17 | 6 | 32 | 7.9 | 35 | 2 | 7.6 | |
| | Sept. 1 | 3 | 17 | 6 | 33 | 0.4 | 34 | 1 | 3.2 | |
| 1 | Jan. 2 | 3 | 17 | 6 | 32 | 10.7 | 34 | 1 | 3.6 | |
| | May 1 | 3 | 17 | 6 | 31 | 11. | 33 | 7 | 5.2 | |
| | Sept. 4 | 3 | 17 | 6 | 31 | 5.5 | 32 | 2 | 2.2 | |
| 2 | Jan. 1 | 3 | 17 | 6 | 31 | 0.2 | 31 | 9 | 2.3 | |
| | May 3 | 3 | 17 | 6 | 30 | 4.7 | 32 | 11 | 8.3 | |
| | Sept. 3 | 3 | 17 | 9 | 31 | 1.3 | 32 | 6 | 4.4 | |
| 3 | Jan. 3 | 3 | 17 | 9 | 31 | 9.6 | 32 | 7 | 2.4 | |
| | May 2 | 3 | 18 | 0 | 30 | 10.5 | 31 | 9 | 2.8 | |
| | Sept. 2 | 3 | 18 | 0 | 31 | 7.9 | 31 | 6 | | 0.5 |
| 4 | Jan. 2 | 3 | 18 | 0 | 33 | 1.5 | 33 | 6 | 1.1 | |
| | May 4 | 3 | 17 | 10½ | 34 | 2.8 | 34 | 4 | 0.2 | |
| | Sept. 3 | 3 | 17 | 10½ | 34 | 2.8 | 34 | 7 | 1.0 | |
| 5 | Jan. 7 | 3 | 17 | 10½ | 34 | 6.2 | 35 | 0 | 1.4 | |
| | May 3 | 3 | 17 | 10½ | 34 | 7.9 | 34 | 11 | 0.7 | |
| | Sept. 2 | 3 | 17 | 6 | 35 | 0.6 | 35 | 4 | | |
| 6 | Jan. 3 | 3 | 17 | 6 | 34 | 4.2 | 34 | 10 | 1.1 | |
| | May 2 | 3 | 17 | 6 | 33 | 11.2 | 34 | 5 | 1.4 | |
| | Sept. 1 | 3 | 17 | 6 | 34 | 2.5 | 34 | 3 | 0.1 | |
| 7 | Jan. 2 | 3 | 17 | 6 | 34 | 6.2 | 34 | 5 | | 0.1 |
| | May 1 | 3 | 17 | 6 | 34 | 0.9 | 34 | 7 | 4.0 | |
| | Sept. 4 | 3 | 17 | 6 | 33 | 9.6 | 35 | 0 | 3.5 | |
| 8 | Jan. 1 | 3 | 17 | 6 | 33 | 9.6 | 35 | 1 | 3.8 | |
| | May 2 | 3 | 17 | 6 | 33 | 9.6 | 35 | 4 | 4.5 | |
| | Sept. 2 | 3 | 17 | 6 | 33 | 9.6 | 35 | 0 | 3.5 | |
| 9 | Jan. 6 | 3 | 17 | 6 | 33 | 9.6 | 34 | 10 | 3.0 | |
| | May 1 | 3 | 17 | 6 | 34 | 0.9 | 35 | 6 | 4.1 | |
| | Sept. 1 | 3 | 17 | 6 | 34 | 6.2 | 35 | 5 | 2.6 | |
| 1790 | Jan. 29 | 3 | 17 | 6 | 34 | 5.9 | 35 | | 1.4 | |
| | May 4 | 3 | 17 | 6 | 34 | 0.9 | 35 | 4 | 3.7 | |
| | Sept. 3 | 3 | 17 | 6 | 34 | 5.9 | 35 | 6 | 2.9 | |

| | Price of Standard Gold per oz. | | | Par of Exchange with Hambro'. | | Course of Exchange with Hambro'. | | Per cent. in favour of London. | Per cent. against London. |
|---|---|---|---|---|---|---|---|---|---|
| | £. | s. | d. | sch. | gr. | | | | |
| 1791 Jan. 4 | 3 | 17 | 6 | 34 | 2.5 | 35 | 6 | 3.7 | |
| May 3 | 3 | 17 | 6 | 34 | 0.9 | 35 | 11 | 5.4 | |
| Sept. 2 | 3 | 17 | 6 | 34 | 7.6 | 35 | 6 | 2.5 | |
| 2 Jan. 3 | 3 | 17 | 6 | 33 | 8.2 | 34 | 6 | 2.4 | |
| May 1 | 3 | 17 | 6 | 33 | 0.4 | 34 | 3 | 3.7 | |
| Sept. 4 | 3 | 17 | 6 | 33 | 1.8 | 34 | 0 | 2.5 | |
| 3 Jan. 1 | 3 | 17 | 6 | 33 | 3.4 | 35 | 4 | 6.1 | |
| May 3 | 3 | 17 | 6 | 34 | 5.9 | 37 | 6 | 8.7 | |
| Sept. 3 | 3 | 17 | 6 | 35 | 0.6 | 36 | 0 | 2.7 | |
| 4 Jan. 3 | 3 | 17 | 6 | 35 | 0.6 | 35 | 9 | 2.0 | |
| May 2 | 3 | 17 | 6 | 35 | 2.3 | 36 | 7 | 4.0 | |
| Sept. 2 | 3 | 17 | 6 | 35 | 3.9 | 35 | 0 | | 1.0 |
| 5 Jan. 2 | 3 | 17 | 6 | 34 | 7.6 | 34 | 6 | | 0.4 |
| May 1 | 3 | 17 | 6 | 35 | 3.9 | 34 | 4 | | 2.8 |
| Sept. 1 | * | | | | | 32 | 6 | | |
| 6 Jan. 1 | | | | | | 32 | 7 | | |
| May 3 | | | | | | 33 | 10 | | |
| Sept. 2 | 3 | 17 | 6 | 33 | 11.2 | 33 | 7 | | 1. |
| 7 Jan. 3 | 3 | 17 | 6 | 33 | 1.8 | 35 | 6 | 7. | |
| May 2 | 3 | 17 | 6 | 32 | 7.9 | 36 | | 10. | |
| Sept. 1 | 3 | 17 | 10½ | 35 | 5.9 | 38 | | 7. | |
| 8 Jan. 2 | 3 | 17 | 10½ | 36 | 1.1 | 38 | 2 | 5.7 | |
| May 1 | 3 | 17 | 10½ | 35 | 2.5 | 37 | 8 | 7. | |
| Sept. 4 | 3 | 17 | 10½ | 35 | 5.9 | 37 | 6 | 5.6 | |
| 9 Jan. 1 | 3 | 17 | 9 | 34 | 10.5 | 37 | 7 | 7.7 | |
| May 3 | 3 | 17 | 9 | 34 | 10.5 | 35 | 6 | 1.8 | |
| Sept. 3 | 3 | 17 | 9 | | | 33 | 4 | | |
| 1800 Jan.†3 | | | | | | 32 | | | |
| May 2 | 4 | 5 | 0 | 34 | 0.4 | 32 | 5 | | 5.3 |
| Sept. 2 | 4 | 5 | 0 | 34 | 0.4 | 32 | 2 | | 5.5 |
| 1 Jan. 2 | 4 | 6 | 0 | 33 | 11.2 | 29 | 8 | | 12.6 |
| May 1 | 4 | 3 | 0 | 31 | 10. | 31 | 6 | | 1. |
| Sept. 1 | | | | | | 31 | 7 | | |

* " Wherever a blank space is left, it shews that no prices of bul-
" lion are quoted of that date, either at Lloyd's, or at the *Bullion*
" *Office* in the Bank of England."

† " From 1800 to 1810, standard gold and silver in bars are not
" regularly quoted. Portugal gold in coin, being nearly of the same
" standard, has in several instances been quoted as standard gold."

| | | Price of Standard Gold per oz. | | | Par of Exchange with Hambro'. | | Course or Exchange with Hambro'. | | Per cent. in favour of London. | Per cent. against London. |
|---|---|---|---|---|---|---|---|---|---|---|
| | | £. | s. | d. | sch. | gr. | | | | |
| 1802 | Jan. 1 | 4 | 3 | 6 | | | 32 | 2 | | |
| | May 4 | | | | | | 32 | 8 | | |
| | Sept. 3 | | | | | | 33 | 3 | | |
| 3 | Jan. 4 | | | | | | 34 | | | |
| | May 3 | | | | | | 34 | 4 | | |
| | Sept. 2 | | | | | | 32 | 10 | | |
| 4 | Jan. 3 | | | | | | 34 | 10 | | |
| | May 1 | | | | | | 35 | 9 | | |
| | Sept. 4 | 4 | 0 | 0 | 34 | 9.3 | 35 | 10 | 3. | |
| 5 | Jan. 1 | 4 | 0 | 0 | 33 | 5.7 | 35 | 6 | 6.0 | |
| | May 3 | 4 | 0 | 0 | 34 | 5.9 | 35 | 5 | 2.6 | |
| | Sept. 3 | 4 | 0 | 0 | | | 35 | 5 | | |
| 6 | Jan. 3 | | | | | | 33 | 3 | | |
| | May 2 | | | | | | 33 | 8 | | |
| | Sept. 2 | | | | | | 34 | 4 | | |
| 7 | Jan. 2 | | | | | | 34 | 8 | | |
| | May 1 | | | | | | 34 | 10 | | |
| | Sept. 4 | | | | | | 34 | 3 | | |
| 8 | Jan. 1 | | | | | | 34 | 4 | | |
| | May 3 | | | | | | 34 | 9 | | |
| | Sept. 2 | | | | | | 34 | 8 | | |
| 9 | Jan. 3 | | | | | | 31 | 3 | | |
| | May 2 | 4 | 11 | 0 | 38 | 0.8 | 30 | 6 | | 19.9 |
| | Sept. 5 | 4 | 9 | 10½ | 36 | 10.9 | 29 | 0 | | 21.4 |
| 1810 | Jan. 2 | 4 | 9 | 10½ | | | 29 | 3 | | |
| | May 1 | | | | | | 31 | 3 | | |
| | Oct. 9 | 4 | 5 | 0 | | | 31 | 0 | | |
| 11 | Jan. 22 | 4 | 7 | 6 | 34 | 9.9 | 26 | 0 | | 25.3 |
| | May 14 | | | | | | 24 | 0 | | |
| | Aug 30 | | | | | | 25 | 6 | | |
| 12 | Jan. 31 | 4 | 18 | 6 | | | 27 | 6 | | |
| | May 22 | 4 | 17 | 0 | 35 | 6.2 | 29 | 0 | | 18.4 |
| | Oct. 2 | 5 | 7 | 0 | | | 28 | 0 | | |
| 13 | Jan. 22 | 5 | 4 | 0 | | | 29 | 0 | | |
| | May 21 | 5 | 3 | 0 | 34 | 11.2 | 28 | 0 | | 24.6 |
| | Oct. 1 | 5 | 8 | 0 | 36 | 2.3 | 26 | 6 | | 29.1 |
| 14 | Feb. 8 | 5 | 8 | 0 | 35 | 6.8 | 29 | 0 | | 14.5 |
| | May 24 | 5 | 3 | 0 | | | 28 | 0 | | |
| | Oct. 4 | 4 | 5 | 0 | 34 | 9.3 | 32 | 10 | | 5.6 |
| 15 | Jan. 3 | 4 | 6 | 6 | 34 | 10.4 | 32 | 4 | | 7.3 |

|  |  | Price of Standard Gold per oz. | | | Par of Exchange with Hambro'. | | Course of Exchange with Hambro'. | | Per cent. in favour of London. | Per cent. against London. |
|---|---|---|---|---|---|---|---|---|---|---|
|  |  | £. | s. | d. | sch. | gr. |  |  |  |  |
| 1815 | May 2 | 5 | 6 | 0 | 36 | 2.3 | 28 | 2 |  | 22.2 |
|  | Sep. 15 | 4 | 9 | 0 | 35 | 10.6 | 32 | 9 |  | 8.7 |
| 16 | Jan. 16 | 4 | 2 | 0 | 36 | 2.8 | 34 | 4 |  | 5.2 |
|  | May 28 | 4 | 0 | 0 | 36 | 2.3 | 35 | 10 |  | 1.0 |
|  | Oct. 1 | 3 | 19 | 0 | 36 | 7.5 | 36 | 11 | 0.8 |  |
| 17 | Jan. 17 | 3 | 19 | 6 | 36 | 6.7 | 36 | 1 |  | 1.3 |
|  | June 6 | 3 | 19 | 0 | 34 | 10.7 | 35 | 0 | 0.3 |  |
|  | Sept. 5 | 4 | 0 | 0 | 35 | 3.9 | 35 | 2 |  | 0.5 |
| 18 | Jan. 9 | 4 | 0 | 6 | 35 | 3.1 | 34 | 6 |  | 2.2 |
|  | May 26 | 4 | 1 | 6 | 34 | 7.3 | 33 | 11 |  | 2.0 |
|  | Sep. 15 | 4 | 0 | 0 | 34 | 9.3 | 35 | 2 | 1.1 |  |
| 19 | Jan. 8 | 4 | 3 | 0 | 35 | 2.9 | 33 | 9 |  | 1.9 |
|  | Mar 23 | 4 | 1 | 0 | 34 | 1.5 | 34 | 4 | 0.6 |  |

No. XIV. EXTRACT from the EVIDENCE of David Hodgson, Esq. before the AGRICULTURAL COMMITTEE of 1821.

*(From the Report of the Committee of the House of Commons on the Agriculture of the United Kingdom, 1821.)*

You are a partner in the house of Cropper, Benson, and Company, at Liverpool? I am.

In what line of business are you engaged? We are in various lines of business, the East India, the American, and the Irish corn trade.

Have you been extensive dealers in foreign corn? We have.

And are now holders of foreign corn in bond? We are.

Have you, with a view to guide your commercial transactions in the article of corn, endeavoured, by any means, to ascertain what has been, of late years, the state of the wheat crops of this country? We have.

Have you any objection to state to the committee, the mode which you have adopted for ascertaining this point? None; but we should prefer, in giving a detail of it, that it was only used for the conviction of the committee, in order that they might decide what importance they might attach to the results; we have been at very considerable expence, and consumed a great deal of time in obtaining the information, and we should prefer that the details of the manner were not made public.

Have the goodness to state the results? We have examined, for the last several years, but more correctly since 1815, a district of the country, comprising about 1,000 miles, and we have endeavoured, as accurately as possible, to take a fair average of the fields examined.

What are the districts of country generally included in this survey of 1,000 miles? We have generally commenced in Kent, and gone down the whole of the east coast to Berwick, and once or twice to Edinburgh, as one part of the survey; the others we have taken from Liverpool, through Cheshire, Shropshire, Worcestershire, Herefordshire, round by Birmingham, and taken in the whole of Warwickshire and Staffordshire, and come round in that circuit home again.

This survey, of course, is taken about the time the harvest is going to begin? Yes; just when we consider the wheat ripe.

Has the result of this survey been such as to afford you satisfactory information for the guidance of your commercial speculations in corn? We have been guided by it, though not always to the result we expected; but latterly it has been becoming more perfect, at the same time there are various contingencies that often disappoint any opinion connected with an article so extensively held, or otherwise, according to the spirit of speculation which may prevail.

You consider the result of the survey to be a material ingredient in forming your conclusions as to the state of the crop, and the probability of the country being in want, or not in want of a foreign supply? Certainly.

And of the probable price of corn in the year following your survey? We do.

Have you any objection to state to the committee, upon any scale you may have formed, what has been the comparative productiveness of the crops of the last six years? None whatever; the crop of 1815, according to the method explained, gave a result of 37 Winchester bushels per acre; 1816 gave $25\frac{3}{10}$; 1817 gave $33\frac{4}{10}$; 1818 gave 32 and $\frac{6}{10}$; 1819, $27\frac{7}{10}$; 1820, $37\frac{3}{10}$; this is the quantity reduced to Winchester bushels, at sixty pounds a bushel, but then it is supposing the whole surface of the acre to produce: we have not any accurate method of knowing what the real produce per acre is, but in making some attempt at a deduction, we have been rather led to believe it would not fall much short of a sixth, but that is estimated entirely ; the loss by hedges, the loss in harvesting, the loss in furrows and by vermin, the waste in machining ; every thing goes out of the quantity stated.

You are of opinion, then, that in order to get at the produce actually brought to market, a deduction of not less than a sixth ought to be made from this acreable return ? —I give it as a very vague estimate ; the data we have had to go upon have been so uncertain ; we had a very small quantity once tried, which made a deduction of about ten per cent. but this I should, myself, think was quite under the mark.

Of course you are aware that the losses some years are much greater than in others ?—Unquestionably.

You have now stated the quantities only, without reference to the quality or state in which the grain is harvested ? —Certainly, I should state, that we have not weighed it wet ; we have reduced it all to what we esteemed the same state of dryness.

But still supposing these to be the quantities, all reduced to an equal state of dryness, the quality or fitness of the produce for converting into flour for the use of the population of this country, must vary materially ?—Very materially, I should think.

And that, also, must be a main consideration in your calculations ?—That is always considered in our estimates ; but these figures are free from all estimate.

Can you state, with respect to those six years, those in which the grain has been considerably injured, and those in which the produce has been generally of a good quality ?— That in 1815 was a very good crop, and we considered it above an average at the time, decidedly ; in 1816 it was very much worse than the survey. I ought to mention with regard to 1815 and 1816, that our examinations were not so perfect as they have been in the four years since, especially 1816; for, from the condition in which it was received, we were so thoroughly satisfied of the deficiency, that we were rather inattentive, and did not weigh nearly the same number; we had gained our point in respect of information, and did not pursue it further; but it was very much worse than the survey; it was nearly rotten. In 1817, the quality was not very good.

In 1818?—In 1818, according to my recollection, the quality was good; I do not perceive that I have made a remark upon it; but I am satisfied, on recollection, it was very good. In 1819, it was very good, not so good as 1818.

The last crop?—The last crop is not very good.

Not so good in quality as in 1819?—No, nor nearly so good as 1818; there is a considerable mixture of mildew in the corn of 1820.

It is generally sound and dry?—Yes; but not equally good with either of the preceding years.

More mildewed than in 1819? —Yes, I think so.

Can you state the average acreable produce of the six years of which you have given us the detail?—The average acreable produce will be about thirty-two.

You have stated, that your survey, though less perfectly carried on, embraced a period of nine years?--It went back to the year 1809, embracing altogether a period of twelve years.

Can you state, as far as your survey was then established, what was the crop of 1813?—We discovered in the year 1814, that the person we had employed in 1813, had made a very gross mistake, which was to take the crown of the ridge, and to select the best ears; so that we reject it in our calculations: but we have every reason to believe it was the greatest crop we have ever known.

When you say, you have every reason to believe it was the greatest crop you have ever known, you have other reasons for that opinion ?—We have other reasons and general observation, from the time that the grain of that season remained, in considerable quantity, in the market; I think two or three years afterwards.

Your survey not extending to Ireland and Scotland, have you any means of giving any information to the committee, as to the state of the crops of those two parts of the United Kingdom for the two last years ?—No, nothing but inference, no survey.

What is your impression ?—My impression is, that the crop of Ireland in 1820 was good; it appeared to be the course of the crop last year to improve towards the west; and I think, there has been a very considerable extension of cultivation in Ireland last year, for a reason I will give by and by.

Do you consider the crop of 1820, as far as ascertained by your survey, to be above an average crop?—Certainly.

How much do you imagine above an average crop?—Upon the average of the six years which I have given, it would appear as about five in thirty-two, between a sixth and a seventh; but if we go further back, and include 1809, 1810, 1811, 1812, and 1814, rejecting 1813, on account of its being uncertain what the real figure was; applying the data of the square yard as actually taken for the last six years, it would give a result for an average crop of 34 in place of 32; of course, in estimating the crop of last year with reference to the acreable produce, it will depend on whether it is called 32 or 34.

Does it appear from the result of this survey, that taking the best year and the worst to which it applies, the fluctuation has been so much as a third ?—Nearly.

AN

# Essay

ON

## THE GENERAL PRINCIPLES

AND

### PRESENT PRACTICE

OF

# BANKING,

IN

England and Scotland;

WITH

OBSERVATIONS UPON THE JUSTICE AND POLICY

OF AN

## IMMEDIATE ALTERATION

IN

The Charter of the Bank of England,

AND THE

MEASURES TO BE PURSUED IN ORDER TO EFFECT IT.

## BY T. JOPLIN.

FOURTH EDITION.

# Dedication.

---

TO NONE CAN IT BE MORE PROPER TO DEDICATE A
WORK OF ANY KIND THAN TO THOSE WHOM IT PRO-
POSES TO SERVE,—THEREFORE,

TO THE MANUFACTURERS, MERCHANTS, AND TRADES-
MEN, OF ENGLAND AND IRELAND, THIS ESSAY IS RE-
SPECTFULLY DEDICATED BY

THE AUTHOR.

# PREFACE.

THE following Essay, though more immediately addressed to the Gentlemen, Merchants, and Others, of Newcastle upon Tyne, Shields, Durham, and Sunderland, and their respective neighbourhoods, is equally applicable to every part of England; and it is to be hoped, that the steps recommended to be pursued, in order to procure an alteration in the Charter of the Bank of England, or similar ones, will be immedately taken, wherever it may be intended to establish Banks on the principles recommended. A simultaneous movement in different quarters, and a general combination in favour of the object proposed, would at once render nugatory any opposition from those who may expect to lose by it.

An effectual opposition, however, in the present state of the public mind, need not be dreaded. The absolute necessity of a change in our Banking System has long been felt, and is quite obvious; but the present Bankers have great influence in Parliament, and might succeed, perhaps, in getting some half-measure adopted, if the public were to shew the least indifference or want of determination on the subject.

A perfect freedom with respect to the System of Banking which it may choose to adopt, more especially since this can be attained without injuring the Bank of England, the country ought to look for, and insist upon. Were the clause in its Charter, for instance, expunged with respect to Country Banks only, as has been done in Ireland, the same defective and insecure principle of Banking would be continued in the metropolis, and the System would still be bad where it ought to be best.

In London, it is requisite that more confidence should be placed in Bankers than in any other part of the kingdom. The circumstances of individuals cannot there be known as in the country, by the observation and report of their neighbours, hence they are obliged to make reference to their Bankers when it is necessary to verify their credit, who can or who will only know the credit they are entitled to, by the goodness of their accounts; and consequently those who have any considerable credit to maintain, are always obliged to keep large balances in their hands. Country Bankers are under the necessity of doing the same, in order to meet the bills upon London, which, in the way of their business they have to draw. A great number of noblemen and country gentlemen of large property, also keep their accounts with them, which together with the great money transactions of foreign nations and governments now negociated in London, with all of which the Bankers have more or less to do, necessarily render the business of the London Banks immense.

The large balances which the merchants in London must keep with their Bankers, would not only with Public Companies be safe, but productive. At present they get nothing for them but their Banker's good word; while with such Companies they would also be allowed three or four per cent. interest.

The Plan recommended to the inhabitants of Newcastle, it will, perhaps, be best to pursue every where. The Deputies of a Company will always have more weight than individuals, however respectable. There can, also, it is trusted, be little doubt of success; and even should any serious opposition arise, by a proper union there need be no great fear of overcoming it. The present System can never be supported a-gainst the united convictions of both government and the country.

# Essay on Banking.

BANKS are by far the most important of all
our commercial establishments. They are the
fountains of our currency, the depositories of
our capital, and at once the wheels and pillars
of our trade. Business to any great extent
could not be carried on without them. All
who have cash transactions of any kind are
more or less dependent upon them. The landed
proprietor finds them a convenient place of deposit for the ready money he possesses, or a
useful resource in case of need. The capitalist,
when he deems them safe, can lodge his money
with them, receive interest for it, and have it
ready when the chances of trade or changes of
property may throw a desirable purchase in his

way. Merchants and traders of every denomination are enabled through them to send money to, and receive it from the most distant places, to raise money when in want of it upon the Bills which they receive from their customers, to have those Bills presented for payment through a channel which in general secures their being duly honoured, and to deposit in them those sums which any particular occasion, or the current demands of their business require. Their Promissory Notes, also, furnish the country with a useful and convenient circulating medium, and are in the hands of every one.

They are, therefore, intimately connected with every class of society. Every person who has any thing to do either with capital or money is interested in their stability. But the capitalist, merchant, manufacturer, and tradesman, and all who have large payments to make and receive, are continually under the necessity of trusting them in amounts, the loss of which might prove their utter ruin. They have besides daily to confide in them for the negotiation of Bills and advances of capital, which, in commercial transactions, are continually required.

On this account, a very deep interest is felt in the welfare of Banks. Nothing can in any way affect them without exciting the immediate attention of the public, and (if it involve their credit) without producing the greatest possible agitation and alarm. Thus when the slightest apprehension is entertained respecting their solvency, however groundless it may sometimes prove, a run upon them immediately takes place. That is, hundreds of people immediately crowd the doors of the Banks, to demand payment of the Notes they hold, or to withdraw that money out of their hands, which they have deposited with them. This puts a stop to their usual Banking operations, and people in trade cannot receive that accommodation upon which they have relied, and upon which the regularity of their payments, and consequently their credit, depends. In the mean time, no person can make remittances without placing their money in a state of peril, which they can only ascertain to be groundless, by waiting until it is over. All is, therefore, confusion; and the whole community is thrown into a state of apprehension and alarm, which may be better conceived than described.

Upon such occasions the greatest exertions are always made to allay the fears, and restore the confidence of the public; and very great risks are sometimes run in doing so. It is not unusual for the friends of a Bank so situated, to issue out Bills or Notices, pledging themselves to the public, to take its Notes in payment, to any amount. By this measure, should the Bank happen to stop, many of them would necessarily be ruined. Within these few years, pledges of this kind were repeatedly issued in favour of the Durham, Stockton, and Sunderland Banks, which* ultimately failed. But, as they were not attended with any serious consequences, it is probable that the Banks did not stop payment immediately when they were issued, or perhaps the public might have overlooked the obligation coutracted, and, from inadvertency, not have called upon the parties to redeem the pledge they had given.

* I have to apologize to the very respectable Banking House of Messrs Hutchinson, of Stockton, for a verbal inaccuracy, in the former Editions, at which they, (no doubt with great justice,) took umbrage, and publicly called for an explanation. Instead of "*which* ultimately failed," it was stated in the former Editions "*all of whom* ultimately failed," from whence it might have been inferred that Messrs H. had failed too. This inference, however, could only have been made where, except by name, they were utterly unknown. The only reason, if I can assign any for the inaccuracy, was, that I had never heard of any pledges having been issued in their favour of the nature referred to, which from Mr Hutchinson's public correspondence upon the subject, I infer must have been the case. In Newcastle, during all the stormy period of the failures that took place around them, their credit was never once doubted.

5

We may, however, form some idea of the inconveniences in which the mercantile world are involved, when people are found wandering so far out of the tract of ordinary prudence as to guarantee the security of establishments with whose affairs they have no intimate acquaintance, and whose insolvency would involve them in certain destruction.

Nothing, in fact, can affect the credit of the Banks without being immediately felt in a corresponding degree by the public ; and the actual stoppage of an extensive Banking concern deranges the whole frame of mercantile affairs, and carries confusion, misery, and ruin, into every department of society.

Great, however, as the inconveniences are which the discredit of Banks, and consequent runs upon them occasion : and great as are the calamities by which their failures are uniformly attended, they are, both in this country and Ireland, of very common occurrence.

By an account printed in the appendix to the Lords' Report upon the Bank resuming Cash Payments, it appears, that in the last twenty years, (that is, twenty years previous to 1818), no fewer than two hundred and thirty commissions of bankruptcy had been issued against Banks ;* an average of failures, pro-

* This statement, not having the Lords' report to refer to, I took from a newspaper, as I mentioned in a note to my

6

portioned to the total number of them, in all probability far exceeding that of any other regular business.

Sometimes, as if epidemically, the Banks of a whole district fail together, as was the case a year or two ago, in the south of Ireland. That part of the country was, in consequence,

first Edition. I have since, however, procured the table referred to, which I here give.

APPENDIX, G 3.

RETURN OF THE PATENTEE FOR THE EXECUTION OF THE LAWS AND STATUTES CONCERNING BANKRUPTS.

| Years. | Commissions. | against Bankers. | Years. | Commissions. | against Bankers. |
|---|---|---|---|---|---|
| 1790 issued | 747 | none. | 1805 issued | 1129 | 9 |
| 1791 | 769 | 1 | 1806 | 1268 | 5 |
| 1792 | 934 | 1 | 1807 | 1362 | 1 |
| 1793 | 1956 | 26 | 1808 | 1433 | 5 |
| 1794 | 1041 | 2 | 1809 | 1382 | 7 |
| 1795 | 879 | 7 | 1810 | 2314 | 26 |
| 1796 | 954 | 6 | 1811 | 2500 | 4 |
| 1797 | 1115 | 3 | 1812 | 2228 | 17 |
| 1798 | 911 | 3 | 1813 | 1953 | 8 |
| 1799 | 717 | 6 | 1814 | 1612 | 29 |
| 1800 | 951 | 8 | 1815 | 2284 | 26 |
| 1801 | 1199 | 3 | 1816 | 2731 | 37 |
| 1802 | 1090 | 8 | 1817 | 1927 | 5 |
| 1803 | 1214 | 8 | 1818 | 1245 | 6 |
| 1804 | 1117 | 6 | | | |

JOSEPH DORIN,
DEPUTY PATENTEE.

*Bankrupt Office, 15th February, 1819.*

involved in the greatest distress; its trade was materially injured, and a shock given to its prosperity, from which it is said not yet to have recovered. The same event happened also in the county of Durham a few years back, when one Durham, two Sunderland, and two Stockton Banks failed within a short time of each other, being five out of the seven Banks then in the county. This part of the country, however, was better able to endure it, though the inconveniences generally felt were great, and the sufferers numerous. Even in this town, to which the evil but partially extended, the want of confidence and the general state of alarm which it produced, must be fresh in the recollection of every one.

Now, while England and Ireland are continually subject to disasters of this kind, it seems an extraordinary fact, that Scotland is totally free from them : the Scotch Banks rarely, if ever, either failing or losing money.

No one, I dare say, will, from this, imagine, that there is any thing different in the nature of their money transactions, or that trade is subject to fewer vicissitudes in Scotland than with us. I believe that trade is pretty much the same in both nations, or if there is any difference, that the merchants of Scotland are the more speculative, and less stable of the two. But the true cause of the difference is to be found in the nature of their respective Banking Establishments : the Scotch Banks being Joint Stock Companies, while the English Banks are private concerns.

The Scotch Banks consist of a great number of Proprietors or Stock Holders, who contribute, some to the extent of one hundred pounds, some of a thousand, and some many thousands. By these means they form a joint capital, establish a Bank, and entrust the management of it to a Committee chosen from their body, called a Court of Directors. The English Banks, on the contrary, never consist of more than six partners, though often fewer, and are for the most part, managed by one, or at the furthest by two of them.

To the uniform success of Joint Stock Banking Companies, history affords but one exception, viz. :—The case of the Douglass, Heron, and Co. (or Ayr) Bank, some account of which is given by Smith, page 58, vol. 2nd, of his Wealth of Nations. If, however, we examine the circumstances which produced that failure, we shall find it attributable to causes which are not likely again to occur, and that as an exception, it merely establishes the rule.

About fifty years ago, this Bank was formed in the West of Scotland, by a number of country gentlemen, totally ignorant of business, and entertaining erroneous views of Banking. Their object was not to make money, but to furnish capital, (which was then scarce,) to the country at large, in order to promote and improve the cultivation of land, &c. This they imagined could be done by means of a few reams of paper, manufactured into Notes. They were unable to see that it was not in the power of any Bank to keep more Notes in circulation than are wanted as a circulating medium by the country, and that the surplus would inevitably be returned upon them for repayment. Conformably to the object of its establishment, the Bank therefore issued its Notes, with great freedom, in permanent loans, which were immediately expended in agricultural improvements, and when they were returned for payment (having been issued in advances which could not be recalled) it had nothing to pay them with ; and was compelled, in a short time, to raise money by improvident expedients, at eight or ten per cent. when it had lent it out to others at five. Such a mode of business was not likely, of course, to be long pursued. The Bank came to a stand in about two years, its proprietors lost money, and it now remains the only exception to the success of such concerns.

It must, however, be understood, that the uniform success of the Scotch Banks, applies only to the Joint Stock Companies. Private Bankers fail in Scotland, as well as in other places. The Private Banks in Scotland, however, are but few, and only one or two of them at present issue notes. They keep the accounts of individuals, and transact business with the Public Banks in the same manner as the Bankers of London transact it with the Bank of England. But the credit requisite even to Private Banks is much greater in Scotland than with us, in consequence of their having to compete with establishments of superior stability, which do business upon the same terms.

The only Bank failures, however, that I have heard of in Scotland, with the exception of the Ayr Bank already spoken of, are the Merchant Banking Company of Stirling, Grace's Bank of Dumfries, and the Falkirk Union Bank. The first two were each of them carried on by an individual, and the last had only three partners. To these must be also added, the Merchant Banking Company of Glasgow, about twenty years ago, a very small concern, which must likewise, I think, have been a Private Bank, as but few particulars are generally known respecting it. Had it been a Public Establishment, a greater degree of publicity would have been given to its affairs.

In consequence of the uniform success of the Public Banks of Scotland, the most unbounded confidence is felt and reposed in them, both by the stock-holders and the public. Every holder of stock, (except with the chartered companies) however small the amount, incurs all the responsibility of a partner, yet that responsibility having been proved by all experience to be merely nominal, has no effect whatever on the sale of it. A person buys a hundred pounds share of the stock of any of the Banks, with the same freedom that he would purchase the same amount of stock in the three per cent. consols, without the responsibility weighing with him one shilling in the purchase.

In addition, however, to their success, some of the Scotch Banks have very considerable capitals, particularly the Edinburgh Banks, which have from five to fifteen hundred thousand pounds each. Hence their credit is almost unbounded, being considered by the Scotch equal to that of the Bank of England itself. The evils, therefore, which we suffer from the feeble and fluctuating credit of most of our Banks, and the disastrous failures of many of them, are nearly unknown to the people of Scotland.

From the very great credit enjoyed by the Scotch Banks, they are enabled to transact business to a much greater extent, and on very different principles, than with us. From this source, still more important, though less obvious benefits arise, and these it may not be improper for us in the first place to consider.

The original and proper business of a Banker is to trade in capital. He ought to be that medium between the borrower and lender in the money market, which a merchant is in other commodities. It is the business of a merchant or trader to buy of the producer on the one hand, and to sell to the consumer or retailer on the other. He acquires a knowledge of both parties, and they of him, and for his credit, capital, labour, and knowledge, he charges a profit upon the commodity which, through his agency, is transferred from the party who has it to sell, to the party wanting to purchase it. Now, what a merchant is in other commodities, the Scotch Banks are in the money market. They borrow of those who have money to lend, and lend to those who want to borrow, acquire a knowledge of both parties, and charge a profit of one per cent. upon the transaction. Any person opening an account with them, receives four per cent.* upon the balance in their hands. He may pay money to the credit of his account when he chooses, and he receives interest for it from the day it is deposited ; he may draw his money out of the Bank when and in such sums as he thinks proper, and only loses

---

* Some of them have lately reduced the interest they give, but others continue to give four per cent. as before.

*Fourth Edition.* They have now, I understand, reduced the interest they give, generally.

interest upon the sum drawn, from the day of receiving it. On the contrary, any person giving proper securities, may open an account with them, and draw to the extent of the security given, for which they will charge him five per cent. upon the fluctuating balance he owes. Consequently, a person who has money to lend is saved all the trouble, not unattended with risk, of mortgages, and may have his money, or any part of it, at any time, should a desirable purchase fall in his way ; whereas with a mortgage he cannot draw his money when he wants it—must take it altogether when he does draw it—or, if the borrower chooses, must take it whether he wants it or not. Their object, however, in borrowing, being to lend, the facilities given to borrowers, are equally great. In the first place, they will discount bills and other mercantile securities, that are perfectly regular and good, at any time, and to any amount. Thus merchants can calculate with certainty upon being accommodated in the course of regular transactions to any extent, which is of infinite service to them, as it would be better for a merchant not to have such assistance at all, than to have any uncertainty respecting it. In the next place, they grant Cash Accounts, that is, any person in business, by giving two sufficient securities, may open an account with them, and overdraw

it to the extent of the security given, for
which, as before stated, he is charged five per
cent. upon the balance he owes. Very great
advances, not to mercantile men only, but to
all classes of persons, are made in this way;
and in the last place, they make advances upon real property, some of them to a very considerable extent. The plan they pursue, I
believe, is, for the proprietor to pledge his
estate, or other property, with the Bank, for a
given amount, open an account with it, and
draw as his occasions may require, to the
amount prescribed. Thus, when any persons
wish to borrow, the facilities held out to borrowers induce them, equally with the lenders,
to make application to the Bank.

As individuals often call in the money they
have lent out on mortgage when they can find
better employment for it, or when the death of
a party produces a division of his property, by
which a great expence to the mortgagee is incurred in procuring a fresh mortgage, Banks
are therefore more to be depended upon, and
borrowers being just as much wanted by them
as lenders, and the money which they lend being rarely, or in fact, never, called in again
until it is the pleasure of the borrower to pay
it off, people, in want of money, will prefer
dealing with the Banks at even a higher per
centage, while lenders, on their part, prefer

dealing with them at a per centage something less than individuals would give. Thus in consequence of the security of their property, and the readiness with which they can at all times obtain it when wanted, a difference of one per cent. is not found to be a sufficient inducement for the borrowers and lenders to pass by the Banks and to transact their business directly with each other. If they did, the gain would, of course, have to be divided between them, and a half per cent. would be no compensation to either party for the additional inconvenience, risk, and trouble, in which they would be involved. Whereas the Bank being open and ready at all times to meet the wants of each party, unless among particular friends, neither party ever thinks of making further enquiries upon the subject, but transacts the business with the Banks as a matter of course. They are, therefore, at once, the great depositories of the money capital of the country, and the source from whence the supplies of it are drawn.

Although considerable advances are made by the Scotch Banks upon real property, it is rather a ground of complaint, that they have been too much in the habit of speculating in the funds, when it might have been more to the advantage of their country that they should have lent out their capital at home ; and while lending their money at home appears to be preferable for a Public Bank, to gambling in the funds, it seems also to be the duty of such an establishment to lend its money at home whenever it can do so with safety.

The failures which continually take place amongst the English, particularly the Country Banks, and the consequent discredit in which they are held, of course almost totally preclude them from trading in capital in the manner pursued by the Banks of Scotland. The London Bankers are the only Bankers, it is generally understood, who at all do so, and they are not considered good mortgagees. Their strictness in requiring powers of sale, &c. to be granted them, which their limited credit renders necessary, in order to be able to call in their money at the shortest notice, should the state of their credit at any time require it, places the mortgager in a state of disagreeable dependence. The business of an English country bank is, however, principally confined to lending out that capital which it raises by the circulation of its Notes, and the comparatively small sums deposited with it, mostly without interest, (its customers seldom depositing more money with it, than their current occasions require) and to buying and selling Bills upon London. The advances of capital which it makes are, of necessity, principally confined to the discounting of such short dated Bills of Exchange as through its London agents can be turned at any time into cash ; as it is always liable to be called upon to pay off its notes, and all the money in its hands, at the shortest notice, it should always be prepared to do so ; and the most prudently managed and best English Banks are those which confine themselves most strictly to the limits which their uncertain credit prescribes to them.

Credit is, in fact, the proper capital of a Bank, without which it is impossible for it to be carried on with any great advantage to the country. For want of this the business of English Banks, extensive as it may appear, is quite inconsiderable compared with that of the Banks of Scotland, and far short of what it would be with a different system.

———

Thus, then, it appears to be the result of experience, that while our Banks are often destructive, at all times dangerous, and at the very best totally inadequate, from want of stability and credit, to perform their proper functions, the Scotch Banks never fail, nor is any danger ever apprehended from them ; and that, in consequence, Banking is carried on in that kingdom to an extent unknown, and, of course, with advantages totally unfelt in our own.

We have stated that the superiority in the success, as well as in the stability and credit of the Scotch Banks, arises from their being public, and not private concerns, which is also proved by our own experience. We have but one Public Bank, the Bank of England, and it has uniformly done well since its first establishment. The same may be also inferred of the Bank of Ireland, the only Public Bank in that country. Lately, when applying for a renewal of its charter, it appeared, that besides its annual dividends, it had made and saved half a million of money, a sum much greater than the Stock-holders had any conception of. This at once proves, that successful management is not at all peculiar to Scotland, or any nation, but is inherent in the system itself.

The cause of this difference proceeds from the charters of the Banks of England and Ireland, which prevent, in their respective countries, more than six persons from entering into a Banking concern, while in Scotland there is no such monopoly, and Banks can be established on the proper principles, and as many people become partners in them as choose.

From the limited number of partners in our Banks, their management has frequently fallen into hands totally incompetent to such a trust.

There is, perhaps, nothing in the theory of Banking very complicated. But to manage a Bank well, requires a degree of firmness, and judgment, which every individual does not possess. If a Banker be too safe and injudiciously cautious in his transactions, he is apt to ruin his business for want of liberality ; if too confident, to ruin himself for want of prudence ; while he must possess firmness sufficient to enable him to refuse the most pressing solicitation of even his friends, when necessary to do so. This knowledge, discrimination, and firmness, not only require natural talent in the person possessing them, but previous practice and experience in the business of the world. Whereas persons are often placed in the management of English Provincial Banks, by some connection or other chance, which usually determines the lot of individuals in the common affairs of life. Or, if they are chosen expressly for their presumed fitness for the trust, their fitness will then depend upon whether the partners who choose them, are themselves sufficiently competent to form such a choice ; independent of which, however, the energy and vigilance of every individual is at times apt to slumber, and we occasionally find the ablest men get very far wrong.

Now, the true reason of the success of Public Banks may be ascribed to their never being managed by any single person, but by a Court of Directors, periodically chosen by the holders of stock; and their fitness for the trust not depending upon the opinion of an individual or two, but of hundreds, founded upon the clear evidence which their successful management of their own affairs has afforded. No man is ever chosen as the director of a joint stock company, where the choice is unbiassed by influence, who has not given sufficient proof in the eyes of the world of his ability for the management, and has not justly inspired his fellow proprietors with that confidence which they repose in him.*

The principal causes which produce the ruin of private Banks may be stated to be,—first, a confusion in their accounts, arising from a bad or relaxed and careless management, so very frequently exhibited in common affairs; but which, in Banking, must ever be fatal; secondly, speculations with the capital in the Bank; and thirdly, and most frequently, accommodating great houses, either from motives of private friendship, or the temptation of extra Banking profits, until they are so involved that they must stand or fall with them. The two great failures which have happened in this part

* Since the publication of this Essay, I have understood that this is far from being always the case.

of the country were Surtees, Burdon, and Co. and the Durham Bank. The first was produced by entering into private speculations with the capital in its hands, and the last by accommodating a great mining concern. But with Public Banks these causes, by which failures are generally produced, cannot exist. In the first place, the vigilant check necessarily kept upon the accountant, and those who have the charge of the books, which must at all times show, without trouble to the Directors, the state of the company's affairs, prevents the possibility of their getting back or into confusion. In the next place, the Directors could not appropriate the money of the Bank to views of private speculation, if they were wishful to do so, as they are a check upon each other. If they were respectable men, they would not attempt it, and if they were not, they would not be there: besides, there is no instance recorded of such a thing. In the third place, they have too little personal interest in the Bank to be tempted by extra profit out of the path of safety, in accommodating great houses: or if any of them were influenced by private friendship to do so, it could never be the case with them all; and they would be also in that respect a check upon each other.

Independent of the general Court of Directors, there is also a Managing Director,

Cashier, Secretary, and Accountant, or sometimes Cashier, Secretary, and Accountant, or
Cashier and Accountant alone, according to
the business done, either the Cashier or Secretary in the latter cases acting as Managing Director, and taking all the practical management;
and if the Directors are careful to choose men
fit for these stations, and see that they do their
duty, the concern will generally succeed.

The Directors having in general business of
their own to attend to, cannot give their whole
attention to the Bank affairs. Their part is more
to deliberate, judge, and determine, than to contrive. Consequently the Managing Director,
or he who is at the head of the executive department, sits with and joins the Directors in
their deliberations, and proposes to them such
views and opinions as his practical knowledge
and undivided attention to the affairs of the
Bank, suggest to him. These they take into
consideration, and approve, alter, or otherwise
direct, as they may think proper. The energetic and profitable management of such a concern, therefore, greatly depends upon the ability of its officers, who are expected to submit
a variety of views and propositions to the Directors, of which there is no fear that they adopt
any which are too speculative. The errors
of Public Banks are generally on the side of
safety, but the concern is apt to flag when the

practical management is not in the hands of men possessed in some degree of ready apprehension, practical energy, and talent for business; and I understand, it is consistent with experience, that when the officers of a Bank are not of this description, the business of the concern is apt to fall off, and to become less profitable.

The business, however, of such a Bank, though it may not be pushed, is seldom neglected. When the Directors can give no attention to the concern, they generally resign, or when it is their turn to go out, are not re-elected. On the other hand, they are not likely to get wrong in taking up sanguine views, by which individuals often mislead themselves. They are responsible in the estimation of the Stock-holders for all that is done, and individually have but little to gain by success; whereas, if their management produced any considerable loss to the concern, they would be turned out of office, and stand committed with the public in a manner that would render them ridiculous, and necessarily produce feelings the most disagreeable and painful.

As, therefore, it thus appears, that the causes which operate in producing the failure of Private Banks are totally prevented by the constitution of Public Companies, we cease to wonder at the uniform success by which the latter are attended. But the risk incurred by Bankers is not, perhaps, so great as we are apt to imagine. With loans on property, or on the personal securities required to establish a Cash account, there is no risk at all. Property is not taken, if not sufficient to cover the loan upon it, and the sureties accepted when a cash account is opened, are each of them required to be sufficiently able to fulfil the obligation of the bond they enter into. Should any thing happen to either of them, another name must be immediately substituted. Independent therefore of the party with whom the account is opened, there are always two perfectly good and sufficient sureties, to make up any deficiency, even to the full amount of the debt, should it be called for.

The greatest risk incurred by a Bank, is in the Discounting of Bills of Exchange, though it is, at the same time, its most desirable business, from being the principal means by which it keeps its Notes in circulation. But with this class of business also, the risk, under proper management, is much less than is supposed. It is said, that the Bank of England, in ordinary times, does not calculate upon a greater loss than one pound in three hundred thousand. Leith is quite a speculating town, and its merchants are subject, in consequence, to considerable vicissitudes. Yet the Branch of the Commercial Bank there, during the first four years of its establishment, did not lose one pound out of many millions of discounts, although, in consequence of having entirely new connexions to form, it rejected no business that it could with any degree of prudence accept. The experience of those also, who live in country towns, where the losses which the Banks sustain are generally known, will point out to them, if they have made the observation, that it is only very rarely that a well managed Bank suffers any loss at all.

The Scotch Banks, in fact, in the arrangements which they make with their agents established in distant towns, assume that there is no risk whatever, and lay it down as a rule, that if they incur any loss, they are to suffer it themselves. The Directors, in general, select for Agents, tried men of business, who have proved, by the manner of conducting their own affairs, their capability of successfully transacting whatever may be confided to them. Securities are required of them, in a town of any business, to the extent, I understand, of not less than ten thousand pounds, and they receive a fixed salary of (say) from two to four hundred per annum, according to the size of the place and business done in it. It is, I believe, generally calculated by the Agent, that if he can make out a case of very unforeseen loss, it will

be partly allowed him ; but the assumed principle is, that there need be none at all.  It is
a most curious circumstance, however, and
completely proves the insecurity of private
management in Bank affairs, that the Banks
lose more money through their agents than in
any other way.

The distance of the town, where the Agent
is established, from the Bank, renders it impossible that any proper judgment can be formed
by the Directors, of the stability of the persons
with whom the Agent does business.  The great
sum, however, required as a security, the business character he possesses, and the risk he himself runs, naturally remove all suspicion as to
the prudence of his transactions.  Should his
affairs become involved, he is, perhaps, sufficiently clever to hide it for a considerable
length of time.  This he probably does with
the hope of recovering himself, until the failure,
perhaps of some house he has imprudently accommodated, or his deficiency is too great for
further concealment, when his own ruin, the
loss of the friends who are security for him, and
the loss of the Bank besides, to perhaps three
times the amount, prove his unfitness for the
trust that has been reposed in him.

This does not unfrequently happen, and no
greater proof of the insecurity of private management could well be afforded.  If Agents,

without the temptation of profit, and under the control of their Banks, cannot keep right, how much more likely are Private Banks to get wrong, without any such control, and with all the usual temptations to influence them?

———

Although our Banking System has been so long in its present state, its effects seem not to have forced themselves on the consideration either of the government or the public, until lately, when the failures in Ireland, and the lamentable effects produced by them, attracted the notice of the whole kingdom, and called the attention of those interested in the welfare of Ireland, to the subject.

In a conversation which, in consequence, took place in the House of Lords, upon the state of commercial credit in Ireland, the Marquis of Lansdowne stated, that *the present* distress in Ireland was principally occasioned by the late failures amongst the Banks in that country, which failures were to be attributed to the law that limited the number of partners in Banking Firms, and he called upon Lord Liverpool, with reference to Ireland, to remedy the evil by an alteration in the law, in order that proper Banks might be established.

In answer to this, Lord Liverpool said, " that
" not only did he agree in the suggestion of
" the Noble Marquis, but it was his anxious
" wish that the number of partners should be
" extended not only in Ireland, but in Eng-
" land," and instanced the hardship of Liverpool, Bristol, &c. being prevented from establishing Banks that would be instrumental to
their prosperity and strength.

Since that time a negociation has taken place
between government and the Bank of Ireland,
in which it has been stipulated, that the Bank
shall give up the restrictive clause in its charter with respect to Country Banks, and it has
done so without an objection.    A bill has consequently passed through parliament, by which,
in the country districts of Ireland, Public Banks
may now be established.

After what has been said by Lord Liverpool,
as well as what has been done for Ireland, there
can be no doubt of the disposition of government on the subject.    It is the declared wish
of Lord Liverpool, who expressed the general sentiment of ministers, (as their subsequent
conduct with respect to Ireland has proved) that
the impediment to the establishment of proper
Banks ought to be removed, and that this country should enjoy the advantages of a better
system.

To again call the attention of government

to the subject, is all that is now, therefore, necessary ; and it will be creditable to the spirit and intelligence of the Gentlemen, Merchants, and others of the town and neighbourhood of Newcastle upon Tyne, to be the first to set the example. The proper plan to pursue is, in the first place to form a company, and then appoint a deputation to wait upon ministers, and the Directors of the Bank of England, and negociate with them respecting the alteration proposed, and at the same time, pursue such other steps as may prove necessary to the ultimate attainment of the object desired.

That such an application must be made by a Company, to be made with proper effect, is evident. A Company will carry with it a weight which no individual can have, while it will prove how much alive the country is to the advantages of a better system, by its readiness to adopt it. It will also evince a proper confidence in the declaration of ministers, as made by Lord Liverpool, that they wished to see a better system of Banking introduced ; and there can be no doubt that the ministry will have every disposition to give to their own declaration the earliest effect.

There is in fact but little doubt that government will use all its influence to get the charter altered, on an application to it for that purpose. There can exist no reason why it should

not. Ministers have declared the clause a great
evil, and are bound by their sense of duty to
endeavour to remove it. They have done so
with respect to Ireland; and can have no motive or apology for not doing so with respect to
us. Ministers, I suppose, will occasionally be
wrong as well as any other set of men. Yet so
far as we can see, they are generally conscienti-
ous. A sufficient ground may sometimes exist
for their opinions and conduct being at vari-
ance; but there is evidently none in the present case, and their co-operation may therefore
be relied upon.

The charter of the Bank of England does
not, however, expire until 1833, and the ob-
noxious clause will require to be immediately
expunged from it. But this can be done without injuring the Bank, and the wishes of ministers, with the directors of the Bank, must necessarily be imperative. Besides, we have nothing
to fear from the directors themselves, who, in
conducting the affairs of the Bank, have always
acted upon disinterested and public spirited
principles. Neither can it be supposed that any
measure for the public welfare, which was con-
ceded by the Bank of Ireland without an objection, would be resisted by the Bank of England. The consent of the directors to any
alteration which benefits the public without
materially injuring the Bank, may, therefore,

also be relied upon. Yet, as to anticipate the worst, is sometimes the best policy, (viewing it as a possible case that the directors may not be at once disposed to accede to the wishes of the nation,) we will examine whether, in that case, parliament ought not to alter the clause without their consent.

The Bank, though intimately connected with government in its transactions, is an independent establishment, governed by directors of its own choosing. It was commenced by individuals as a speculation, and was chartered by government on the grounds of its public utility. Upon the same principle it has been continued a Bank by its proprietors, and the charter renewed by government to the present day. It would be absurd to suppose that the Bank proprietors would have carried on the Bank merely to serve the public, had they not thereby served themselves, or that the public would have conferred upon them, A. B. and C. the holders of Bank Stock, any exclusive privilege from time to time, except upon the ground of public advantage.

That the Bank is held to be as much a public institution as a private speculation, is evinced by the interference of Parliament in its affairs. This interference is quite opposed to the common law of the land, yet it is perfectly justifiable with respect to the Bank of England, in consequence of its enjoying privileges as much for the public benefit as for that of its proprietors. The Bank is in fact an engine of the state ; and acts of parliament are continually made for regulating its affairs, without any reference to the proprietors, but solely for the public convenience ; and the right of parliamentary interference in its affairs, when the public good is involved, is clearly established by this usage.

It must, however, be kept in view, that though the affairs of the Bank have been regulated by the independent authority of parliament, its substantial interests have never been infringed upon. At each renewal of its charter a pecuniary fine, or loan at a reduced rate of interest, has generally been exacted, by which it has fairly purchased the profit to be made by its charter during the term of it. Hence the pecuniary emoluments which were intended to be secured to it, have never been curtailed. Mr Pitt, when he persisted in drawing the specie from the Bank, protected it from the consequences of his doing so, by an act of parliament to suspend the payment of its notes. From this restriction it derived great advantage ; and although when the Bank was ordered, by act of parliament, to return to cash payments, the measure was contrary to its interests, it only restored the contract to its original footing.

Now the exclusive right of Banking, as a Joint Stock Company, in this kingdom, is of no advantage whatever to the Bank, except in London and Lancashire, and the latter is probably the result of chance. The advantage it derives from it, is the monopoly which it secures in those districts to the circulation of its notes. Private Bankers, in London, are not prevented, any more than Country Banks, from issuing notes, if they thought proper, but they would be continually liable to runs upon them, from the never-ending rumours' of the metropolis. In the country, a Banker's property is seen ; his economical habits, and prudent management, if he possess those qualities, are generally known, and a run upon him without some cause, cannot so easily happen. In London, on the contrary, the public at large, or even the customers of a Bank, have hardly any means of forming a knowledge as to the management, prudence, or property of its partners. Hence its credit would be totally at the mercy of every offended or malignant individual, runs would continually happen upon one Bank or another, and the town would be in a continual commotion. No Bank, therefore, whatever may be its present credit, would find its interest in issuing notes, and it is probable that as the charter, and the present system of Private

Banking now stands, it is perfectly effectual in securing the Bank the monopoly of London.

In the country, however, with the exception of Lancashire, Bank of England Notes have no circulation at all. Country Banks issue their Notes, in general, upon the same terms as the Bank of England; making no other charge than the interest upon the Bills they discount. The Bank of England having no means of issuing its Notes out of London, the Country Banks entirely possess the country circulation. Independent of this, Bank of England Notes would not pass in most parts of the kingdom, as, where Local Notes can be had, no person in the more Northern Counties, will take a Bank of England Note if he can help it. The signatures of Country Notes are, generally, written in a legible and distinct uniform character, peculiar to the writer, and well known to the public. Hence every person can, at least, attempt, to form a judgment, whether a note is forged or not. Should his observation upon hand-writing not be sufficient to enable him to distinguish any discrepancies in it, or between it and a printed fac-simile, the notes have, in general, some little figure or etching, with which he is familiar, and in which he might discover any slight variation from the original. But, in consequence of the number of Bank of England Notes to be signed, from their not being more than once issued, the signing clerks and signatures are so numerous, and the latter are written so hastily, that nothing can be ascertained from them; and the object of the signature is totally defeated. I never remember having once seen a person look at the signature of a Bank of England Note, in order to ascertain whether or not it was a forgery. The rest of the Note is also little more than a piece of plain printing, and presents (at least to a person in the country,) nothing by which a forgery can be distinguished. Country Notes, therefore, are always preferred.

In Lancashire, however, there seems to be a prejudice in favour of Bank of England Notes, which is rather surprising. The Banks there do not, in consequence, issue their own, but Bank of England paper, and to compensate this supposed disadvantage, charge a commission upon their discounts; which method must render their business a great deal less hazardous, and more profitable. Hence also they are never subject to runs, and when they discount a Bill, are sure of their commission of 5 or 10s. per cent. Banks in other districts, on the contrary, that charge no commission, constantly have their Notes returned upon them through other Banks, the next day after issuing them; and, by this means, where the Lancashire Bankers would gain a handsome profit, they often do not make a farthing. By this prejudice, however, the Bank of England also enjoys the almost exclusive circulation of Lancashire.

It has been very usual to consider the derangement and loss by the circulating medium, particularly to the poor, the greatest evil attending the failure of Banks. This is, however, an erroneous view of the matter; for Country Notes are, upon the whole, a better currency than Bank of England paper. A good deal of present inconvenience may occasionally for a short time be sustained where the Banks of a country fail all together (as was before mentioned of Ireland); but the loss by the Notes in actual circulation is widely spread, and, comparatively speaking, little felt. The evil would be trifling if it extended no further than to the Notes which are in the hands of individuals; that proportion which is held by the lower classes, even taking it in the aggregate, can never be considerable, more especially since the Savings' Banks were established; it will probably seldom exceed a pound to a hand, and even in that case, the Bank ought to fail on Saturday, the day on which wages are generally both paid and spent. The circulation is principally in the hands of tradesmen, and the richer classes, few of whom would not prefer the risk attending Country Paper, if it were three times as great as it is, rather than incur the plague, trouble, and inconvenience which they suffer from the fear of forgeries, so prevalent with Bank of England Paper, as well as the loss by them, which there is no avoiding. This is incontestably proved by the decided preference which is actually given to the paper of Country Banks wherever it is circulated.

Upon considering the generally acknowledged superiority of Country Notes, it seemed at first natural to think that the prejudice existing in Lancashire against them must have originated with the Bankers in that part of the country themselves, as it was apparently their interest to support it. I had even formed a conjecture to this effect, until I observed in the papers of the day an account of the transactions and resolutions of a meeting, held on the 1st of September last, by the Merchants and Manufacturers of Manchester, on the subject. By the proceedings at this meeting, it seems that the Bankers of that town, not content with the present profits of their trade, have had it in contemplation to issue notes, expecting, no doubt, to enjoy their present commissions, and the advantage to be gained from the circulation of the country besides. This scheme, it is likely, in the end, they would have found impracticable ; for in the free competition of this country, the profits of no trade can be kept for any length of time above their natural level, and the ruin of their commissions, from the competition of other Banks, would most probably have been the result. But the merchants and manufacturers met for the purpose of resisting the attempt, and refused to take the notes which it was thus proposed to issue. A great deal of very ingenious arguments were used by the proposers of the resolutions entered into at this meeting. The statement, however, which probably carried the most conviction and unanimity along with it, was the fact, that fewer of those Banks fail which do not issue Notes, than of those which do. Now, as there is no reason why Banks that issue notes, and get smaller profits, should undertake greater risks than those who have more temptations of profit to influence them; as also there can be nothing in the mere issuing of their own notes very materially different from that of issuing those of any other establishment; and lastly, since though they may stop payment by a run, they seldom become bankrupts when they are not insolvent : the difference mentioned must principally arise from the issuing of notes being attended with the same risk, but with much less profit. It is inconceivable that the issuing of notes should make any other difference than that which arises from reducing the commission upon discounts. Bankers who circulate notes may, from the fear of runs, be obliged to circumscribe their business, and without great profits, may indulge in great expence; or should they have lent out their money too freely, they may also, it is true, be brought to a stand by a run upon them; but if they are solvent, any loss which may be thus caused will of course fall upon themselves.

The superior safety of those Banks which do not issue notes, can, therefore, I apprehend, only arise from their business paying them better; and if the merchants and manufacturers of Manchester will continue to pay Messrs Jones and Co., or Messrs Heywood and Co., the same commission as before, they may be safely allowed to do as they think proper. But if the Bankers take the very sensible advice of Mr Wood, they will make no further attempt to alter their present system. The fear of runs might compel them to curtail their business, and they may be sure the profits of Banking in Manchester, as in other places, would find their level. The probability therefore is, that if they were to issue notes, they would discover, in the end, that in grasping at the circulation, they had only illustrated the fable of the Dog and the Shadow.

The apprehensions expressed at this meeting, that persons of no property would issue notes, and maintain a circulation in competition with

Bankers of stability and credit, is supposing what is contrary to experience, and could never happen. But in this case there is little doubt that, in time, the trade of Banking would not be so profitable in Manchester, and the business would be done upon more liberal terms; if the Banks issued notes, the present bankers might go out of the business, others would not make so much money, and they would consequently not be so safe as the rich Bankers in question. In that view of the subject, therefore, the meeting was right in the resolutions it adopted. But to pay a Banker an extra profit, in order to render you safe in transacting with him, is the same as giving a premium for insurance against a sea risk. It is prudent, at any rate, perhaps, to insure, though the premium may be high, but it becomes a question for serious consideration, whether you cannot get your insurance effected at a cheaper rate.

The circulation of the Bank of England notes in Lancashire, is evidently founded upon a view of the subject taken up by the manufacturers and merchants in Manchester alone, and in consequence it is only enjoyed by a kind of chance. To give the Bank that circulation was evidently, therefore, not the intention of the charter, while the tenure by which it is held is too frail to be relied upon, and therefore can neither be argued upon as a matter of right conferred by the charter, nor depended upon as a source of profit.

The right, consequently, of the Bank to prevent more than six partners entering into a Banking Concern, is, with respect to the whole kingdom except London, a right which confers no advantage upon it, while it loosens the whole frame of commercial credit, of which Banks are the pillars and support. To call it, therefore, a right, with respect to the country, is improper; legally it may be so termed, but equitably it is nothing but a wrong.

It seems also by the act which conferred it, that this privilege was first granted by a mistake. By stat. 6 Anne, c. 22, it was enacted that "*for securing the credit of the Bank of* "*England,*" no other Banking Company in England should consist of more than six partners. Now it did not secure the credit of the Bank of England in the smallest degree. The credit of the Bank of England depended upon the amount of its capital and the state of its affairs. This act merely ruined the credit of every other Bank; and it is almost certain that had the true object of the bill been stated, and had the preamble run thus "*for the intent and purpose of ruining the credit of all the unchartered Banks in England, it was enacted, &c.*" it may be safely affirmed, that no such act would have been passed by any British Parliament, at least since the Revolution. The error then committed, has been continued to the present day; but when the practical evils produced by it have been so severely felt, and are become so evident, it is the duty of parliament to correct it.

Parliamentary interference in the affairs of the Bank, is, as we have endeavoured to shew, a right which practice has conferred; but, admitting, for the sake of argument, our conclusions on that view of the subject to be erroneous, it must be obvious to the commonest apprehension, that there is a right in any government to take from any body of men, a monopoly which does them no good, while it does the country a great deal of harm. An indefeasible right of inflicting a wrong, would be a new principle in our institutes.

The only permanent and substantial good which the Bank derives from the clause in its charter is the monopoly of the circulation of London, and its neighbourhood. The circulation of Lancashire, as we have seen, cannot be depended upon.

Now, a worse way of securing the circulation of London cannot be conceived. The object is to prevent the Bankers of London from issuing Notes; and the manner of doing it is to weaken their credit, and keep it so low that they cannot. Nothing could be more simple, nor more effectual, than to prevent them from issuing Notes, by enacting that they should not do so. Instead of that, the object is accomplished by taking from them their credit, the vital principle of their trade. It would be just as proper to bleed a horse in order to diminish his speed; to take from him his strength in order to reduce his action; instead of an additional bridle and curb, to restrain his pace by the weakness produced from the frequent use of the lancet; you would, no doubt, thereby effectually reduce his fire and check his speed, but you would also ruin his constitution, and the probability is, in such a case, that upon the slightest trip, both horse and rider would tumble into the ditch. Nothing, in fact, can be more absurd than the present manner in which the monopoly is secured, while its baneful influence extends to every part of the country. The constitutions of our Banks are unequal to the burthens they have to support; and it may be truly said, that the Banks and the country are continually, in some part or other, tumbling together into a ditch, and often one so deep that they never get properly out again.

It must be admitted that the restriction is productive of less apparent ill consequences in London than in the country. The reason of this is, that the business of Banking is more profitable in London, (where all business is generally better managed) than it is in the country; for it is principally in the hands of old houses, conducted by acting partners, who have been all their lives in the houses which they manage, and who have raised themselves by their industry, experience, and talents.

All, therefore, that the country requires is, that the monopoly of the Bank of England be secured to it, in a more simple and direct manner. That in lieu of the clause enacting, that not more than six partners shall enter into other Banking concerns, it be enacted that no Banks shall issue notes within the boundaries of the present monopoly. In doing this, there is no infringement of the rights of the Bank. The object of its charter is to give it an exclusive privilege, which, by this alteration, will be the more effectually preserved; for it is merely incidentally secured by the present terms of it.

Government have no right to do the Bank an injury, but they have surely a right to remove from its charter any impediment to the public welfare, upon granting it an equivalent. This is nothing more than the principle upon which all Acts of Parliament are passed, for making roads, canals, &c. through private property. The individual is fully compensated for the loss he sustains, and substantial justice being done him, his inclinations are not consulted in the matter.

If an argument in favour of the present system should be drawn from the circulation enjoyed by the Bank in Lancashire, the merchants and manufacturers of Manchester have it in their power, effectually to destroy its efficacy. They have but to encourage, instead of suppressing Local Notes; and whether the present Banks issue them or not, they will, no doubt, by the competition of trade from other quarters, find their way into circulation.

It is, however, equally the interest of the Bank, to have its monopoly secured in a more direct and less questionable manner. Any person may, at present, issue Notes in London, and nothing but want of credit, prevents Private Banks from doing it. If any plan, however, should be thought of, to give the Notes of Private Banks sufficient credit, there would, doubtless, be found Banks to issue them, and there can also be little question that the public would, as in the country, give them a preference.

Without entertaining any wish to deprive the Bank of its monopoly, but to show that it does not stand upon the securest footing, how easy would it be for Private Banks in London to adopt the plan proposed by the Chancellor of the Exchequer two or three years ago, with respect to country establishments. If, for instance, a private Bank were to issue half a million of paper, it might purchase stock to that amount, and assign it to trustees, and these trustees might indorse and guarantee the notes, holding the stock to meet their payment, should they be ever called upon by the failure of the Bank. There would then not only be value in the funds sufficient to pay them with, which could not be applied to any other purpose, but the holders of the Notes, should it be necessary, would have a claim upon the estate of the Bank to the full amount of their value, and thus no apprehension respecting them could possibly be entertained. A renewal would, of course, from time to time, be requisite, but the trustees would take care, for their own sakes, before they endorsed a new Note, that an old one of the same value should be cancelled.

Many other plans might, I have no doubt, be contrived to attain the same object, and render the Notes of private Bankers perfectly safe to the public, by which they need not as now apply to the Bank of England for Notes, but issue their own, and in that case the charter of the Bank would be rendered almost useless. The alteration proposed, therefore, is as much the interest of the directors and proprietors of the Bank, as of any set of men in the kingdom. The charter of the Bank does not expressly confer a monopoly, nor could it be discovered from the charter itself, that the monopoly of a circulation of Notes was intended. But if a monopoly was intended, there needed to have been no fear of expressing it in words ; and it would now be desirable to the Bank for it to have that monopoly which it has paid for, clearly expressed and secured to it. Thus there can be but little doubt that we shall meet with the ready co-operation as well of the directors as of parliament and ministers, in the measure.

The only persons who will be injured by it, will be the present Bankers. But no set of men can expect a country to continue voluntarily to submit to an evil after it has discovered the cause and can apply the remedy. They must take the fate incident to all rights or institutions, founded in error : as soon as truth appears, the fabric, for want of its foundation, must be destroyed. But on none can a loss fall more lightly. If a Banker be not independent of his trade, he ought not to be a Banker. He has gained a credit that he is not entitled to ; and to deprive him of a business he should not, and could not carry on, if the public were aware how little security he afforded them, is nothing more than an act of justice. If he be independent of his business, which the great majority of Bankers are, he may lose, but cannot feel his loss very severely.

The Clerks and Managers of those Banks whose business may be curtailed, will find as good, if not better situations than they had before, with the New Companies, who will, as a matter of common sense, be anxious to employ them, for the sake of their practical knowledge. Hence we may safely calculate, that the amount of positive injury to individuals, produced by the loss of the means of support, from the proposed change, will not be great; and by no means equal to what the failure of any one considerable Banking Concern would occasion, under the present system, if it be continued.

In order that we may form an idea of the profit to be made by establishing a public Bank in this town, we will next examine the success that has attended those which we propose for our models.

The stock of many of the Local Banks of Scotland has sold much higher than the stock of the Edinburgh Banks. The Edinburgh Banks, however, are those to which we shall more particularly refer, as the business of this town and neighbourhood is sufficiently extensive to require an establishment of equal magnitude.

There are four Banks in Edinburgh: The Royal Bank of Scotland, The Bank of Scotland, The British Linen Company, and The Commercial Bank. The last established was the Commercial Bank, in 1810 ; it commenced with a subscribed capital of Six Hundred Thousand Pounds ; it has divided from 6 to 8 per cent., and its stock is at present at 50 per cent. premium. It has had to contend in a ground completely pre-occupied, and the most ruinous times in our mercantile history ; and in struggling to form connexions, it has been led into the midst of the failures that have happened, and has met with considerable losses. The Directors have, in consequence, reduced the dividend from 8, which they had paid the first few years, to 6 per cent. Its stock, however, has not fallen in consequence. It has never, I understand, been higher than it is at present ; and there is little doubt, that had it continued to divide 8 per cent., the stock would by this time have doubled its original value. The Directors, it is supposed, will not again divide more than six per cent., until they have accumulated such a reserved fund as that, in future, when the dividends are increased, there may never be a necessity for their being reduced again. The success upon the whole of this concern, considering the opposition it has encountered, which was very great, and the bad times it has met with, which were equally so, has not, I have heard, disappointed its Stock-holders.

The Bank of Scotland, and Royal Bank Stock, are at a premium, I understand, upon the original capital advanced, of from about 90 to 140 per cent. But their capitals are, I believe, a million and a half each, being unnecessarily large for the Trade of Edinburgh. Their credit would be as good, and their business as extensive, if they were to pay off half their capitals, each Stockholder would then get as much profit upon half his present stock as he now does upon the whole of it. All that a Bank can gain by capital is credit, and when its capital is sufficiently large to put that upon the most solid basis, it is as large as there is any occasion for. More only incumbers it, and would be as well in the hands of the original Stock-holders, many of whom would probably turn it to better account.

The most successful, however, of the four establishments, has been the British Linen Company. It commenced originally with one hundred thousand pounds, which afterwards, either by an accumulation of profits, or by a further advance of capital, was doubled. Upon this capital it annually made very handsome dividends, and also accumulated a reserved fund, which, about eight or nine years ago, amounted to nearly three hundred thousand pounds, making its capital, in all, nearly half a million. It was not then a Chartered Company, but it applied to Government for a charter, and got one, the proprietors having, it is understood, subscribed a small deficiency necessary to raise their capital to five hundred thousand pounds. Since then they have gone on, notwithstanding the precarious and disastrous state of the mercantile world, with almost unparalleled success, so that now their half million of stock is worth a million and a half; it meets a ready sale at not less than two hundred per cent. premium. I do not imagine that their charter has contributed much, if any thing, towards this increase of value. The only advantage the charter gives, is to free the Stock-holders from responsibility beyond their respective shares in the capital of the Bank. This, however, can be no advantage in Scotland, where the very idea of danger, beyond a capital of half a million, would be considered as one of the absurdest chimeras that could be entertained. I do not suppose the stock of the Commercial Bank, which is not chartered, sells for a pound less on that account. It is, in proportion to the interest paid upon it, nearly about the same price as the 3 per cent. consols, and it is not likely a charter would raise it higher. I therefore imagine that the value of the British Linen Company's stock arises altogether from the ability with which the Bank is managed, and the amount of dividends it consequently makes. It must be also considéred, that government could not, with justice to the public, and therefore would not, grant a charter, if it was really any thing more than a name. It would never agree to exonerate any set of men who enjoyed a certain gain, from the loss incident to it, and throw it upon the unsuspecting public. It is only when the capital of a Bank is sufficiently great to satisfy the most sceptical doubt with regard to the safety of the public, that a charter can ever be granted. Besides which, if the freedom from personal responsibility conferred by the charter on the Stock-holders of the British Linen Company, had been of any real use in freeing them from risk, it must have destroyed their trade. Nobody would make permanent deposits in a Bank, whose partners, by any peculiar privilege, were freed from the loss which their own transactions involved. They would naturally have dealt with those that had no charter, in preference, or with the other Chartered Banks that had three times the capital. Had the charter not, in every respect been a mere dead letter, it must have injured the concern.

It is evident, that if Banking is carried on at all, it must be with a profit more than adequate to the risk incurred; and those who gain the profit must take the risk they are paid for. The reason why the charges of Bankers are so small is, that they are found, with judicious management, to cover all risk, besides leaving a sufficient profit.

The business for a Bank in this town and neighbourhood, I should think by no means inferior to that of either the Commercial Bank or the British Linen Company. In the present state of the country, however, as it is far from being certain that government may not be compelled to reduce the interest of the national debt,* it is not necessary to make out a case of extravagant profit, in order to induce capitalists to enter into such a concern. Equal interest with greater safety would of itself be a sufficient inducement. But with the chance, which experience has reduced to a certainty, of increasing their capital at least 50 per cent. what probability is there of capitalists turning their money at present to such account in any other way?

As this Bank will be the first of the kind, it will also, with equal management, be the best. There is no connexion more stable than the connexion of a Bank. When a person once opens an account with it, if he does his business creditably, he never has occasion to leave it; and if he does not, he could gain nothing by the change. Hence it generally happens that merchants adhere through life to the Bank

* Since the meeting of parliament all fears, on this head, seem to be removed.

they begin with, provided it stands. When, however, in addition to this, we consider the fine field which this great mining and commercial district presents, we may be a little more sanguine in our calculations. I should think we have a right to expect as great a profit as has ever been made by any public Bank yet established.

Where public Banks have not been established, and I may say, also, where private Banks have, there appears always to have existed a prejudice on the subject of Banking. On this account, at the first formation of public Banks, we generally find it has been considered politic to encourage them, by granting charters. That there exists at present in this country a great prejudice against Banks and Banking, from the disasters they have produced both to the partners in them and the public, there can be no question. As also there can be little doubt that when the present impediment is removed, government will be disposed, for the benefit of commerce, and for the general convenience derived from public Banks, to encourage them, I should suppose that where a sufficient capital is subscribed, there will be no objection to granting a charter, if it is required. I would therefore propose, that the Bank in question be commenced with a capital sufficient to command a charter, if one was desired, or to make it a matter of perfect indifference in the event of government declining to grant charters, whether one was to be had or not. It is also reasonable to suppose, that in granting charters, government will only require such an amount of stock, to be possessed by each Bank, as the business of the place where they may be established, shall seem to render necessary. The capital required for a Bank in Manchester or Liverpool, where mercantile transactions are so large, could not be employed in a small town like Sunderland, and would never pay in a town like Newcastle.

Considering the business of this town and neighbourhood, however, we should suppose that government would not grant us a charter under half a million of capital, if it would even grant a charter at all with a less sum ; and we should think, that with such a capital, it would be immaterial whether we had a charter or not. The most sceptical, whatever their prejudices on the subject might be, could never imagine any danger with such a security, either to the public with a charter, or to the private property of the Stock-holders without.

So large a capital, however, would warrant a greater extension of business than our own town affords. The Edinburgh Banks have agencies, and do business to a great amount, in all the principal towns of Scotland, which no doubt is on the aggregate found to pay them. In that respect it is proposed, with reference to the neighbouring towns at least, that we shall follow their example : but while we do this, we must also endeavour to improve by their experience. And the following is the plan we beg to submit :—

1. That a Bank with a capital of £500,000 be established in Newcastle, with Branches at Durham, Sunderland, Shields, and any other place which may be hereafter determined upon.

2. That no individual shall be allowed to hold more stock than to the amount of two thousand pounds.

3. That the capital be subscribed as follows : —Two hundred thousand in Newcastle and neighbourhood ; one hundred thousand in Sunderland ; fifty thousand in Durham ; fifty thousand in Shields, and their respective neighbourhoods, and the other hundred thousand as may be hereafter determined upon.

4. That the Bank in Newcastle be governed by four Directors, three of them chosen by the Newcastle Stock-holders, and the fourth to be their Chairman, and be chosen by the other three. One of these Directors to go out annually, and not for one year be eligible to be re-elected. That the Chairman be elected annually, and be eligible to be re-elected.

5. That the Branches be governed by three Directors, chosen by their respective Stockholders, and a Chairman chosen by the three Directors in the same manner as with the main branch in Newcastle.

6. That the Branches be under the general management and control of the Court of Directors in Newcastle, who shall receive daily or weekly accounts of their transactions.

7. That the Chairman of the Branches form with the Newcastle Directors a Committee of General Management, and come into Newcastle every month to examine the affairs of the establishment, and consult and decide with the Newcastle Directors all questions and rules of General Management, which it may be necessary from time to time to lay down.

8. That none but the Chairman, and the Newcastle Directors, have any inspection of the particular transactions of each Branch ; but that a general meeting of the whole Directors shall be periodically held for the purpose of making laws, or may at any time be called to consult upon any given question, either with respect to the transactions of any Branch with an individual, or upon any specific point of management which may be proposed to it, and its decision to control and bind the Committee of General Management with respect to that

point ; and two Directors to have at any time the power of calling a general meeting.

9. That there also be a Governor and Deputy-Governor, the latter of whom to be chosen by the Committee of General Management, and the former either by the Directors at large, or the Stock-holders. The Governor to be principally an honorary appointment, and to be a member of one of the two houses of parliament, and the Deputy-Governor some gentleman resident in Newcastle, who has leisure and inclination to give his attention to the affairs of the Bank, and preside at the monthly meetings.

10. That the executive officers of the Establishments consist of a Cashier and Accountant, with a Secretary, if required; and such other Clerks as are necessary for each Branch, and a Managing Director in Newcastle.*

11. That the division into Branches extend only to the division of the capital and management, and not to the profits, which shall be divided equally.

This gives a general outline, and I need not go further. The first step that the Company will have to take must necessarily be to appoint

---

* It seems also the general opinion, that there ought to be a couple of salaried Directors.

a Committee to procure all the laws and regulations of the Public Banks of England and Ireland, and the leading Public Banks of Scotland.
They must examine into their comparative success, and the cause of it, and from their rules
draw out such a constitution, as, adapted to the
peculiarities of our local situation, shall be the
best fitted to secure both the safest and most
profitable management.   In proposing this outline, my object is principally to suggest the enquiry, and not by any means to presume that a
better plan may not be adopted.   That the
constitutions of some of the present Public
Banks are not so good as they might be, and
not suited to such a town as this, I am pretty
well convinced; and as it is difficult to
make a change after a constitution is once acted upon, it will be evidently proper to consider
the subject well beforehand.   The outline
which I have given, I shall, however, take the
liberty of illustrating by a few explanatory observations.

In the first place, the capital proposed will at
once have the effect of giving the concern stability, and of securing the unlimited confidence necessary to be reposed in it by the public, in order to render it equally profitable and
useful.   In the next place, limiting the amount
of stock held by each individual, will keep the
concern in the hands of the public.   It is very

usual with Private Bankers and other wealthy individuals, to buy largely of the Stock of the Public Banks in Scotland, which is a disadvantage to them, as the greater the number of persons interested in supporting such a concern, the better. There are two individuals who each hold upwards of a hundred thousand pounds of the British Linen Company's Stock, neither of whose accounts with it are so profitable, nor, in all probability, is their influence in its favour nearly so advantageous as the transactions and influence of a respectable tradesman, or merchant, would be, who was in a situation to hold £2000 Stock independent of the capital of his trade. One of them is, in fact, himself a Banker, and issues notes, so that he must be a rival, as far as his business extends, and not a friend to the Bank. By this means, it is deprived of at least a hundred interested supporters, which, by our plan, it would have, and the profit of the smaller Stock-holder is diminished in a corresponding degree. There is also another practical evil, of still greater importance, which would be avoided. The Private Bankers in Edinburgh who do not issue Notes, keep an account with one of the Public Banks, in the same manner as the London Bankers do with the Bank of England, and discount with it, or draw upon it for the cash they require. They have, generally, made it their policy, to buy largely of the Stock of the Bank they do business with, so that by the amount of their stock, together with their private influence as Bankers, they might get themselves chosen Directors. By that means they not only gain an undue preference in their transactions with the Bank, but, as it has been proved, have, sometimes, for years together, contrived to render the Bank totally subservient to the extension and profit of their own private business.

Where great Public Banks are established, there will always be trade to a certain extent for such Bankers. They draw upon London, act as Bill Brokers, charging a commission upon their discounts, &c. and when capital is scarce, by their superior credit and influence in obtaining discounts, contrive sometimes to do business to considerable extent. We may consequently expect that the same, in a greater or less degree, will be the case in this town, and as such Bankers here will have the same interest to prompt them as in Edinburgh, they may be expected to endeavour to take the same steps. But by limiting the amount of Stock held by each individual to £2,000, no monopoly can take place, and one Stock-holder cannot possess any advantage over another.

Such persons generally, no doubt, get possession of the Stock by giving the best price for it ; and by thus limiting the competition, individual sellers will not get, at the moment, quite as much as it would otherwise bring. By a strict adherence, however, to the rule, the profit of the concern will be improved, and instead of a holder having to sell his Stock with a dividend of 10 per cent., it may leave a dividend of $12\frac{1}{2}$. Thus though he may not get so much for it when it comes into the market, as with a free competition, yet he will evidently get more for it than if, from the consequence of such competition, the dividends were $2\frac{1}{2}$ per cent. less.

It may be said that £2000 stock is not a sum large enough to give any Directors a sufficient interest in the management. To this it may be answered, nor yet would three times the amount, if they felt no interest in the management independent of the profit of their stock. The Directors in general will be wealthy individuals, with whom that profit can be of little importance.

With respect to the division into Branches, there can be no doubt that by thus effectually embracing the business of the different towns wherein they are established, the profit of the concern will be materially increased, and that capital, which might be too large for Newcastle alone, become only proportioned to a plan so much more comprehensive. But there will be also great advantages derived from it in the system of management which it affords.

There are two objects to be aimed at in planning the constitution of a Bank. First, its safety : and next, its success. And though safety is a natural consequence of success, yet there may be great safety where the success is but small. They are, in fact, partly opposed to each other. That constitution which would best secure the one might be very liable to di- minish the other. In a multitude of Directors there would be safety, but the chances would not be so much in favour of success. It is commonly said, and with truth, " What is every body's business is nobody's ;" and this in some degree would be the case with a multi- tude of Directors. The common routine of transactions would be done by the officers of the institution ; but no able or energetic, and successful management, would be attempted. The responsibility lies with the Directors at large. No individual director would conse- quently take any step of the least importance himself. Nothing would be done without a ma- jority present, and too little interest would be felt by the majority for it ever to attend. Be- sides, when many people meet, they talk more than they act : and if they differ in opinion, are apt to do nothing, leaning always to the safe side. Little being therefore done, and always that little with superlative safety, the business of the concern would be liable to flag, if not fall off altogether. It will sometimes happen, as with the Bank of England, where a considerable business is necessarily done, that with a number of Directors a good arrangement may be adopted, and the management go on tolerably well. But the Bank of England derives its business from its monopoly, in spite of its Directors, and not from its superior management. Four and twenty Directors could never successfully compete with the management of a smaller body. This is partly proved by its own experience. It does business upon the same principles as the Private Banks, yet notwithstanding its superior credit, it gets little or nothing to do, beyond the circulation of its notes, and keeping the accounts of government. On the contrary, were the Directors fewer, the interest they felt would be greater. The whole credit of the management would attach solely to them ; they would acquire a better knowledge of it, do it with more ease and pleasure, and give that spirit and energy to the direction by which the business of the concern would be extended, and its profits increased. There is also another disadvantage arising from too many Directors. Few people like their cash transactions to be known, and none, that they should come under the review and cognizance of their neighbours, who might sometimes *even* be their rivals in trade. This will always be particularly the case with borrowers, who are as good customers, and as necessary to a bank, as lenders : and when there is a great number of Directors, people are apt to feel that privacy is almost out of the question. This, I dare say, is one of the principal causes which gives business to the Private Bankers in Edinburgh ; and it will always induce many *country gentlemen* (more particularly those with whom a few shillings per cent. is less an object) to do their business with Private Banks in preference, if they possess the requisite credit, or can give them the accommodation they require.

Now, by the plan propôsed, we shall combine all the advantages of both public and private management, without the drawbacks of either.

For these reasons, the fewer the Directors the better : but there could not well be fewer than four ; and, indeed, perhaps no Bank could be safely trusted to the management of so small a number. By the Branches being under the control of the Newcastle Directors, however, while they will enjoy all the advantages of the most private management, they will have all the security of the most public. The same will be the case with the management at Newcastle : it will regularly come under the inspection and control of the Chairman of the Branch Directors, and any thing wrong in the management will immediately be discovered, and corrected or exposed. By this means, no doubt, the transactions of individuals with the Bank will be reviewed by more than four Directors. They will, however, generally be strangers; and people have a much greater objection to be immediately under the cognizance of their neighbours, and those they are known to, in money matters, than they have to their affairs being reviewed by persons who do not know them, and who only stand in the relation towards them of A. to B.

A declaration, however, if not an oath publicly made, ought to be required from every Director, that he would never make the transactions of the Bank a subject of conversation to any but those concerned in the management; and from the Committee of General Management, that their individual communications to the Branch Directors, should embrace only points of general management, unless a general meeting is to be called, and any question to be discussed which shall involve the detail of any particular transactions. By this means the public might be continually *reminded and assured* that their transactions would have the greatest privacy possible, an assurance which there can be little doubt, would be of consider‑ able benefit to the business of the Bank.

Another great advantage of this plan is the superior activity which the comparing and in‑ specting of each others management will natu‑ rally produce. While the Directors at New‑ castle will require a good account of the ma‑ nagement of the Branches, they will naturally be anxious to give as good an account to the Branch Directors, in return. Thus by being poised against each other, an emulation will be excited, which, by keeping the interest and attention of all parties continually alive, must prove of incalculable service in promoting the interest of the establishment : for a falling off in the time, trouble, and attention given by those who are entrusted with the management, is the easily besetting sin of the Directors of all public concerns.

If the public could be equally assured of the goodness of the management, it would be bet‑ ter that the Directors once chosen should never be changed. The secrets of the Bank ought to be kept in as small a compass as possible.

The management of a Bank also requires a practical knowledge, which, of so great a busi‑ ness, must take some time to acquire. Of this the Scotch are aware, and though some of the Directors go out every year, they generally re‑ elect such as have been Directors before, so

that the same set of persons, whom experience
has rendered the most fit, are continually in
the management.

In order, therefore, not to have more changes
than necessary, and to introduce no strange
faces that can be dispensed with, it is proposed
that but one Director shall go out each year by
rotation, and that the order of rotation be not
imperative. If to retain a Director, whose usefulness is such, that his brother Directors think
he ought not to retire, or if to permit one to
go out who may have found that he cannot give
the attention required, the Directors choose to
alter it, so much the better. In so small a
number, it would neither be desirable to lose a
good Director, nor to retain a bad one ; and of
their respective qualifications and usefulness,
the Directors will themselves be the best judges.
It will also generally happen, that there is some
one individual who has more time, takes more
pleasure and interest in, and gives more attention to, the management than the rest, and the
object in giving the Directors the choice of the
fourth member themselves is, that they may
choose this person for their Chairman. He will
always have the most knowledge of the transactions of his particular branch, and will be the
fittest to give any explanations respecting it,
at the monthly meetings of the Committee of
General Management, and will have the most

tact and fitness for that inspection and judgment which he will be called upon to exercise
on the transactions of the other branches, that
will come under his review.

The monthly meetings of the Chairmen of
the Branches, with the Newcastle Directors, being for the purpose of scrutinizing and control-
ling each others management, it is possible
that differences of opinion may sometimes arise.
In order, however, to prevent such differences
from ever producing any disunion (which varie-
ties of opinion, when people are earnest in a
pursuit, have been known to cause) it is proposed, that the Deputy Governor who presides
at these meetings, shall have nothing to do with
the particular management of any Branch. Being chosen by the Committee, whose respect
and confidence he will in consequence naturally enjoy, he will possess sufficient influence to
prevent any such event from ever happening.
It is likely, however, from the character and
respectability of the parties, that a misunder-
standing is merely a possible, but not at all a
probable event.

The Governor having merely an honorary station, should be chosen in a manner calculated
to convey the greatest compliment, and should
always be a member of one of the Houses of
Parliament, both in order that he may be a
man of undoubted rank, and in order to secure

a parliamentary interest and co-operation in promoting any measure, or procuring any act which may hereafter be wanted.

The superior power of control possessed by the general court of Directors, does not involve its interference in the details of the concern, and will not, consequently, in the least degree, embarrass its operations, which might be the case if it were called upon to take a practical management. It will merely be a superior court of appeal, to which reference may be made upon any particular question or point, by the Committee of General Management, or any two of its members. Its judgment and interference will be merely occasional, and never exercised without being specially called for, which it is probable will rarely be the case. The existence of the power may be useful, however, though never exercised.

Independent of these different checks, the Managing Director ought to make periodical visits, more particularly at the commencement of the concern, to aid, with his advice and assistance, the Directors of the Branches. By thus diffusing his practical knowledge into every department, a general uniformity and harmony in the direction of affairs, will subsist throughout, which will render the positive application of any one of the checks, an event rarely called for.

By this plan, therefore, I should imagine, that there would be every probability of the establishment being conducted both with safety and success. The whole management, in a short time, would become a very well understood routine. Any appeals would merely take place on particular occasions, by the Directors of the Branches requiring the additional authority of the Committee of General Management; or by the Committee of General Management, on any important point, requiring the additional authority of the General Court of Directors, to relieve themselves from responsibility.

Branches may also be established at Berwick, Carlisle, Stockton, &c. upon the same principles, but the distance would be too great to require the monthly attendance of their Chairmen. If they came once or twice a year, to ascertain, for the benefit of their constituents, the general state of the concern, it would be sufficient. In any large town, however, where an Agent was appointed, and any considerable business done, it would be better to have a Board of Directors. No business could be done to any extent, without a discretionary power exercised upon the spot; and the experience of the Scotch Banks has proved, that it is not safe to entrust such a power to an Agent. With these few observations, we will leave the plan to the consideration of the public.

SUPPLEMENTARY

# OBSERVATIONS

TO

## THE THIRD EDITION

OF

### AN ESSAY

ON THE

GENERAL PRINCIPLES AND PRESENT PRACTICE

OF

## BANKING, &c.

SUPPLEMENTARY

# OBSERVATIONS.

THE general conviction which this Essay has
produced, and the active steps which, in
other more important commercial towns, it has
already given rise to, leave no room to doubt
the accomplishment of the change in our Banking system, which it recommends. No apology, I trust, will therefore be necessary for my
hazarding a few observations on the mode of
proceeding which it will be proper to adopt,
both here and in other places similarly situated,
in order to set the proposed Banks on foot.

The objection to this, and almost every important change in the general business of mankind is, that some must lose by it. It cannot
be denied that a great Public Bank, established
in this town and neighbourhood, must materi-

ally diminish the business of the very respectable private establishments which we now have. The present system of Private Banking, however, is opposed to the welfare of the whole community, and the interest of six or seven persons can never be maintained against that of sixty or seventy thousand.

No Banks, on the present system, could stand higher in the estimation of the country than the Banks of this town, and there can be no doubt that they possess a great many friends, who would be very willing to exert themselves in opposing the establishment about to be formed, had they any reasonable grounds to go upon.

Could it be maintained, for instance, that the existing Banks possessed sufficient credit to enable them to conduct the business of the country on the principles of the joint stock companies, so as to render them unnecessary? Or, could it be contended, that they would always be as well managed as they are at present, whatever changes may take place in their partners? Or, could any reasonable guarantee be held out that other Banks, less entitled to public confidence, would not set up in this town, force themselves into credit, and abuse it? Or even could all this be maintained, other places could not be prevented from taking those steps which they are about to take in order to procure the alteration proposed in the Bank of

England's Charter, and any such exertions would consequently be useless.

Opposition to a measure of this nature by the present Banks, would evidently be totally unavailing. To expect their mercantile friends, therefore, out of mere compliment, to forego any advantage which may arise from purchasing the stock of the proposed concern, would be perfectly unreasonable. Such a compliment might even be subject to misconstructions.

In carrying the proposed Bank into effect, there are two points of view in which it will have to be considered : first, as a public institution, and next, as a speculation to individuals. It has been said that half a million is too large a capital to be raised in this district ; but that can only be known by experiment, which remains to be tried. As a public institution, it is necessary that it should have a capital sufficiently large to secure it the credit it requires ; and it is of no consequence to the public whether it be raised in this district or not, if it only be raised. When we want a machine or engine which cannot be made at home, we do not go without it on that account, but send for it to where it can be had. The same must be done with the capital of this Bank. If there are not people here sufficient to supply the amount required, let people at a distance be invited to make up the deficiency. A man who deposits his money in such a Bank will consider the half million of security held out as good to him, if it comes from a distance, as if it were raised at home.

The question then to be first determined is, whether half a million of capital is necessary to establish the unbounded credit required for a public Bank in this district or not? If decided in the affirmative, which so far as I can gather, has already been done, then let those set up the Bank who can furnish it. I am, however, very much disposed to think, that when subscriptions are opened, there will be found more capital in Newcastle, Shields, Sunderland, and Durham, than they have credit for possessing.

As soon as this Bank divides six per cent. with the prospect of its permanently continuing to do so, its stock at the present value of money, will be at 50 per cent. premium ; and this will only be dividing five thousand per annum above the interest of its capital, out of the Banking Profits of four considerable towns, besides an extensive commercial and mining district, in which are two great shipping ports. We should suppose that in this district there are a very great many millions of capital at present not near so well employed.

But its capital will only be required by slow degrees. No Bank could take up half a million of money at once. If ten per cent. were paid down, and after that ten per cent. every six months, it would be advanced as quickly as it could perhaps with prudent management be required.

Now the steps which it is proposed to pursue both in Newcastle and the neighbouring towns, are as follow. It is intended that two hundred thousand pounds be subscribed in Newcastle and the neighbourhood. It is also desirable that it should be subscribed by those who are likely to be the best supporters to the establishment. Although the respectability and character of our present Bankers is such, as to render any fears of ungentlemanly or splenetic conduct equally groundless and improbable, yet it must happen that many are so connected with them that they would not wish to run any risk of disobliging them by taking a share, however groundless such an idea may be. It is therefore proposed to take subscriptions to the extent of one half in the first instance, which will include those who are less dependent upon the Banks, and the other half after it is set on foot, when those who are more dependent upon them need not dread inconvenience from their displeasure.

If there should be a considerable demand for

the stock, it will be proper that the shares be the smaller, in order that all may be supplied. No set of persons ought to be allowed a monopoly. If the amount which each is allowed to subscribe be too large to include all who are entitled to shares, those who come first only can be supplied ; whereas if they are too small, they can easily be increased upon. It is, therefore, on the safe side to take only moderate subscriptions at first. They may be increased afterwards, if necessary. It is consequently proposed that no person be allowed to subscribe in the first instance more than a thousand pounds.

When the hundred thousand pounds are subscribed, or as large a sum as is likely, with the above limitation, a meeting will be called, and a committee of subscribers chosen to prosecute the measure, and one per cent. be paid down to meet the expences which will be incurred.

If the hundred thousand pounds be not all subscribed, the committee will have to determine the proportions in which those who have taken shares may increase the amount of them ; or should there be found, as has been suggested, any difficulty in raising either the first or last half of the capital in this district, monied men from a distance might then be allowed to take up the surplus. There will be no risk, I presume, in engaging that such men will be readily found, though, for my part, I am disposed to think that no such men are at all likely to be wanted.

In procuring the first subscribers, no great discrimination can be used, for no one is properly entitled to make the selection. Any who are willing to subscribe must be allowed to do so. By this, no doubt, it may happen that the amount will be made up before many have the opportunity of putting down their names, who, from their business, are more particularly intitled to subscribe; but this there is no avoiding. When, however, the second subscription comes to be taken, the committee will have the power of discriminating; and it will be the interest of the first subscribers, and the duty of the committee, who represent them, to apportion out the remaining shares in the manner best calculated to further the interests of the establishment.

I do not think, that if the shares are in demand, they should be sold to the highest bidder; that would be neither wise nor liberal. The shares will be principally retained for the benefit of those, whose connexion with the present establishments is such, that they would be good customers to any concern, and yet the nature of that very connexion prevents them running the risk of being put to any inconvenience by incurring the displeasure of the old Banks, before they have the new one to go to. As, however, the second subscribers are thus particularly favoured, and are not called upon, in the first instance, either to subscribe to the expence, or take any share in the trouble, of establishing the concern, I think it would be perfectly fair that their shares should be subject to a small premium of, say 5 or $7\frac{1}{2}$ per cent. This, I dare say, they will pay without any objection, as an acknowledgement for the consideration with which they will be treated. By this arrangement a sum will be raised sufficient to purchase offices, pay the expences which must be incurred in setting the Bank on foot, and enable it to begin its operations with a clear and untouched capital.

It has been objected that the smallness of the shares does not hold out sufficient inducement for gentlemen and men of large property to enter into the concern. The private property of the share holders is, however, a matter of no importance. The capital ought to be sufficiently large to give the Bank the credit it requires, did none of the partners possess more property than the capital which they advance ; and it is presumed that half a million is sufficient for that purpose. No person of property will in fact enter into the concern, if his property be necessary to its credit. No man of common sense will put his fortune in danger for the sake of making a thousand pounds or two. It is only in consequence of the capital being so great that no danger can be apprehended, that he will subscribe at all.

When, however, the capital of a Bank is sufficiently large to hold out the requisite security, its credit for any practical purpose cannot be improved either by enlarging the capital, or by taking into account the private property of its stock holders. A person who deposits money in a Bank gains nothing by the great wealth of its proprietors. All that he desires is to be satisfied that it is safe ; and capital enough to render that obvious and palpable, is all that is necessary.

Of the four Edinburgh Banks, the British Linen Company holds out the least security. It has half a million of capital ; but is a chartered Bank, and the private property of its stockholders is not liable to the public. The other two chartered Banks have three times the capital, and the Commercial Bank, which has no charter, to a capital of six hundred thousand pounds, adds the further security of the property of its stock-holders, which probably amounts to many millions. The credit of the British Linen Company is, however, as good as any of the other three, and its business, if we may judge by the superior profits which it has made, a great deal better. Therefore I apprehend there can be no doubt that half a million of capital in this district is sufficiently great to render the property of individuals ·a matter of no importance whatever to the credit of the Bank.. It must, at the same time, be equally obvious, that if the property of an individual can add nothing to its credit, by the same rule his property can never be endangered by it.

The stock ought to be principally distributed with a view to the business of the parties. It will no doubt, however, be very desirable that the neighbouring country gentlemen, should give the Bank their countenance and support, by taking shares in it. This they will probably do upon principles of public spirit. They can never be tempted by the magnitude of their shares, to do so upon any other grounds; otherwise many more efficient supporters of the concern would have to be left out.

It appears to be a general opinion, that two thousand pounds stock is too small an amount for the Directors to be confined to. I beg, therefore, to suggest that after they are chosen they may be allowed to hold shares to the amount of five thousand pounds. The first Directors will make the most benefit by this privilege, but it will be a very cheap way of rewarding them, and it is unquestionable that having every thing to arrange from the commencement, they will have the most trouble.

I still, however, cannot help thinking that after the annual profits of the Bank have become stationary, and the stock attained its value in the money market, the small difference which could be made on any stock that a Director may be allowed to hold, would not be a consideration worth the attention of such men as it is most probable will be always at the head of this concern. If they do not undertake the office as a public trust, execute it as a public duty, and have a pleasure in doing so, they are not the proper persons to fill the important office to which they will be elected. A Director, whose strongest motive for the performance of his duty is 50 or 100 pounds per annum extra, which he may gain by the stock he possesses, holds a station he ought not to hold. In fact, if such men only were chosen Directors, there can be no doubt that the Bank would be totally neglected. They would soon find that they could make much more money by confining the attention required by the Bank, to their own private affairs.

After the subscribers have chosen a Committee, one of the first steps to be taken will be to promote a petition to parliament for an alteration in the charter of the Bank of England. In this almost every person not connected with the existing Banks, whether they are subscribers to this Bank or not, will feel interested, and join. It is a measure which will have the good wishes of every one, and the public voice will be unanimous in its favour.

The most decided and fairest mode of giving expression to public opinion, is by a meeting of the town to petition parliament, held under the sanction of the magistrates, when the merits of the question might be fairly discussed, and the objections to it made known. By presenting a requisition to the mayor, such a meeting would no doubt be called. But in towns like this, where the Bankers are intimate with all the principal inhabitants, the proper persons to take a lead in such a meeting might feel a delicacy in doing so. It will perhaps, therefore, be as well to set a petition on foot without a meeting, and let it be numerously signed. It is a question that admits of but one opinion, and there can be no doubt that the petition will be held to convey the unanimous sentiments of the public.

There will always be the most difficulty in setting a public Bank on foot in small towns : the influence of the Banks being always greater in proportion to the smallness of the place. The first, however, is the only difficult step in the business, and almost any one independent and respectable person is competent to undertake it. For instance, we will suppose Stockton, Darlington, Richmond, and Stokesley, towns not far distant from each other, in each of which there are Banks, to form a proper district for a public company, with, say two hundred thousand pounds capital. In any one of those places, any respectable person might open a subscription for, say five and twenty thousand pounds stock, being half the proportion to be subscribed in the town where he resides. When the subscription is full, the subscribers might then meet, deposit a per centage on their shares, to cover the expences which may be incurred, and appoint a committee to stir up and co-operate with the other towns, or such other towns as are disposed to join them, in carrying the measure into effect. A committee being thus appointed, whose interest and whose duty it is to bestir itself, there can be no doubt of such a Bank being speedily established. One of the Branches will have, like Newcastle, to be the centre of the system. It is not, however, necessary that this Branch should be in the principal town, the most central and convenient would evidently be the best for it.

Nor, is it necessary that the shares should be a thousand pounds each; there can be no objection to take subscriptions for a hundred pounds, and probably five hundred pound shares would be as far as subscribers in the first instance ought to be permitted to go. That is, however, altogether a local question, which will have to be determined by the numbers and class of persons likely to give their support to the measure. No general rule can be laid down. What is a large subscription in one town may be a small one in another, and *vice versa.*

That public Banks have not hitherto existed, more especially in London and Lancashire, seems to have arisen from the want of a proper knowledge of the principles of Banking, rather than from the charter of the Bank of England, which I find does not prevent public Banks for the deposit of capital from being established. I hope it will not be considered as an attempt to arrogate merit to myself, when I say that I have not been able to discover any correct views extant upon the subject. The disserta-tions which I have met with, have generally consisted, of what has been said by Smith in his Wealth of Nations, the History of the Trans-actions of the Bank of England with Govern-ment, and a Eulogy of the Present System. In the same manner as the rules for epic poetry have been deduced from the writings of Homer, so have the principles of Banking been deduced from the practice of the Bank of England. That Banks ought to be the permanent depo-sitories of the capital of the country, is an idea which no writer has hitherto entertained, and the silent operations of the Scotch Banks have eluded observation.

It has in fact always been hitherto considered, that the proper business of a Bank was to issue notes and discount bills at short dates. This is very strikingly exemplified, by the clause in the charter of the Bank of England, which restricts other Banks to six partners.

12—" And to prevent any doubts that may
" arise concerning the privilege or power given
" by former acts of parliament, to the said go-
" vernor and company of *exclusive Banking*,
" *and also in regard to the erecting any other*
" *Bank or Banks by parliament, or restraining*
" *any other persons from Banking*, during the
" continuance of the said privilege, granted to
" the governor and company of the Bank of
" England, as before recited, It is hereby fur-
" ther enacted and declared by the authority
" aforesaid, that it is the true intent and mean-
" ing of this act, that *no other Bank shall be*
" *erected, established, or allowed by parliament*,
" and that it shall not be lawful for any body
" politic or corporate whatsoever, erected, or
" to be erected, or for any other persons united
" or to be united in covenants or partnerships,
" exceeding the number of six persons, in that
" part of Great Britain called England, *to bor-*
" *row, owe, or take up, any sum or sums of*
" *money on their bills, or notes payable on de-*

" *mand, or at any less time than six months* from
" the borrowing thereof, during the continu-
" ance of such said privilege to the said go-
" vernor and company ; who are hereby de-
" clared to be and remain a corporation *with*
" *the privilege of exclusive banking* as before
" recited, subject to redemption on the terms
" and conditions before-mentioned."—21 *Geo.*
3. *c.* 60. *sec.* 12.

It is quite evident that the framers of the
above clause considered the business pursued
by the Bank of England, the only proper
Banking. It appeared to them that preventing
Banks with more than six partners, from issuing bills at short dates, or notes payable on demand, was altogether conferring on the Bank
the privilege of exclusive Banking as a public
company. This, it did, no doubt according to
their definition of the term, but it still leaves
the most important part of Banking open to
the public.

There is at this moment no legal impediment
to the establishment of joint stock companies
for trading in real capital. Both the letter and
spirit of the charter has reference to the circulation of bills and notes alone. A Bank which
traded only in capital, would not in the least
touch upon the monopoly of the Bank of England, nor be any infringement of its charter.
Now in London and Lancashire, the Banks do

principally trade in capital. In London, however, they accept bills, and in Lancashire they draw them, which such Banks, without an alteration in the charter, could not do. But I apprehend there is a great deal of drawing upon London from Lancashire, and consequently of accepting in London, which would be quite unnecessary with a better system.*

Such a Bank, though it could not draw upon London, could sell to those who wanted such bills as it had discounted for others, and as I should imagine the balance of trade would, on the average, be in favour of Lancashire, it would not be many Bankers bills that would be wanted. These could easily be procured from other Banks, or the London agents of the concern might appoint a person in Lancashire

---

* I understand that most of the bills in Lancashire are made payable in London, which must arise from the demand for capital in that great manufacturing and commercial district, under the present system of Banking, being greater than the supply. By the bills being made payable in London, they can be discounted there; and some of the Banks have branches in London, which, it is probable, were originally established to save the expence of agency. Instead of saying that the Lancashire Banks trade in capital, it would, perhaps, be more proper to designate them Bill Brokers, on a large scale. Public Banks would, of course, from the investments of capital made with them, be able to discount bills, payable at home, by which the present expence of paying in London would be saved.

to draw such bills upon them as the Bank required. As to accepting of bills, by the London Banks, it is a part of their business, which, I understand, is not much valued. It would, however, be needless to go into the details of management, which would have to be pursued by a public Bank established with the charter as it now stands. There is no reasonable ground of probability that the directors of the Bank of England will oppose the required alteration. Sufficient, therefore, for our argument, is it, that the establishment of Joint Stock Companies without such alteration is perfectly legal.

# APPENDIX

## TO THE

# Essay on Banking.

# APPENDIX.

———

No. I.   Letters from The Times Newspaper.

## JOINT STOCK BANKING COMPANIES.

*To the Editor of The Times.*

Sir,—As the important advantages to be derived from the alteration of the Bank Charter and the establishment of Joint Stock Companies seem little understood, permit me to offer a few observations on the subject.

Experience has shown, that Joint Stock Companies never fail, and from the nature of the management to which they are subject, have been rarely known to ever lose money.   By the confidence which this security inspires, and their liberal mode of transacting business, they become permanently, to large amounts, the depositories of the actual capital of the country. This they lend out again, not only upon short dated bills, but in permanent advances, upon sufficient personal and other securities, to merchants, manufacturers, and agriculturists, with great advantage, as has been proved in Scotland, to the agriculture and commerce of the country. Provincial private banks (in London they are more stable) are unable, from the frail nature of their credit, to transact in this manner. Not only are people deterred from keeping capital in their hands, but the banks dare not re-issue that which is deposited with them, except upon short dated bills, and such available securities as, in the event of a run upon them, can, through their London agents, be turned into money at any time. Comparatively speaking, therefore, the accommodation afforded to trade by private banks is merely casual, while an encouragement is given to bill transactions, which often leads to and is productive of the most fatal consequences. To agriculture, where bills are not current, they can give no accommodation at all.

The proposed alteration of the Charter is, in fact, brought forward by ministers as a measure of agricultural relief: and when properly considered, it will be seen, that no proposition made this session of parliament for that purpose, can in point of magnitude or efficacy, be compared with it.

It is understood, that ministers are very serious in their intention of carrying it through, and will be supported on both sides of the house; but it is also supposed, that on both sides of the house, from the great connexions of country bankers in parliament, a great deal of indirect influence will be opposed to it. This, it is reported, government have already met, even in the directors of the bank of England, who have admitted the principle, but wish to defeat it in practice. Not only have they stipulated that no Charters shall be granted, (a stipulation of not the slightest importance to the Bank of England,) but it is understood, that they wish to prevent any alteration of the law with respect to Joint Stock Banks, which renders a company liable for the obligations in the name of its firm entered into by any of its partners. This, of course, would completely prevent any such banks being established, and can have nothing else for its object. By thus quibbling with the nation, the Directors may serve their friends, but they most seriously commit the interests of their constituents. The Bank is founded upon public opinion, and, perhaps, it is not too much to say, even upon public prejudice. If, however, it is thus foolishly opposed to the interests of the nation, opinion and prejudice may take a turn, and it may never have its Charter renewed again.

AN OBSERVER.

## TO THE DIRECTORS OF THE BANK OF ENGLAND.

Gentlemen,—At a meeting of the Bank Proprietors, it was agreed to permit the establishment of Joint Stock Companies at the distance of sixty-five miles from London, upon having the Charter of the Bank renewed for ten years. This agreement was a favourable one, inasmuch as for resigning a privilege worth nothing, you were to receive a valuable consideration. The circulation of Lancashire you have been for some time desirous of discontinuing : to give it up was, therefore, making no sacrifice.

Now, it is the interest of the Company, and your duty, who are intrusted with the care of its interests, to get this agreement carried into effect. Report, however, states (how truly you best know,) that instead of doing so, you have attempted to defeat this measure.

You must know what Joint Stock Companies are. The Bank of England is a Joint Stock Company. You must also know very well, that by the laws of this country, it is not practicable to establish these Companies without some bill, which shall free them from being responsible for the acts of individual partners, which shall also make their stock transferable without a formal dissolution of partnership, and contain other regulations of a similar nature.

Now, when the Bank Proprietors agreed to their establishment, they agreed also to such regulations as a matter of course. If, however, you have quibbled about them, with a view to get rid of the arrangement, I leave it to your constituents and you to determine how far you have done your duty.

AN OBSERVER.

BANKING SYSTEM.

*To the Editor of The Times.*

Sir,—I have read with some surprise two letters

that have appeared in your journal from a correspondent who signs himself " An Observer ;" and as you invited, in a former journal, discussion on the subject to which your correspondent has alluded, I trouble you with a few remarks. Your correspondent is evidently very angry with the Bank Directors, for not promoting this new scheme of Joint Stock Companies. Let me first ask, what is the object of these Joint Stock Companies? And I believe a fair answer to this inquiry will be, that their design is to extend the circulating medium, and thereby enhance prices. Now, if your correspondent had taken a comprehensive view of the subject, he would see the unpleasant, and I may say dangerous, situation the Bank Directors will be placed in; for it must be remembered, that the same paper which is issued, and will cause the rise of the price of corn, will also cause the rise of the price of gold; and is it to be expected the Bank Directors can permit Joint Stock Companies to issue all over England their paper, and cause the rise of the prices of all commodities (remember, gold included), and yet the Bank Directors be bound by an act of parliament to supply the public with one commodity (gold) at a fixed price, viz. 3*l*. 17*s*. 10½*d*. per oz.? One of two things must ensue: either ruin to the Bank of England from such an unequal trade, or a corresponding withdrawal of their paper to the extent of the issues of the Joint Stock Companies, to keep paper and gold at par. Where then will be the use of these new companies?

Should, however, any arrangement be made by a breaking in upon Mr Peel's bill, and making the bank note a legal tender, to increase the issue of paper, this would be nothing more than a complete robbery of the 5 per cent. fund-holder. He has had 20 per cent. deducted from his income, and one principal argument to reconcile him to it has been, " Never " mind ; you can now purchase the same quantity of " commodities for 80l. you used to do for 100l., and " therefore you are no worse off." But issue fresh paper, and let prices increase, and then the poor fundholder will have again high prices, and 20 per cent. income less.

That this will be the case, I appeal only to the operation of the paper system in 1816, and I must say that any infraction whatever of Mr Peel's bill, after the arrangement that has just been made with the public creditor, is neither more nor less than a fraud upon the fund-holder, and all who have had deductions made from fixed salaries or rents, since the passing of that bill.

Respecting the establishing of Joint Stock Companies, I shall then say, that more evil is likely to arise to the community than good. One month a large issue of paper will be made, and prices will rise; another month, a withdrawing by the Bank of England, and prices will fall; it will keep property in a complete state of vacillation as to price, and the merchant will also be liable to great fluctuation in his commodities. There is no want of circulating medium, according to the present value of property at this moment; why then make any alteration in the existing law, which we were told, when made, was " to set the question " at rest for ever ?" Let it be remembered, that nothing is more dangerous to the well-being of a country than tampering with the currency; and after the solemn engagement the legislature has entered into, by unanimously passing a bill to return *bona fide* to cash payments, I should hope the integrity of our government will never be again compromised by allowing any new paper projects, although they may be called " Joint Stock Companies."　　　　　J. F.

May 23, 1822.

---

## JOINT STOCK COMPANIES.

*To the Editor of The Times.*

Sir,—In reply to the letter of J. F., in your paper of yesterday, I beg to say, that I have no wish to impute improper motives to the Directors of the Bank of England, yet their conduct cannot appear otherwise than extraordinary.

The reasons against the establishment of Joint Stock Companies must either have been known before the meeting of proprietors took place, or have been discovered since. If they were known before, why was the meeting called, and the measure agreed to? The directors can have no faith in the soundness of their own arguments, or they never would have acted in such direct opposition to them. If, on the other hand, they have been discovered since, allow me to say they are mere lame apologies for equivocal conduct.

The apprehensions professed to be entertained are, that by the establishment of these companies, the circulation will be extended, and the relative price of gold and paper thereby altered—that is to say, while a note is worth twenty shillings, a sovereign may rise to twenty-two shillings; and a demand be created for gold which must fall upon the Bank of England, and either ruin it or undermine its circulation.

Now, without disputing about the unqualified assumption, first, that the circulation would be increased to so great an extent; and next, that it would, in the present state of the country and our exchanges, alter the relative prices of gold and paper, let us admit such to be the result of experience. Must it not then appear to be a marvellous circumstance, that the Bank of England, previous to the restriction act, had a note in circulation at all? The principle laid down is, that the over issues of country banks contract those of the Bank of England; yet, as country banks have always issued as much as they could, and often more than they found profitable, it is really quite surprising that the Bank of England has not, long ere this, ceased to exist.

I am unable to say, at this moment, whether by the law as it now stands, country banks will not be obliged to pay in gold as well as the Bank of England. However, let the law be restored to the state in which it stood before the restriction act was passed, and the relative situation of the banks will be precisely the same. Each bank will enjoy the circulation of that district the business of which it transacts, and any improvidence in its issues will recoil upon itself.

Your correspondent inquires, what is the object of these Joint Stock Companies? It may be replied—to supply to the country, banks with capital, where there are now banks with none, and to give a security and steadiness to its money transactions which they do not now possess.   How far they may contribute to extend the circulation, and counteract the ruinous consequences which its great contraction has produced, I shall leave to more competent judges to determine.   I trust it will in some degree assist the views of ministers in relieving the distresses of the country, though it may not altogether realise the apprehensions of the Bank Directors with regard to the holders of five per cent. stock.

It does not, however, appear to me, that the original promoters of these establishments had any such views as those with which their present advocates are charged.   I quote the following from a paper publishing in Newcastle, where the idea of establishing these companies, founded upon the encouragement held out last year by government, originated :—

" It is the result of experience that public banks or
" Joint Stock Companies, in consequence of the un-
" bounded credit which they naturally possess, and
" their liberal mode of doing business, receive great
" *permanent* investments of capital.   They are, in con-
" sequence enabled to re-issue it in *permanent* advan-
" ces to those who can give proper security.   Where-
" as private banks, for want of the necessary credit,
" have not such large sums deposited with them ; nor
" dare they, for fear of runs, to which they are so
" subject, make advances, except upon bills, and such
" available securities as can, in case of need, be turn-
" ed into money through their London correspondents
" at any time.

" The consequence is, that the latter principle of
" banking is purely mercantile, and can afford no use-
" ful assistance to agriculture whatever. An advance
" of money is of no use to the agriculturist without he
" is allowed years to re-pay it. Whereas the dubious
" credit of private banks renders it necessary that they
" should principally limit their advances to the dis-
" counting of bills at two or three months.

" With Joint Stock Companies, however, this is
" not the case. If a farmer can produce two persons
" in sufficient credit to be his securities, he can open
" a cash account, draw out of the bank the sum for
" which he gives security, and repay it by degrees, as
" the returns of his farm, or success of the improve-
" ments in which he has expended it, may enable him.
" It very often happens, that many valuable perma-
" nent improvements are totally prevented from want
" of capital on the part of both landlord and tenant.
" The landlord is very willing to allow for such im-
" provements by a gradual deduction from the rent,
" and the tenant to make them if he had the means;
" but the want of this on both sides puts an entire stop
" to the improvements contemplated. With a Joint
" Stock Bank, however, in the neighbourhood, this
" would not be the case; the landlord would have no
" objection to become security to the bank for that
" money which he had himself ultimately to pay. It
" could, therefore, be immediately raised for the
" purpose required, and would be discharged by de-
" grees, as the rents came round. Even if the land-
" lord did not pay for the improvements himself, were
" a tenant to show how capital might be expended
" with advantage, his landlord could have no objec-

" tion to become security for the money spent in the
" improvement of his own property, the tenant en-
" gaging to re-pay it before the expiration of his
" lease. Thus, such a bank would be a source and
" main-spring of improvement and fertility to the
" neighbourhood in which it was placed, while the
" business thus done by it would be a source of great
" profit to the concern.

" Hence the establishment of Joint Stock Compa-
" nies is a matter of great importance to the landed
" interest, independent of remedying the positive evils
" which have arisen out of the present system ; and
" most of the intelligent country gentlemen, who have
" been consulted upon the subject, are decidedly fa-
" vourable to the measure."

The simple principle that these banks bring actual
capital to the aid of the practical agriculturist, who can
give security for it, is what is here proposed, and it
must be obvious that no advance of exchequer bills,
or any temporary expedient that can be devised, could
be either so practicable or so extensively useful to the
country.

Not only, however, will the proposed change in our
Banking System be of great service both to commerce
and agriculture, but an extensive evil will be thereby
remedied. During the last thirty years, nearly three
hundred Private Banks, principally provincial, have
failed. What an immense mass of misery does this
present to the imagination. Each failure was an earth-
quake to the neighbourhood where it took place. The
savings of the labourer, the capital of the tradesman,
the dependence of the widow, all swallowed up in its
dreadful vortex. Could a spectator but see the gene-

ral alarm, the anxious inquiry, the frantic look, and the domestic misery produced, he would be disposed to class such an event amongst the greatest calamities to which mankind are subject. Can a desire possibly exist in any quarter, then, of perpetuating that system from which these evils have sprung?

AN OBSERVER.

London, May 5th.

No. II. Letter, from The Newcastle Courant, referred to in the last Letter from The Times.

## BANKING IN CONNECTION WITH AGRICULTURE.

*To the Editor of The Newcastle Courant.*

By the Pamphlet which you have more than once favoured with your notice, it is shewn to be the result of experience, that public Banks or Joint Stock Companies, in consequence of the unbounded credit which they naturally possess, and their liberal mode of doing business, receive great *permanent* investments of capital. They are, in consequence, enabled to re-issue it in *permanent* advances to those who can give proper security. Whereas private Banks, for want of the necessary credit, have not such large sums deposited with them; nor dare they, for fear of runs, to which they are so subject, make advances, except upon bills, and such available securities, as can, in case of need, be turned into money, through their London correspondents, at any time.

The consequence is, that the latter principle of banking is purely mercantile, and can afford no useful assistance to Agriculture whatever. An advance of money is of no use to the Agriculturist without he is allowed years to repair it. Whereas the dubious credit of private Banks renders it necessary that they should principally limit their advances to the discounting of bills at two or three months.

With Joint Stock Companies, however, this is not

the case. If a Farmer can produce two persons in sufficient credit to be his securities, he can open a cash account, draw out of the Bank the sum for which he gives security, and re-pay it by degrees, as the returns of his farm, or success of the improvements in which he has expended it, may enable him. It very often happens, that many valuable permanent improvements are totally prevented from want of capital on the part of both landlord and tenant. The landlord is very willing to allow for such improvements by a gradual deduction from the rent, and the tenant to make them if he had the means; but the want thereof on both sides, puts an entire stop to the improvements contemplated. With a Joint Stock Bank, however, in the neighbourhood, this would not be the case, the landlord would have no objection to become security to the Bank for that money which he had himself ultimately to pay. It could therefore be immediately raised for the purpose required, and would be discharged by degrees, as the rents came round. Even if the landlord did not pay for the improvements himself, were a tenant to shew how a few hundred pounds might be expended with advantage, his landlord could have no objection to become security for the money spent in the improvement of his own property, the tenant engaging to re-pay it before the expiration of his lease. Thus such a Bank would be a source and main spring of improvement and fertility to the neighbourhood in which it was placed, while the business thus done by it would be a source of great profit to the concern.

Hence the establishment of Joint Stock Banking Companies, is a matter of great importance to the landed interest, independent of remedying the positive evils which have arisen out of the present system; and most of the intelligent country gentlemen who have been consulted upon the subject, are decidedly favourable the measure.

It has consequently been suggested that petitions from the counties of Northumberland and Durham, for the alteration of that clause in the charter of the Bank of England, which restricts Banks to six partners, ought to be set on foot, in order to permit the establishment of such Banks.

By the Pamphlet above mentioned, it will be seen that the clause in question is a mere error in legislation, and that error too a verbal one, and that the alteration proposed not only offers no injury to the Bank of England, but puts its monopoly upon a better footing. Consequently opposition on any rational principle cannot be offered to the measure, admitting for a moment that the interests of a Bank could be maintained against that of a kingdom. This point, however, as well as the subject generally, is very fully discussed in the Pamphlet alluded to, which has been very generally circulated, and may be also had in all the principal towns of the two neighbouring counties.

Independent of the great national advantages to be derived from the system of banking recommended, the gentlemen of the county of Durham are particularly called upon to express themselves, by the positive injuries from the present system which the county has, within these few years, sustained. It is but a short time since five banks, viz. two at Stockton, two at Sunderland, and one in the city of Durham, failed nearly together, by which at least a million of money was lost. No stronger argument than the evidence of this fact could be offered, both for the necessity and duty of every gentleman in the county joining to promote any steps that may be necessary to prevent the recurrence of evils so dreadful as these failures produced to hundreds of individuals.

Nor can it be less necessary for the gentlemen of the county of Northumberland to bestir themselves. They have recently had an indication of those evils which Durham has suffered, while the failure of Messrs Surtees, Burdon, and Co. cannot be forgotten. The credit of the present Banks, it must be admitted, leave little room to doubt, that it will be some time before any more disasters can happen of a similar nature ; yet, the Banks referred to, and the latter in particular, had a credit as good as the present, or any private Bank, could possess.

No one can feel a greater respect for our present bankers, both as gentlemen and men of business, than I do; and I am very well assured, that even they will not contend, that if we could discover (to speak allegorically) a clear and safe North West Passage, we ought to send our ships to China by the present route, and encounter the hurricanes of the Indian ocean, merely that they might purchase their mutton at the Cape.     T.

## No. III.    Resolutions at Durham.

AT a meeting of Gentry, Clergy, Magistrates, and others, of the county of Durham, held at the Grand Jury Room, on Wednesday the 17th of April,

## THE RIGHT HON. LORD VISCOUNT BAR-RINGTON, IN THE CHAIR,

*Resolved*,—That this meeting are convinced of the superior security afforded by Joint Stock Banking Companies, beyond that derived from private Banks, as well as of their more extensive influence in promoting the Commercial and Agricultural prosperity of a country.

*Resolved*,—That for the purpose of promoting the establishment of Joint Stock Companies, a committee be appointed, to correspond with other persons impressed with the same sentiments.

*Resolved*,—That Lord Viscount Barrington, William Thomas Salvin, Francis Johnson, Edward Shipperdson, John Ralph Fenwick, Richard Scruton, and John Ward, Esquires, be a committee for that purpose.

*Resolved*,—That these resolutions be published in the Newcastle and Durham newspapers.

BARRINGTON, CHAIRMAN.